Teaching Grammar

A Reader and Workbook

Edited by
Julie Ann Hagemann

DeVry University DuPage

Boston • New York • San Francisco
Mexico City • Montreal • Toronto • London • Madrid • Munich • Paris
Hong Kong • Singapore • Tokyo • Cape Town • Sydney

Series Editor: *Aurora Martínez Ramos*
Series Editorial Assistant: *Beth Slater*
Senior Marketing Manager: *Elizabeth Fogarty*
Composition and Prepress Buyer: *Linda Cox*
Manufacturing Buyer: *JoAnne Sweeney*
Production Editor: *Paul Milhailidis*
Editorial-Production Service: *Modern Graphics, Inc.*
Electronic Composition: *Modern Graphics, Inc.*

For related titles and support materials, visit our online catalog at www.ablongman.com

Between the time Website information is gathered and then published, it is not unusual for some sites to have closed. Also, the transcription of URLs can result in unintended typographical errors. The publisher would appreciate notification where these errors occur so that they may be corrected in subsequent editions.

Library of Congress Cataloging-in-Publication Data

Teaching grammar : a reader and workbook / edited by Julie Ann Hagemann.
    p. cm.
  Includes bibliographical references and index.
  ISBN 0-205-34386-4
    1. English language–Grammar–Study and teaching. 2. English language–Grammar–Study and teaching–Problems, exercises, etc. 3. English language–Rhetoric–Study and teaching. 4. English language–Rhetoric–Study and teaching–Problems, exercises, etc. 5. College students' writings–Evaluation–Problems, exercises, etc. I. Hagemann, Julie Ann,

PE1404.T285 2002
428.2'071'1–dc21

2002071684

Contents

Preface

> *The question is* not *a simple dichotomy, 'to grammar or not to grammar?' Rather, the question is, 'What aspects of grammar can we teach to enhance and improve students' writing, and when and how can we best teach them?' 'In the context of writing' is our short answer, but we keep learning more ways as we keep taking risks as teachers.*
>
> —C. Weaver, C. McNally, and S. Moerman
> To Grammar or Not to Grammar:
> That Is *Not* the Question!"
> *Voices from the Middle* (March 2001)

Chances are, if you've picked up this book, you're someone like me: someone interested in knowing more about teaching grammar. Perhaps you're a preservice teacher, a practicing teacher, a parent. Perhaps you have questions about what to teach, about how to teach it, about whether to even teach grammar at all. Perhaps you wonder about the relationship of grammar to the other language arts: reading, writing, speaking, listening, and visual interpretation. Perhaps you wonder about how to deal with all the irksome grammatical mistakes in the writing you read on a daily basis—student writing or adult, academic or non. Perhaps you wonder about how best to respond to a speaker of a nonmainstream dialect of English or a non-native speaker learning English.

These are the questions I've wrestled with for almost twenty years of teaching writing, mainly basic writing, to ESL and urban students on the college level. These are the issues I explored as I studied applied linguistics, composition theory, and literacy studies. These are the dilemmas raised by the English language arts preservice and practicing teachers in my writing methods classes. These are the issues I've brought the best thinkers and practitioners of grammar pedagogy together to debate in this reader and workbook.

A Reader and Workbook

As the title suggests, there are two main parts to this text: it's a reader—a collection of readings—and a workbook—a collection of student writings. The readings were chosen to raise critical issues about the teaching of grammar and, at the same time, offer readers pragmatic advice about classroom practice and curriculum development. They draw on the experience and expertise of teachers at the middle school, high school, and college levels. The various pieces of student writings were chosen to illustrate some of the issues raised in the published readings. The student writers were in elementary, middle school, high school, and college at the time they created their pieces. I chose this range so that you can see how writers develop as they get older and more experienced. My students have taught me how important it is to understand this whole range because without it, teachers can't know where students have come from and where they're going.

They've also taught me it's important to engage issues on both an abstract and a concrete level, and that's why this book includes these two sections. My students generated richer discussions when they could reflect on various ideas raised in the published readings and when they could see how these concepts were enacted by developing writers. (In addition, they liked the extra practice in responding to student writing, because practicing and preservice teachers alike agree that evaluating student writing is often the hardest part of their jobs.) I believe you'll find both sections equally rewarding, though of course, as a reader, you may use the book to suit your own needs.

Chapter Formats

The central focus of each chapter is a previously published reading about teaching grammar. In the introduction to each chapter, I lay out the pedagogical issue(s) raised in the reading by contextualizing it with discussions of related articles and studies. I wanted to bring together in a single resource collection the experts that have had such an influence on my thinking. I also wanted to create a resource bibliography of quality thinking about grammar.

When appropriate, I connect the issue(s) to curricula and text being used in today's classrooms. For my readers who aren't familiar with current texts and commercially available programs, these discussions introduce them to new materials and model for them ways to critique various approaches. For readers who are familiar with these materials, I may perhaps discuss them in a new light. As Patterson (2001) points out, it's important to understand critically what, why, and how we're teaching. I examined a number of (English) language arts textbook series published by the major publishing houses, but I scrutinized three in particular:

- *Elements of Language: Introductory Course*, Odell, Vacca, Hobbs, and Irvin (2001, Holt, Rinehart and Winston).
- *English*, Rueda, Saldivar, Shapiro, Templeton, Terry, and Valentino (2001, Houghton Mifflin).
- *Glencoe Writer's Choice: Grammar and Composition: Grade 6* (2001, Glencoe/McGraw-Hill).

I chose these three because their presentation of grammar and writing represents a range from fairly traditional to somewhat innovative. They were also texts being considered by my local school district at the time of this writing. I also spotlight four quality curriculum programs available as supplements or substitutes to the text series. Readers may not be familiar with these programs, but may find them helpful.

Issues Raised

The chapters are divided into four parts. Part I introduces the debate over the traditional grammar. The readings in this section challenge the traditional grammar curriculum, explaining why such a curriculum doesn't achieve its often stated goal of improving student writing. The readings propose instead alternative curricula that help students see academic writing in a larger context and better motivate them to work on improving their writing.

Chapter 1 examines various definitions of grammar and their implications. It also reviews some key principles of linguistics, sociolinguistics, and language acquisition. No doubt, you've studied the structure of English (and perhaps know it intuitively as a native speaker). Perhaps you've had classes in how children learn their first language, how children and adults learn second languages, how and why dialects of English occur. If so, the ideas in Harvey A. Daniels' "Nine Ideas about Language" will be familiar to you. We begin with these definitions and this refresher because we'll return to these ideas again and again as we explore grammar pedagogy.

Chapter 2 challenges the traditional grammar curriculum—the isolated study of the seven (or eight) parts of speech and the four kinds of sentences—by reviewing several studies which show that such a curriculum doesn't lead to improved student writing. Nancy G. Patterson's "Just the Facts: Research and Theory about Grammar Instruction" summarizes five such studies.

Chapter 3 offers an alternative to traditional grammar: grammar in the context of real language, especially writing and literature. In "To Grammar or Not to Grammar: That Is *Not* the Question!" Weaver, McNally, and Moerman explain how students can use grammatical knowledge to comprehend texts, as well as generate, revise, and edit them.

Part II introduces the idea of rhetorical judgment. These are judgments we make about which words to use in which order to meet our readers' expectations and achieve our purpose(s) (Kolln, 1999). Rhetorical judgment is part of a native speaker's intuitive sense of language.

Chapter 4 explores some of the strategies writers use to develop their sense of rhetorical judgment. Key among them is the ability to identify salient features of various genres of texts so that writers can visualize what readers need and expect from a piece of writing. Another is the ability to notice significant gaps between what the writer has written and what the reader expects so that writers can revise. Teachers can help students identify these features and these gaps by the kinds of comments they make to students—either in conferences or in written comments—as they evaluate their writing. Most teachers, myself included, say that evaluating writing is the hardest—most anxiety-producing—part of their jobs. So Richard Straub's advice in "Guidelines for Responding to Student Writing" about how to make thoughtful comments is comforting.

Chapter 5 explores grammatical and mechanical "error" in student writing—that is, the gap between what's on the page and what the reader expected. Lois Matz Rosen's "Developing Correctness in Student Writing: Alternatives to the Error Hunt" discusses not only why students make errors when they write, but also how to help students recognize and correct those errors on their own.

Part III explores more fully some of the salient features of written texts that should be a part of every writer's rhetorical knowledge. The chapters also suggest ways to make grammar instruction more rhetorical. Such instruction combines theories of (socio)linguistics and rhetoric to teach students how to form more effective sentences, paragraphs, and essays. These are lessons all writers—regardless of linguistic, ethnic, or socioeconomic background—need to know.

Chapter 6 points out the differences between oral language, which most students are quite comfortable with, and written, academic language, which most students need to learn explicitly. Such differences can help students sort out which oral language experiences can transfer to writing and which need to be learned specifically for the written medium. Although Walt Wolfram, Carolyn Temple Adger, and Donna Christian's "Dialects and Written Language" focuses on student writers who speak a vernacular dialect of English, they begin with a discussion of the differences between oral and written language that all students must come to understand in order to become academically literate.

Chapter 7 discusses how students come to develop a sense of the sentence, and thus, how to punctuate sentences effectively. Punctuation is one feature of written English that doesn't correspond well to oral English, and as a result, developing writers make numerous mistakes in punctuating sentences—both at their boundaries and within the sentence. In "Run-ons, Comma Splices, and Native-Speaker Abilities," Rei Noguchi struggles to understand why students make mistakes in punctuation and then suggests ways to help students understand punctuation more fully.

Chapter 8 discusses research—and resulting curricula—on sentence structure to understand more clearly how writers develop longer, denser, more complex sentences. The goal is not only to help students add structures to their repertoire, but to understand when and how to use these structures effectively in their writing. This is what Kolln and Funk refer to as rhetorical grammar, and what they discuss in "Rhetorical Grammar."

Part IV suggests ways to work with language minority writers, that is, with writers whose home language(s) aren't Standard English and, as a result, who struggle as writers. These writers may be speakers of a vernacular dialect of English or they may be speakers of another language in the process of learning English. The readings in this section focus on language minority writers because they're the students most likely to need special attention in learning academic English. In addition to learning the lessons discussed in Chapters 6 through 8, they also need to learn Standard English. This means they have additional lessons to learn that other students can take for granted and easily transfer.

Chapter 9 discusses strategies for working with students whose home language is a vernacular dialect of English. In this chapter, we see again how important it is to help students sort out which experiences with vernacular English can transfer and which cannot. In "A Bridge from Home to School: Helping Working Class Students Acquire School Literacy," Julie Hagemann shows ways teachers can actively contrast home language and school language to make that sorting easier.

Chapter 10 discusses strategies for working with students whose home language is a language other than English. Many mainstream teachers feel inadequately prepared to help English language learners in their classrooms, but this chapter suggests that they can use a number of strategies already in their repertoire—at least to some extent. This chapter explains how ELLs develop their writing abilities and why they make the errors they do. In "Teaching Students to

Self-Edit," Dana Ferris offers concrete suggestions for helping students master their errors.

If you're interested in seeing how developing writers deal with the grammatical issues explored in this reader, then read the sixteen pieces of student writing in Part V. The authors range from fourth-graders to a college upperclassman, and the pieces represent a variety of genres, from stories to a literary analysis. Some are first drafts; some are finished drafts. Some authors were willing to provide multiple drafts. Together, they're a wonderful collection of voices.

Acknowledgments

I thank my editor Aurora Martinez and her assistant Beth Slater for their helpful advice in guiding me through the writing process. I couldn't have done it without them. I'd also like to thank the following reviewers: Anne Bliss, University of Colorado at Boulder; Pamela Sissi Carroll, Florida State University; Robert W. Funk, Eastern Illinois University; F. Todd Goodson, Kansas State University; Holly Johnson, Texas Tech University; Hugh Thomas McCracken, Youngstown State University; Stephen Wilhoit, University of Dayton; and Melvin R. Winninger, DePauw University. Their careful reading and sound criticism made this book better than I imagined it myself.

I thank the students in my writing and grammar methods classes as well as my basic writing classes. I would also like to thank my colleagues Matt Gordon, Mel Wininger, Jocelyn Riley, Kathryn Flannery, Barry Kroll, Myron Tuman, Julia Austin, Marilyn Cleland, Judith Burdan, Carolyn Boiarsky and the Northwest Indiana Writing Project, Christine Lewinski, Lori Danley, and Diana Lopez-Colon. My gratitude returns only a tiny measure of all that you've taught me about language and literacy and learning.

I also thank Susan Friedberg, Sandra Graham, and Pam Grady at DeVry University DuPage for their interest in and support of this project. Even though they learned about it halfway through the writing, they adopted it as their own.

Last, I thank Toni Mitchell Wesson, Rosie Carroll, Megan Donelli, Barbara Cantrell, Barbara Lamar, Kateri Noone, Susan Chang, Lalu Palamattam, and all the others who were so helpful in securing permissions to publish the readings and the student writing.

But most of all, I especially thank Ajay Singh and my family, whose faith in me never wavered.

J. A. H.

Contributors

Carolyn Temple Adger is the Director of the Center for Applied Linguistics in Washington, D.C.

Donna Christian is the President of the Board of Trustees of the Center for Applied Linguistics in Washington, D.C.

Harvey A. "Smokey" Daniels is currently a professor at the Center for City Schools at National-Louis University in Chicago. He directs the Best Practice Network as well as the Walloon Institute summer seminar.

Dana Ferris is a professor of English and the coordinator of the ESL program at California State University in Sacramento.

Robert Funk is retired from the English department at Eastern Illinois University.

Julie Hagemann directs the Academic Support Center at DeVry University DuPage in Addison, Illinois.

Martha Kolln is professor emeritus of English at Pennsylvania State University.

Carol McNally is a literacy specialist at Springfield Middle School in Battle Creek, Michigan.

Sharon Moerman is an eighth-grade teacher at Watervliet, Michigan, Middle School.

Rei R. Noguchi is currently a professor at California State University in Northridge, where he teaches classes in linguistics and the applications of linguistics to writing.

Nancy G. Patterson is a Portland, Michigan, middle school teacher.

Lois Matz Rosen is currently Professor of English and Director of the Thompson Center for Learning and Teaching at the University of Michigan–Flint.

Richard Straub is currently an associate professor of English at Florida State University.

Constance Weaver is a professor at Western Michigan University, where she teaches courses in English education and linguistics.

Walt Wolfram is William C. Friday Distinguished Professor of English at North Carolina State University where he researches the dialects of North Carolina under the aegis of the North Carolina Language and Life Project.

List of Figures

Part I

Debating the Grammar Curriculum

One of the most controversial school subjects is grammar, and the stakeholders in the debate are many and varied: English language arts teachers and students, linguists and rhetoricians, and the general public. The three chapters in this section explore this debate. They address the following questions:

- What is grammar? What do various stakeholders generally mean when they use the term *grammar?*
- How should grammar be taught? Is the *traditional* or *formal* grammar approach that most of us are familiar with the best one? If not, then which other approach(es) is(are) better and why?

1

Defining Grammar

We know the goal: To help students learn to use their spoken, written, and visual language knowledgeably, reflectively, creatively, and critically to achieve their own purposes and to participate fully in a number of different language communities. This is a summary of the goals described in the Standards for the English Language Arts (National Council of Teachers of English [NCTE], 1996b) and the ESL Standards for Pre-K–12 Students (Teachers of English to Speakers of Other Languages [TESOL], 1997).

We know whom we want to help students achieve this goal: teachers who recognize, value, and draw on the diverse linguistic and communicative competencies of their students; who understand the integral part that language and literacy play in students' lives; and who are skillful at creating opportunities for growth in themselves and their students. This is the profile described in Guidelines for the Preparation of Teachers of English Language Arts (NCTE, 1996a).

What we can't seem to agree on is a curriculum to achieve this goal. Whole language or phonics. Writing process or written product. Standard English or Ebonics. Bilingual education or English language immersion. The English language arts curriculum is passionately debated in the public sphere as perhaps no other school subject is.

One of the most controversial elements in this debate is grammar. How does it contribute to our goal of lifelong readers and writers? Should we teach it? If so, what should we teach? And why? We can't even agree on what it is. The stakeholders in this debate—English language arts teachers, linguists, the general public—can't agree—either among themselves or with each other.

Defining Grammar

The debate about grammar begins at the level of basic definition. Linguists, English language arts teachers, and the general public tend to have different ideas in mind when they use the word *grammar*. Members of the same field may even have different ideas. These different definitions are teased out by Patrick Hartwell (1985) in his now classic article "Grammar, Grammars, and the Teaching of Grammar."

Hartwell begins with what is perhaps the broadest definition of grammar. What he labels Grammar 1 is the internal set of rules of the language shared by its speakers. These rules—which tell speakers how to pronounce syllables (phonology), how to form words (morphology), how to structure sentences (syntax), and what style of language to use in a given context (pragmatics)—are generally absorbed by children from the language community(ies) they're raised in. These rules are so intuitive that it's hard for speakers to articulate them or even to be aware they're using them. You yourself may have been in a situation in which you know something is ungrammatical—it sounds "funny" or "awkward" or "wrong" to you—but you can't say why. Your grammatical judgment is at work, but you can't articulate the rules it's based on. Or you may feel you learned more about English grammar in your foreign language classes than you did in English classes. This is because most adolescents and adults learn a second language consciously through the use of rules. When you learned the rules of another language, you became more conscious of the rules of your first.

A conscious attempt to articulate the rules native speakers know intuitively is the definition of Hartwell's Grammar 2. The field of English linguistics is based on professionals who systematically and scientifically attempt to describe English—to articulate what native speakers actually say. In some ways, this definition is narrower than the first. Individuals know so much more about language, about how and why it works, than linguists can put into words. In other ways, it's broader. The field of linguistics as a whole knows more about language than any one individual does.

As with all descriptive systems, the framework that linguists use has an impact on the resulting description. While linguists have adhered to various theoretical positions in the last century, there have been several important challenges to traditional grammar: among them, structuralism and transformational-generative grammar. It has also been challenged by sociolinguistics.

The purposes of traditional grammar evolved over the centuries. At first, traditional grammar was used mainly to prepare students to study Latin, the language of instruction in medieval and Renaissance universities. Later it was used to help standardize a language emerging as a national and international force. Scholars looked to the literary masters and classical grammarians to determine the rules of English. What developed was a prescription for writing formal Standard English.

Structuralist linguistics and transformational-generative grammar, on the other hand, are two branches of linguistics developed in the twentieth century to challenge traditional grammar. Both systems are descriptive in nature, looking to the speech of ordinary people to determine the rules of English. Structuralists focus on creating a more accurate depiction of the structure of English, while transformational-generative grammarians seek to understand people's biological abilities to learn language. What developed was a description of how natives speak English.

Sociolinguistics adds a sociocultural dimension to the description (Spolsky, 1998). Coming of age thirty or more years ago, sociolinguistics explores the relationship between language use and the society(ies) language users live in. It seeks to discover how natives speak in a variety of contexts using a variety of dialects of English.

Grammar 2's contribution to the theoretical foundation of the English language arts is vast, but its contribution to school curriculum is mixed. Because of its pedagogical focus, traditional grammar is firmly entrenched in schools. But because neither structuralist linguistics nor transformational-generative grammar has an overtly pedagogical focus, neither has had much impact in the schools. Sociolinguists have perhaps made more in-roads because there has been an increasing interest in raising awareness of the sociolinguistic factors that influence students' language and their degree of success in school (See Chapters 3, 9, and 10).

Nevertheless, a narrow view of grammar is still often presented in schools. This is Hartwell's Grammar 3, and it's the grammar that usually comes to mind when the general public hears the term. For most of us, grammar is the decontextualized study of the seven (or eight) parts of speech and the four kinds of sentences. You may remember middle school work sheets in which you underlined nouns and circled verbs. You also may have parsed or diagrammed sentences. People usually have a love–hate relationship with this kind of study. They seldom remember it with fondness—they found the grammar terminology off-putting, the lessons boring, the diagrams confusing, the whole enterprise vastly different from their normal use of language—and yet they often insist that the next generation have such classes. They believe these classes will help students improve their speaking and writing abilities.

Often taught alongside Grammar 3 is Grammar 4, which some call *usage*. While Grammar 3 is analytical—focused on identifying and labeling the parts of language—Grammar 4 is prescriptive—focused on determining what people should say to speak "proper English." By implication, those who fail to follow this linguistic etiquette are held in low esteem.

But as entrenched as Grammars 3 and 4 are in the schools, they nevertheless have their challengers. For decades, English language arts teachers have known that traditional grammar instruction has little impact on students' writing and speaking abilities (Braddock, Lloyd-Jones, & Schoer, 1963; Weaver, 1996). Nor does it, we've recently come to realize, do much to motivate vernacular English speakers to learn Standard English (Wolfram, Adger, & Christian, 1999). And yet, English language arts teachers continue to teach it, in part because they can't agree on what kind of curriculum should take its place (Lester, 2001a). (See Chapters 2 and 3 for more about the challenge to traditional grammar.)

However, an increasingly influential group of teachers and applied (socio)linguists employs grammar as a vocabulary for metalinguistic discussions of language in general and writing in particular (Kolln, 1996; Weaver, 1996). This is Hartwell's Grammar 5. For these teacher-scholars, grammar is a way to talk to writers about purpose, audience, and style. Grammar can be used to generate content, to revise paragraphs, to edit sentences. It draws on the intuitions of writers (Grammar 1) and the insights of linguistics (Grammar 2). It values a range of genres, styles, and dialects. (See Chapters 4 through 10 for a discussion of grammar from the point of view of developing writers.)

Hartwell's five definitions of grammar are summarized in Figure 1.1.

This chapter explores these various definitions as well as the positions of the various stakeholders in the debate about grammar in a number of ways. First, in the reading for this chapter, Harvey Daniels lays out some fundamental beliefs of linguists about what language is, how it works, and how children learn it. Second, the survey about grammar and language attitudes you're asked to take yourself will give you some insight into what (preservice) teaching professionals believe. (Chapters 2 and 3 will further explore positions held by English language arts teachers.) This survey will also help you understand what the general public believes. Third, the questions at the end of this chapter ask you to research some of the opinions of conservative and liberal syndicated columnists available on the Internet, also giving you some sense of the general public's views of language. Because traditional grammar is generally the status quo, each of these positions reacts explicitly or implicitly to traditional grammar.

FIGURE 1.1   *Theoretical Foundation: Hartwell's Five Definitions of Grammar*

Hartwell (1985) identifies five different definitions of grammar used in the debate about what language structures and conventions to teach in school.

1. The set of rules of a language known intuitively by its speakers—native speaker grammatical competence.
2. The scientific and systematic attempt to describe Grammar 1—the field of linguistics.
3. The rules of the language taught in schools—in the case of English, these rules tend to be drawn from masterfully written literary texts, so they tend to reflect the formal, written, standard version of English.
4. An emphasis on discrete rules, usually elements about which the rules of Standard English and vernacular dialects disagree—often called usage by teachers; the general public usually sees the standard version as "correct" or "proper" while the vernacular is seen as "wrong," "vulgar," or "uneducated"; often derided by linguists as "linguistic etiquette."
5. Terms used to identify sentence structures, often used to create a common vocabulary for talking about writing and its aesthetic and persuasive effects on the reader—often called style.

Exploring Your Own Language Experience

1. Before you begin the reading, spend five minutes or so writing in your journal about the following:

   a. What do you already know about the teaching of grammar? Where did you acquire this knowledge?

   b. How can the study of linguistics and writing help you to be a better teacher of grammar?

2. Our beliefs about curriculum tend to reflect our attitudes about the subject matter, so it's important to be conscious of what we believe. Figure 1.2 presents several statements about grammar. Rate how strongly you agree or disagree with each one. Then answer the questions that follow. In general, what are your feelings about grammar? Do you feel it's an important subject? Why?/Why not? Do you feel that correcting grammar is an important part of the job of an English language arts teacher?

FIGURE 1.2   *Survey: Survey of Beliefs about Grammar and Grammar Teaching*

Please complete the following survey about your beliefs about grammar and grammar teaching. Your responses will be anonymous. They'll be used by students studying to be English language art teachers to learn about the general public's feelings about grammar. Please also include some general information about yourself. Thank you.

How old are you? _____   Are you _____ Male or _____ Female?
Which language(s) do you speak/write? _____
How many years of schooling have you had? _____
Have you taken any linguistics classes? _____ No _____ Yes. How many? _____
How confident do you feel about your grammar? your writing skills?

What do you think most contributed to your knowledge of grammar?

1. Children should be taught grammar in school because that's how they learn to speak/write correctly.

                    strongly agree | | | | | strongly disagree

   Comments:

FIGURE 1.2   *Continued*

2. The version of English used in school (i.e., Standard English) is the only proper dialect of English. Other versions of English use "bad grammar"—they're "slang" or "street talk" or they're incorrect and ungrammatical.

strongly agree | | | | | | strongly disagree

Comments:

3. These inferior versions of English shouldn't be allowed in the classroom.

strongly agree | | | | | | strongly disagree

Comments:

4. There's a right way to speak/write, and you can find out what it is by consulting dictionaries, handbooks, grammar books, etc.

strongly agree | | | | | | strongly disagree

Comments:

5. The English language is in decline. Today's young people don't speak/write as grammatically as previous generations did.

strongly agree | | | | | | strongly disagree

Comments:

6. It's the job of English and language arts teachers to teach students correct English.

strongly agree | | | | | | strongly disagree

(continued)

FIGURE 1.2   *Continued*

Comments:

7. Teachers should correct students who learn bad grammar at home.

strongly agree | | | | | strongly disagree

Comments:

8. What is grammar?

9. Give some examples of "good" grammar and of "bad" grammar.

10. What are some characteristics of good writing? What connection do you see between grammar and good writing?

11. How much grammar should the average person know?

12. Should grammar be taught in school? Why? Should it be a required subject for everyone?

---

3. Give the same survey to at least four other people. Try to aim for a wide range of respondents. Based on your—admittedly small, admittedly un-scientific—survey, what conclusions can you draw about the general public's attitudes toward grammar?

Nine Ideas about Language

Harvey A. Daniels

> In "Nine Ideas about Language," Harvey A. "Smokey" Daniels presents nine fundamental ideas about language that modern linguists generally agree on. His purpose in writing this chapter is to

dispel many language myths held by the general public. This reading is adapted from Daniels' book Famous Last Words: The American Language Crisis Reconsidered *(1983, Southern Illinois Press).*

Assuming we agree that the English language has in fact survived all of the predictions of doom which occupy the previous chapter, we also have reason to believe that current reports of the death of our language are similarly exaggerated. The managers of the present crisis of course disagree, and their efforts may even result in the reinstatement of the linguistic loyalty oath of the 1920s or of some updated equivalent ("I promise to use good American unsplit infinitives") in our schools. But it won't make much difference. The English language, if history is any guide at all, will remain useful and vibrant as long as it is spoken, whether we eagerly try to tend and nurture and prune its growth or if we just leave it alone.

Language critics today recognize that language is changing, that people use a lot of jargon, that few people consistently speak the standard dialect, that much writing done in our society is ineffective, and so forth—but they have no other way of viewing these phenomena except with alarm. But most of the uses of and apparent changes in language which worry the critics *can* be explained and understood in unalarming ways. Such explanations have been provided by linguists during the past seventy-five years.

I have said that in order to understand the errors and misrepresentations of the language critics, we need to examine not only history but also "the facts." Of course, facts about language are a somewhat elusive commodity, and we may never be able to answer all of our questions about this wonderfully complex activity. But linguists have made a good start during this century toward describing some of the basic features, structures, and operations of human speech. This chapter presents a series of nine fundamental ideas about language that form, if not exactly a list of facts, at least a fair summary of the consensus of most linguistic scholars.

1. *Children learn their native language swiftly, efficiently, and largely without instruction.*

Language is a species-specific trait of human beings. All children, unless they are severely retarded or completely deprived of exposure to speech, will acquire their oral language as naturally as they learn to walk. Many linguists even assert that the human brain is prewired for language, and some have also postulated that the underlying linguistic features which are common to all languages are present in the brain at birth. This latter theory comes from the discovery that all languages have certain procedures in common: ways of making statements, questions, and commands; ways of referring to past time; the ability to negate, and so on.[1] In spite of the underlying similarities of all languages, though, it is important to remember that children will acquire the language which they hear around them—whether that is Ukrainian, Swahili, Cantonese, or Appalachian American English.

In spite of the common-sense notions of parents, they do not "teach" their children to talk. Children *learn* to talk, using the language of their parents, siblings, friends, and others as sources and examples—and by using other speakers as testing devices for their own emerging ideas about language. When we acknowledge the complexity of adult speech, with its ability to generate an unlimited number of new, meaningful utterances, it is clear that this skill cannot be the end result of simple instruction. Parents do not explain to their children, for example, that adjectives generally precede the noun in English, nor do they lecture them on the rules governing formation of the past participle. While parents do correct some kinds of mistakes on a piecemeal basis, discovering the underlying rules which make up the language is the child's job.

From what we know, children appear to learn language partly by imitation but even more by hypothesis-testing. Consider a child who is just beginning to form past tenses. In the earliest efforts, the child is likely to produce such incorrect and unheard forms as *I goed to the store or I seed a dog*, along with other conventional uses of the past tense: *I walked to Grandma's*. This process reveals that the child has learned the basic, general rule about the formation of the past tense—you add *-ed* to the verb—but has not yet mastered the other rules, the exceptions and irregularities. The production of forms that the child has never heard suggests that imitation is not central in language learning and that the child's main strategy is hypothesizing—deducing from the language she hears an idea about the underlying rule, and then trying it out.

My own son, who is now two and one-half, has just been working on the *-ed* problem. Until recently, he used present tense verb forms for all situations: *Daddy go work?* (for: *Did Daddy go to work?*) and *We take a bath today?* (for: *Will we take a bath today?*) Once he discovered that wonderful past tag, he attached it with gusto to any verb he could think up and produced, predictably enough, *goed, eated, flied*, and many other overgeneralizations of his initial hypothetical rule for the formation of past tenses. He was so excited about his new discovery, in fact, that he would often give extra emphasis to the marker: *Dad, I swallow-ed the cookie*. Nicky will soon learn to deemphasize the sound of *-ed* (as well as to master all those irregular past forms) by listening to more language and by revising and expanding his own internal set of language rules.

Linguists and educators sometimes debate about what percentage of adult forms is learned by a given age. A common estimate is that 90 percent of adult structures are acquired by the time a child is seven. Obviously, it is quite difficult to attach proportions to such a complex process, but the central point is clear: schoolchildren of primary age have already learned the great majority of the rules governing their native language, and can produce virtually all the kinds of sentences that it permits. With the passing years, all children will add some additional capabilities, but the main growth from this point forward will not so much be in acquiring new rules as in using new combinations of them to express increasingly sophisticated ideas, and in learning how to use language effectively in a widening variety of social settings.

It is important to reiterate that we are talking here about the child's acquisition of her native language. It may be that the child has been born into a community of standard English or French or Urdu speakers, or into a community of nonstandard English, French or Urdu speakers. But the language of the child's home and community is the native language, and it would be impossible for her to somehow grow up speaking a language to which she was never, or rarely, exposed.

2. Language operates by rules.
As the *-ed* saga suggests, when a child begins learning his native language, what he is doing is acquiring a vast system of mostly subconscious rules which allow him to make meaningful and increasingly complex utterances. These rules concern sounds, words, the arrangement of strings of words, and aspects of the social act of speaking. Obviously,

children who grow up speaking different languages will acquire generally different sets of rules. This fact reminds us that human language is, in an important sense, arbitrary.

Except for a few onomatopoetic words (*bang, hiss, grunt*), the assignment of meanings to certain combinations of sounds is arbitrary. We English speakers might just as well call a chair a *glotz* or a *blurg*, as long as we all agreed that these combinations of sounds meant *chair*. In fact, not just the words but the individual sounds used in English have been arbitrarily selected from a much larger inventory of sounds which the human vocal organs are capable of producing. The existence of African languages employing musical tones or clicks reminds us that the forty phonemes used in English represent an arbitrary selection from hundreds of available sounds. Grammar, too, is arbitrary. We have a rule in English which requires most adjectives to appear before the noun which they modify (*the blue chair*). In French, the syntax is reversed (*la chaise bleue*), and in some languages, like Latin, either order is allowed.

Given that any language requires a complex set of arbitrary choices regarding sounds, words, and syntax, it is clear that the foundation of a language lies not in any "natural" meaning or appropriateness of its features, but in its system of rules—the implicit agreement among speakers that they will use certain sounds consistently, that certain combinations of sounds will mean the same thing over and over, and that they will observe certain grammatical patterns in order to convey messages. It takes thousands of such rules to make up a language. Many linguists believe that when each of us learned these countless rules, as very young children, we accomplished the most complex cognitive task of our lives.

Our agreement about the rules of language, of course, is only a general one. Every speaker of a language is unique; no one sounds exactly like anyone else. The language differs from region to region, between social, occupational and ethnic groups, and even from one speech situation to the next. These variations are not mistakes or deviations from some basic tongue, but are simply the rule-governed alternatives which make up any language. Still, in America our assorted variations of English are mostly mutually intelligible, reflecting the fact that most of our language rules do overlap, whatever group we belong to, or whatever situation we are in.

3. All languages have three major components: a sound system, a vocabulary, and a system of grammar.

This statement underscores what has already been suggested: that any human speaker makes meaning by manipulating sounds, words, and their order according to an internalized system of rules which other speakers of that language largely share.

The sound system of a language—its phonology—is the inventory of vocal noises, and combinations of noises, that it employs. Children learn the selected sounds of their own language in the same way they learn the other elements: by listening, hypothesizing, testing, and listening again. They do not, though it may seem logical, learn the sounds first (after all, English has only forty) and then go on to words and then to grammar. My son, for example, can say nearly anything he needs to say, in sentences of eight or ten or fourteen words, but he couldn't utter the sound of *th* to save his life.

The vocabulary, or lexicon, of a language is the individual's storehouse of words. Obviously, one of the young child's most conspicuous efforts is aimed at expanding his lexical inventory. Two and three-year-olds are notorious for asking "What's that?" a good deal more often than even the most doting parents can tolerate. And not only do children constantly and spontaneously try to enlarge their vocabularies, but they are always working to build categories, to establish classes of words, to add connotative meanings, to hone and refine their sense of the semantic properties—the meanings—of the words they are learning. My awareness of these latter processes was heightened a few months ago as we were driving home from a trip in the country during which Nicky had delighted in learning the names of various features of the rural landscape. As we drove past the Chicago skyline Nicky looked up at the tall buildings and announced "Look at those silos, Dad!" I asked him what he thought they kept in the Sears Tower, and he replied confidently, "Animal food." His parents' laughter presumably helped him to begin reevaluating his lexical hypothesis that any tall narrow structure was a silo.

Linguists, who look at language descriptively rather than prescriptively, have different definitions of *grammar*—and unfortunately there are two main ones. The first, which I am using, says that grammar is the system of rules we use to arrange words into meaningful English sentences. For example, my lexicon and my phonology may provide me with the appropriate strings of sounds to say the words: *eat four yesterday cat crocodile the*. It is my knowledge of grammar which allows me to arrange these elements into a sentence: *Yesterday the crocodile ate four cats*. Not only does my grammar arrange these elements in a meaningful order, it also provides me with the necessary markers of plurality, tense, and agreement. Explaining the series of rules by which I subconsciously constructed this sentence describes some of my "grammar" in this sense.

The second definition of *grammar* often used by linguists refers to the whole system of rules which makes up a language—not just the rules for the arrangement and appropriate marking of elements in a sentence, but all of the lexical, phonological, and syntactic patterns which a language uses. In this sense, *everything* I know about my language, all the conscious and unconscious operations I can perform when speaking or listening, constitutes my grammar. It is this second definition of grammar to which linguists sometimes refer when they speak of describing a language in terms of its grammar.

4. Everyone speaks a dialect.

Among linguists the term *dialect* does not have the pejorative connotation which it retains in general use. It simply designates a variety of a particular language which has a certain set of lexical, phonological, and grammatical rules that distinguish it from other dialects. The most familiar definition of dialects in America is geographical: we recognize, for example, that some features of New England language—the dropping r's (*pahk the cah in Hahvahd yahd*) and the use of *bubbler* for *drinking fountain*—distinguish the speech of this region. The native speaker of Bostonian English is not making mistakes, of course; he or she simply observes systematic rules which happen to differ from those observed in other regions.

Where do these different varieties of a language come from and how are they maintained? The underlying factors are isolation and language change. Imagine a group of people which lives, works, and talks together constantly. Among them, there is a good deal of natural pressure to keep the language relatively uniform. But if one part of the group moves away to a remote location, and has no further contact with the other, the language of the two groups will gradually diverge. This will happen not just because of the differing needs of the two different environments, but also because of the inexorable and sometimes arbitrary process of language change itself. In other words, there is no likelihood that the language of these two groups, though identical at the beginning, will now change in the same ways. Ultimately, if the isolation is lengthy and complete, the two hypothetical groups will probably develop separate, mutually unintelligible languages. If the isolation is only partial, if interchange occurs between the two groups, and if they have some need to continue communicating (as with the American and British peoples) less divergence will occur.

This same principle of isolation also applies, in a less dramatic way, to contemporary American dialects. New England speakers are partially isolated from southern speakers, and so some of the differences between these two dialects are maintained. Other factors, such as travel and the mass media, bring them into contact with each other and tend to prevent drastic divergences. But the isolation that produces or maintains language differences may not be only geographical. In many American cities we find people living within miles, or even blocks of each other who speak markedly different and quite enduring dialects. Black English and mid-western English are examples of such pairs. Here, the isolation is partially spatial, but more importantly it is social, economic, occupational, educational, and political. And as long as this effective separation of speech communities persists, so will the differences in their dialects.

Many of the world's languages have a "standard" dialect. In some countries, the term *standard* refers more to a *lingua franca* than to an indigenous dialect. In Nigeria, for example, where there are more than 150 mostly mutually unintelligible languages and dialects, English was selected as the official standard. In America, we enjoy this kind of national standardization because the vast majority of us speak some mutually intelligible dialect of English. But we also have ideas about a standard English which is not just a *lingua franca* but a prestige or preferred dialect. Similarly, the British have Received Pronunciation, the Germans have High German, and the French, backed by the authority of the Académie Française, have "Le Vrai Français." These languages are typically defined as the speech of the upper, or at least educated, classes of the society, are the predominant dialect of written communication, and are commonly taught to schoolchildren. In the past, these prestige dialects have sometimes been markers which conveniently set the ruling classes apart from the rabble—as once was the case with Mandarin Chinese or in medieval times when the English aristocracy adopted Norman French. But in most modern societies the standard dialect is a mutually intelligible version of the country's common tongue which is accorded a special status.

A standard dialect is not *inherently* superior to any other dialect of the same language. It may, however, confer considerable social, political, and economic power on its users, because of prevailing attitudes about the dialect's worthiness.

Recently, American linguists have been working to describe some of the nonstandard dialects of English, and we now seem to have a better description of some of these dialects than of our shadowy standard. Black English is a case in point. The most important finding of all this research has been that Black English is just as "logical" and "ordered" as any other English dialect, in spite of the fact that it is commonly viewed by white speakers as being somehow inferior, deformed, or limited.

5. Speakers of all languages employ a range of styles and a set of subdialects or jargons.

Just as soon as we get past the often unappetizing notion that we all speak a dialect, it is necessary to complicate things further. We may realize that we do belong to a speech community, although we may not like to call it a dialect, but we often forget that our speech patterns vary greatly during the course of our everyday routine. In the morning, at home, communication with our spouses may consist of grumbled fragments of a private code:

Uhhh.
Yeah.
More?
Um-hmm.
You gonna . . . ?
Yeah, if . . .
'Kay

Yet half an hour later, we may be standing in a meeting and talking quite differently: "The cost-effectiveness curve of the Peoria facility has declined to the point at which management is compelled to consider terminating production." These two samples of speech suggest that we constantly range between formal and informal styles of speech—and this is an adjustment which speakers of all languages constantly make. Learning the sociolinguistic rules which tell us what sort of speech is appropriate in differing social situations is as much a part of language acquisition as learning how to produce the sound of /b/ or /t/. We talk differently to our acquaintances than to strangers, differently to our bosses than to our subordinates, differently to children than adults. We speak in one way on the racquetball court and in another way in the courtroom; we perhaps talk differently to stewardesses than to stewards.

The ability to adjust our language forms to the social context is something which we acquire as children, along with sounds, words, and syntax. We learn, in other words, not just to say things, but also how and when and to whom. Children discover, for example, that while the purpose of most language is to communicate meaning (if it weren't they could never learn it in the first place) we sometimes use words as mere acknowledgements (Hi. How are you doing? Fine. Bye.). Youngsters also learn that to get what you want, you have to address people as your social relation with them dictates (Miss Jones, may I please feed the hamster today?). And, of course, children learn that in some situations one doesn't use certain words at all—though such learning may sometimes seem cruelly delayed to parents whose offspring loudly announce in restaurants: "I hafta go toilet!"

Interestingly, these sociolinguistic rules are learned quite late in the game. While a child of seven or eight does command a remarkably sophisticated array of sentence types, for example, he has a great deal left to learn about the social regulations governing language use. This seems logical, given that children *do* learn language mostly by listening and experimenting. Only as a child grows old enough to encounter a widening range of social relationships and roles will he have the experience necessary to help him discover the sociolinguistic dimensions of them.

While there are many ways of describing the different styles, or registers, of language which all speakers learn, it is helpful to consider them in terms of levels of formality. One well-known example of such a scheme was developed by Martin Joos, who posited five basic styles, which he called *intimate, casual, consultative, formal,* and *frozen.*[2] While Joos's model is only one of many attempts to find a scale for the range of human speech styles, and is certainly not the final word on the subject, it does illuminate some of the ways in which day-to-day language varies. At the bottom of Joos's model is the *intimate* style, a kind of language which "fuses two separate personalities" and can only occur between individuals with a close personal relationship. A husband and wife, for example, may sometimes speak to each other in what sounds like a very fragmentary and clipped code that they alone understand. Such utterances are characterized by their "extraction"—the use of extracts of potentially complete sentences, made possible by an intricate, personal, shared system of private symbols. The *intimate* style, in sum, is personal, fragmentary, and implicit.

The *casual* style also depends on social groupings. When people share understandings and meanings which are not complete enough to be called intimate, they tend to employ the *casual* style. The earmarks of this pattern are ellipsis and slang. Ellipsis is the shorthand of shared meaning; slang often expresses these meanings in a way that defines the group and excludes others. The *casual* style is reserved for friends and insiders, or those whom we choose to make friends and insiders. The *consultative* style "produces cooperation without the integration, profiting from the lack of it."[3] In this style, the speaker provides more explicit background information because the listener may not understand without it. This is the style used by strangers or near-strangers in routine transactions: co-workers dealing with a problem, a buyer making a purchase from a clerk, and so forth. An important feature of this style is the participation of the listener, who uses frequent interjections such as *Yeah, Uh-huh* or *I see* to signal understanding.

This element of listener participation disappears in the *formal* style. Speech in this mode is defined by the listener's lack of participation, as well as by the speaker's opportunity to plan his utterances ahead of time and in detail. The *formal* style is most often found in speeches, lectures, sermons, television newscasts, and the like. The *frozen* style is reserved for *print*, and particularly for literature. This style can be densely packed and repacked with meanings by its "speaker," and it can be read and reread by its "listener." The immediacy of interaction between the participants is sacrificed in the interests of permanance, elegance, and precision.

Whether or not we accept Joos's scheme to classify the different gradations of formality, we can probably sense the truth of the basic proposition: we do make such adjustments in our speech constantly, mostly unconsciously, and in response to the social situation in which we are speaking. What we sometimes forget is that no one style can accurately be called better or worse than another, apart from the context in which it is used. Though we have much reverence for the formal and frozen styles, they can be utterly dysfunctional in certain circumstances. If I said to my wife: "Let us consider the possibility of driving our automobile into the central business district of Chicago in order to contemplate the possible purchase of denim trousers," she would certainly find my way of speaking strange, if not positively disturbing. All of us need to shift between the intimate, casual, and consultative styles in everyday life, not because one or another of these is a better way of talking, but because each is required in certain contexts. Many of us also need to master the formal style for the talking and writing demanded by our jobs. But as Joos has pointed out, few of us actually need to control the frozen style, which is reserved primarily for literature.[4]

Besides having a range of speech styles, each speaker also uses a number of jargons based upon his or her affiliation with certain groups. The most familiar of these jargons are occupational: doctors, lawyers, accountants, farmers, electricians, plumbers, truckers, and social workers each have a job-related jargon into which they can shift when the situation demands it. Sometimes these special languages are a source of amusement or consternation to outsiders, but usually the outsiders also speak jargons of their own, though they may not recognize them. Jargons may also be based on other kinds of affiliations. Teenagers, it is often remarked by bemused parents, have a language of their own. So they do, and so do other age groups. Some of the games and chants of youngsters reflect a kind of childhood dialect, and much older persons may have a jargon of their own as well, reflecting concerns with aging, illness, and finances. Sports fans obviously use and understand various abstruse athletic terms, while people interested in needlecrafts use words that are equally impenetrable to the uninitiated. For every human enterprise we can think of, there will probably be a jargon attached to it.

But simply noting that all speakers control a range of styles and a set of jargons does not tell the whole story. For every time we speak, we do so not just in a social context, but for certain purposes of our own. When talking with a dialectologist, for example, I may use linguistic jargon simply to facilitate our sharing of information, or instead to convince him that I know enough technical linguistics to be taken seriously—or both. In other words, my purposes—the functions of my language—affect the way I talk. The British linguist M. A. K. Halliday has studied children in an attempt to determine how people's varying purposes affect their speech.[5] Halliday *had* to consider children, in fact, because the purposes of any given adult utterance are usually so complex and overlapping that it is extremely difficult to isolate the individual purposes. By examining the relatively simpler language of children, he was able to discover seven main uses, functions, or purposes for talking: *instrumental, regulatory, interactional, personal, heuristic, imaginative, and representational.*

The *instrumental* function, Halliday explains, is for getting things done; it is the *I want* function. Close to it is the *regulatory* function, which seeks to control the actions of others around the speaker. The *interactional* function is used to define groups and relationships, to get along with others. The *personal* function allows people to express what they are and how they feel; Halliday calls this the *here I come* function. The *heuristic* function is in operation when the speaker is using language to learn, by asking questions and testing hypotheses. In the *imaginative* function, a speaker may use language to create a world just as he or she wants it, or may simply use it as a toy, making amusing combinations of sounds and words. In the *representational* function, the speaker uses language to express propositions, give information, or communicate subject matter.

Absent from Halliday's list of functions, interestingly, is one of the most common and enduring purposes of human language: lying. Perhaps lying could be included in the representational or interactional functions, in the sense that a person may deceive in order to be a more congenial companion. Or perhaps each of Halliday's seven functions could be assigned a reverse, false version. In any case, common sense, human history, and our own experience all tell us that lying—or misleading or covering up or shading the truth—is one of the main ends to which language is put.

As we look back over these three forms of language variation—styles, jargons, and functions—we may well marvel at the astounding complexity of language. For not only do all speakers master the intricate sound, lexical, and grammatical patterns of their native tongue, but they also learn countless, systematic alternative ways of applying their linguistic knowledge to varying situations and needs. We are reminded, in short, that language is as beautifully varied, and fascinating as the creatures who use it.

6. Language change is normal.

This fact, while often acknowledged by critics of contemporary English, has rarely been fully understood or accepted by them. It is easy enough to welcome into the language such innocent neologisms as *astronaut, transistor, or jet lag.* These terms serve obvious needs, responding to certain changes in society which virtually require them. But language also changes in many ways that don't seem so logical or necessary. The dreaded dangling *hopefully*, which now attaches itself to the beginning of sentences with the meaning *I hope*, appears to be driving out the connotation *full of hope*. As Jean Stafford has angrily pointed out, the word *relevant* has broadened to denote almost any kind of "with-it-ness." But these kinds of lexical changes are not new, and simply demonstrate an age-old process at work in the present. The word *dog* (actually, *dogge*), for example, used to refer to one specific breed, but now serves as a general term for a quite varied family of animals. Perhaps similarly, *dialogue* has now broadened to include exchanges of views between (or among) any number of speakers. But word meanings can also narrow over time, as the word *deer* shrank from indicating any game animal to just one specific type.

The sounds of language also change, though usually in slower and less noticeable ways than vocabulary. Perhaps fifty years ago, the majority of American speakers produced distinctly different consonant sounds in the middle of *latter* and *ladder*. Today, most younger people and many adults pronounce the two words as if they were the same. Another sound change in progress is the weakening distinction between the vowels *dawn* and *Don*, or *hawk* and *hock*. Taking the longer view, of course, we realize that modern pronunciation is the product of centuries of gradual sound changes.

Shifts in grammar are more comparable to the slow process of sound change than the sometimes sudden one of lexical change. Today we find that the *shall/will* distinction, which is still maintained among some upper class Britishers, has effectively disappeared from spoken American English. A similar fate seems to await the *who/whom* contrast, which is upheld by fewer and fewer speakers. Our pronouns, as a matter of fact, seem to be a quite volatile corner of our grammar. In spite of the efforts of teachers, textbooks, style manuals, and the SAT tests, most American speakers now find nothing wrong with *Everyone should bring their books to class* or even *John and me went to the Cubs game*. And even the hoary old double negative (which is an obligatory feature of degraded tongues like French) seems to be making steady, if slow progress. We may be only a generation or two from the day when we will again say, with Shakespeare, "I will not budge for no man's pleasure."

While we may recognize that language does inexorably change, we cannot always explain the causes or the sequences of each individual change. Sometimes changes move toward simplification, as with the shedding of vowel distinctions. Other changes tend to regularize the language, as when we de-Latinize words like *medium/media* (The newspapers are one media of communication), or when we abandon *dreamt* and *burnt* in favor of the regular forms *dreamed* and *burned*. And some coinages will always reflect the need to represent new inventions, ideas, or events: *quark, simulcast, pulsar, stagflation*. Yet there is plenty of language change which seems to happen spontaneously, sporadically, and without apparent purpose. Why should *irregardless* substitute for *regardless*, meaning the same thing? Why should handy distinctions like that between *imply* and *infer* be lost? But even if we can never explain the reasons for such mysterious changes—or perhaps *because* we can't—we must accept the fact that language does change. Today, we would certainly be thought odd to call cattle *kine*, to pronounce *saw* as *saux*, or to ask about "thy health," however ordinary such language might have been centuries ago. Of course, the more recent changes, and especially the changes in progress make us most uncomfortable.

But then our sense of the pace of language change is often exaggerated. When we cringe (as do so many of the language critics) at the sudden reassignment of the word *gay* to a new referent, we tend to forget that we can still read Shakespeare. In other words, even if many conspicuous (and almost invariably lexical) changes are in progress, this doesn't necessarily mean that the language as a whole is undergoing a rapid or wholesale transformation. But once we start looking for language change, it seems to be everywhere, and we are sorely tempted to overestimate its importance. Sometimes we even discover changes which aren't changes at all. Various language critics have propounded the notion that we are being inundated by a host of very new and particularly insidious coinages. Here are some of the most notorious ones, along with the date of their earliest citation in the *Oxford English Dictionary* for the meaning presently viewed as modern and dangerous: *you know* (1350); *anxious* for *eager* (1742); *between you and I* (1640); *super* for *good* (1850); *decimate* for *diminish* by other than one-tenth (1663); *inoperative* for nonmechanical phenomena (1631); *near-perfect* for *nearly perfect* (1635); *host* as in *to host a gathering* (1485); *gifted*, as in *He gifted his associates* (1600); *aggravate* for *annoy* (1611).[6]

If we find ourselves being aggravated (or annoyed) by any of these crotchety old neologisms, we can always look to the Mobil Oil Corporation for a comforting discussion of the problem. In one of its self-serving public service magazine ads, Mobil intoned: "Change upsets people. Always has. Disrupts routine and habit patterns. Demands constant adaptation. But change is inevitable. And essential. Inability to change can be fatal."[7] And Mobil inadvertently gives us one last example of a language change currently in progress: the increasing use of sentence fragments in formal written English.

7. Languages are intimately related to the societies and individuals who use them.

Every human language has been shaped by, and changes to meet, the needs of its speakers. In this limited sense, all human languages can be said to be both equal and perfect.

This does not mean, however, that any given language will work "perfectly" or be "equal" to any other in a cross-cultural setting.

There is a related question concerning the differences between languages. Many linguists have tried to determine the extent to which our native language conditions our thought processes. For all the talk of similarities between languages, there are also some quite remarkable differences from one language to another. The famous studies of American Indian languages by Benjamin Lee Whorf and Edward Sapir have suggested, for example, that Hopi speakers do not conceptualize time in the same way as speakers of English.[8] To the Hopi, time is a continuing process, an unfolding that cannot be segmented into chunks to be used or "wasted." The words and constructions of the Hopi language reflect this perception. Similarly, some languages do not describe the same color spectrum which we speakers of English normally regard as a given physical phenomenon. Some of these name only two, others three, and so on. Are we, then, hopelessly caught in the grasp of the language which we happen to grow up speaking? Are all our ideas about the world controlled by our language, so that our reality is what we *say* rather than what objectively, verifiably exists?

This question becomes especially important when cross-cultural differences in language serve as a basis for social, economic, or political decision making. We may believe that Indians have "no sense of time" and will therefore never make good, punctual employees, however we attempt to train them. Or we may argue that the speech patterns of Eskimos are so alien to the language of modern, industrial societies that these people can never be expected to participate in our environment. The best judgment of linguists on this subject comes down to this: we are conditioned to some degree by the language we speak, and our language does teach us habitual ways of looking at the world. But on the other hand, human adaptability enables us to transcend the limitations of a language—to learn to see the world in new ways and voice new concepts—when we must. While it is probably true that some ideas are easier to communicate in one language than another, both languages and speakers can change to meet new needs. The grip which language has on us is firm, but it does not strangle; we make language more than language makes us.

It is also important to realize that a language is not just an asset of a culture or group, but of individual human beings. Our native language is the speech of our parents, siblings, friends, and community. It is the code we use to communicate in the most powerful and intimate experiences of our lives. It is a central part of our personality, an expression and a mirror of what we are and wish to be. Our language is as personal and as integral to each of us as our bodies and our brains, and in our own unique ways, we all treasure it. And all of us, when we are honest, have to admit that criticism of the way we talk is hard not to take personally. This reaction is nothing to be ashamed of: it is simply a reflection of the natural and profound importance of language to every individual human being.

8. Value judgments about different languages or dialects are matters of taste.

One of the things that we seem to acquire right along with our native tongue is a set of attitudes about the value of other people's language. If we think for a moment about any of the world's major languages, we will find that we usually have some idea—usually a prejudice or stereotype—about it. French is the sweet music of love. German is harsh, martial, overbearing. The language of Spain is exotic, romantic. The Spanish of Latino Americans is alien, uneducated. Scandinavian tongues have a kind of silly rhythm, as the Muppet Show's Swedish chef demonstrates weekly. British English is refined and intelligent. New York dialect (especially on Toity-Toid Street) is crude and loud. Almost all southern American speakers (especially rural sheriffs) are either cruelly crafty or just plain dumb. Oriental languages have a funny, high-pitched, singsong sound. And Black English, well, it just goes to show. None of these notions about different languages and dialects says anything about the way these tongues function in their native speech communities. By definition—by the biological and social order of things—they function efficiently. Each is a fully formed, logical, rule-governed variant of human speech.

It is easy enough to assert that all languages are equal and efficient in their own sphere of use. But most of us do not really believe in this idea, and certainly do not act as if we did. We constantly make judgments about other people and other nations on the basis of the language they use.

Especially when we consider the question of mutually intelligible American dialects, we are able to see that most ideas about language differences are purely matters of taste. It isn't that we cannot understand each other—Southerners, Northerners, Californians, New Yorkers, blacks, whites, Appalachian folk—with only the slightest effort we can communicate just fine. But because of our history of experiences with each other, or perhaps just out of perversity, we have developed prejudices toward other people's language which sometimes affect our behavior. Such prejudices, however irrational, generate much pressure for speakers of disfavored dialects to abandon their native speech for some more approved pattern. But as the linguist Einar Haugen has warned:

> And yet, who are we to call for linguistic genocide in the name of efficiency? Let us recall that although a language is a tool and an instrument of communication, that is not all it is. A language is also a part of one's personality, a form of behavior that has its roots

in our earliest experience. Whether it is a so-called rural or ghetto dialect, or a peasant language, or a "primitive" idiom, it fulfills exactly the same needs and performs the same services in the daily lives of its speakers as does the most advanced language of culture. Every language, dialect, patois, or lingo is a structurally complete framework into which can be poured any subtlety of emotion or thought that its users are capable of experiencing. Whatever it lacks at any given time or place in the way of vocabulary and syntax can be supplied in very short order by borrowing and imitation from other languages. *Any scorn for the language of others is scorn for those who use it, and as such is a form of social discrimination.* [Emphasis mine][9]

It is not Haugen's purpose—nor is it mine—to deny that social acceptability and economic success in America may be linked in certain ways to the mastery of approved patterns of speech. Yet all of us must realize that the need for such mastery arises *only* out of the prejudices of the dominant speech community and not from any intrinsic shortcomings of nonstandard American dialects.

9. *Writing is derivative of speech.*

Writing systems are always based upon systems of oral language which of necessity develop first. People have been talking for at least a half million years, but the earliest known writing system appeared fewer than 5,000 years ago. Of all the world's languages, only about 5 percent have developed indigenous writing systems. In other words, wherever there are human beings, we will always find language, but not necessarily writing. If language is indeed a biologically programmed trait of the species, writing does not seem to be part of the standard equipment.

Although the English writing system is essentially phonemic—an attempt to represent the sounds of language in graphic form—it is notoriously irregular and confusing. Some other languages, like Czech, Finnish, and Spanish, come close to having perfect sound–symbol correspondence: each letter in the writing system stands for one, and only one, sound. English, unfortunately, uses some 2,000 letters and combinations of letters to represent its forty or so separate sounds. This causes problems. For example, in the sentence: *Did he believe that Caesar could see the people seize the seas?* there are seven different spellings for the vowel sound /e/. The sentence: *The silly amoeba stole the key to the machine*, yields four more spellings of the same vowel sound. George Bernard Shaw once noted that a reasonable spelling of the word *fish* might be *ghoti*: *gh* as in *enough*, *o* as in *women*, and *ti* as in *nation*. In spite of all its irregularities, however, the English spelling system is nevertheless phonemic at heart, as our ability to easily read and pronounce nonsense words like *mimsy* or *proat* demonstrates.

Writing, like speech, may be put to a whole range of often overlapping uses. And shifts in the level of formality occur in writing just as they do in talk. An author, like a speaker, must adjust the style of her message to the audience and the occasion. A woman composing a scholarly article, for example, makes some systematically different linguistic choices than those she makes when leaving a note for her husband on the refrigerator. Both writers and speakers (even good ones) employ various jargons or specialized vocabularies that seem comfortable and convenient to the people they are addressing. Rules change with time in both writing and speech. Most obviously, changes in speech habits are reflected in writing: today we readily pen words which weren't even invented ten or a hundred years ago. And even some of the rules which are enforced in writing after they have been abandoned in speech do eventually break down. Today, for example, split infinitives and sentence fragments are increasingly accepted in writing.

Our beliefs about writing are also bound up with our literary tradition. We have come to revere certain works of literature and exposition which have "stood the test of time," which speak across the centuries to successive generations of readers. These masterpieces, like most enduring published writing, tend to employ what Joos would call formal and frozen styles of language. They were written in such language, of course, because their authors had to accommodate the subject, audience, and purpose at hand—and the making of sonnets and declarations of independence generally calls for considerable linguistic formality. Given our affection for these classics, we quite naturally admire not only their content but their form. We find ourselves feeling that only in the nineteenth or sixteenth century could writers "really use the language" correctly and beautifully. Frequently, we teach this notion in our schools, encouraging students to see the language of written literature as the only true and correct style of English. We require students not only to mimic the formal literary style in their writing, but even to transplant certain of its features into their speech—in both cases without reference to the *students'* subject, audience, or purpose. All of this is not meant to demean literature or the cultivation of its appreciation among teenagers. It simply reminds us of how the mere existence of a system of writing and a literature can be a conservative influence on the language. The study, occasionally the official worship, of language forms that are both old and formal may retard linguistic changes currently in progress, as well as reinforce our mistaken belief that one style of language is always and truly the best.

The preceding nine ideas about language are not entirely new. Many of them have been proclaimed by loud, if lonely, voices in centuries long past. It has only been in the last seventy or eighty years, however, that these ideas have begun to form a coherent picture of how language works, thanks to the work of the descriptive and historical linguists. It is their research which has been, I hope, accurately if broadly summarized here.

Our earlier look at the history of past crises offered a general kind of reassurance about the present language panic. It suggested that such spasms of insecurity and intolerance are a regular, cyclical feature of the human chronicle, and result more from social and political tensions than from actual changes in the language. It shows us that our language cannot "die" as long as people speak it; that language change is a healthy and inevitable process; that all human languages are rule governed, ordered, and logical; that variations between different groups of speakers are normal and predictable; that all speakers employ a variety of speech forms and styles in response to changing social settings; and that most of our attitudes about language are based upon social rather than linguistic judgments.

And so, if we are to believe the evidence of historical and linguistic research, our current language crisis seems rather curious. This is a crisis which is not critical, which does not actually pose the dangers widely attributed to it. If anything, the crisis is merely a description of linguistic business as usual, drawn by the critics in rather bizarre and hysterical strokes. It seems fair to ask at this point: What's the problem?

Notes

1. Victoria Fromkin and Robert Rodman, *An Introduction to Language* (New York: Holt, Rinehart and Winston, 1978), pp. 329–42.
2. Martin Joos, *The Five Clocks* (New York: Harcourt, Brace and World, 1962).

3. Ibid., p. 40.

4. Ibid., pp. 39–67.

5. M. A. K. Halliday, *Explorations in the Functions of Language* (London: Edward Arnold, 1973).

6. With many thanks to Jim Quinn and his *American Tongue and Cheek* (New York: Pantheon, 1981).

7. "Business Is Bound to Change," Mobil Oil advertisement, *Chicago Tribune*, January 5, 1977.

8. See Edward Sapir, *Culture, Language, and Personality* (Berkeley: University of California Press, 1949).

9. Einar Haugen, "The Curse of Babel," in Einar Haugen and Morton Bloomfield, *Language as a Human Problem* (New York: W. W. Norton, 1974), p. 41.

Questions for Discussion

1. Daniels wrote this article in order to dispel the "errors and misrepresentations" of the general public about language, and yet, doesn't specifically say what those myths are. Identify as many of the myths Daniels addresses as you can infer. Compare your list to the findings of your class survey of attitudes about grammar. To what extent does Daniels' list compare to yours?

2. How does Daniels define "grammar"? Compare his definition to your definition, the definitions you gathered in your survey, and to Hartwell's definitions. To what extent does it matter how grammar is defined? Why?

3. Compare the answers of your respondents to those of your classmates and their respondents. To what extent is there consensus? Is there a correlation between attitudes and certain variables, such as age, gender, level of school, or linguistic background?

4. Consult the archives of the major newspaper(s) in your area (many are available via the Internet), especially the editorial section. What positions do the paper's editorial writers, columnists (both local and nationally syndicated), and letters to the editors take on issues such as grammar, language arts curriculum, standardized tests, and Ebonics?

2

Challenging Traditional Grammar

According to Mark Lester (2001a), author of *Grammar and Usage in the Classroom*, the state of grammar instruction (Hartwell's Grammar 3 [p. 00]) in American elementary and secondary schools has been in chaos since the 1960s. An influential research report published at that time questioned the value of the grammar curriculum (which has now come to be known as *traditional grammar* or *formal grammar*). Many teachers found the report convincing and were willing to abandon the existing curriculum, but there was no universally accepted curriculum to take its place.

Traditional grammar, or the systematic study of the parts of speech and the kinds of sentences, was developed centuries ago and hasn't changed much in hundreds of years. Perhaps you recognize the grammar instruction you had as a child in Constance Weaver's (1996) description:

> When people talk about "teaching grammar," . . . [t]hey mean teaching grammar as a system, and teaching it directly and systematically, usually in isolation from writing or the study of literature. They mean studying parts of speech and their functions in sentences, various types of phrases and clauses, and different sentence types, perhaps accompanied by sentence diagramming and usually followed by a study of such concepts as subject–verb agreement and pronoun reference. (p. 7)

However, in the 1960s, both the fields of linguistics and English language arts called traditional grammar instruction into question. In 1963, the National Council of Teachers of English (NCTE) issued a report by Richard Braddock, Richard Lloyd-Jones, and Lowell Schoer, in which they stated:

> In view of the widespread agreement of research studies based upon many types of students and teachers, the conclusion can be stated in strong and unqualified terms: the teaching of formal grammar has a negligible or, because it usually displaces some instruction and practice in actual composition, even a harmful effect on the improvement of writing. (p. 37–38)

This report, simply called the Braddock Report, had some impact on teachers, which earlier research reports did not. Thirty years earlier, the Curriculum Commission of the NCTE had recommended that "all teaching of grammar separate from the manipulation of sentences be discontinued . . . since every scientific attempt to prove that knowledge of grammar is useful has failed" (as quoted in Weaver, 1996, p. 9). That report went virtually unheeded as traditional grammar continued to flourish.

Traditional Grammar

Perhaps what made the Braddock Report more influential was that it came at a time when the field of linguistics was openly critical of traditional grammar as well. According to *The Cambridge Encyclopedia of the English Language* (Crystal, 1995), linguists had long been frustrated by the legacy of traditional grammar for two main reasons:

- *Traditional grammar analyzed English sentences using rules based on Latin.* Because English is a Germanic language, the rules didn't always fit well.
- *Traditional grammar insisted that only certain styles—formal, written, literary Standard English—were worth studying.* This excluded a great many of the contexts in which English was used, namely English used informally for everyday occasions spoken in a vernacular dialect.

But these features, so at odds with modern linguistics, were the reasons traditional grammars were created. They had developed from the fifteenth through the eighteenth centuries in an effort to stabilize and standardize the language (Finegan, 1992; J.J. Smith, 1992). English had come into its own as a political, social, and literary language. Moreover, there was a growing public eager to read English, since the printing press made mass ownership of books—and mass literacy—possible. Defining a standard grammar became imperative, in part because both printers and readers came to expect consistent spelling, punctuation, and grammar. For example, which spelling should a printer use if there were many pronunciations of English words—because there were many dialects of English? What might seem like a close sound-symbol relationship to one set of speakers might not to others. How should sentences be punctuated? Which grammar rules should a printer use? People increasingly turned to grammarians to answer these questions, and they in turn looked to literary masters, of both English and Latin, to dictate what people should say.

Traditional grammar had another, more pedagogical, purpose: to prepare students to study Latin (Lester, 1990). Even though English was increasingly used in public arenas, in schools, universities, and churches, the language was still Latin. Young boys (and sometimes girls) would go to so-called grammar schools to learn to read and write in English, but those students destined to go on to high school and college also studied grammar. If they learned the grammar of English, it was believed, they would have the necessary tools for learning Latin at a later time.

It made sense that grammarians would look to literary masters of Latin for models, because written texts were their only connection to Latin speakers. By the medieval times, classical Latin had evolved into the various Romance languages, and there were no longer any native speakers of the language. It also made sense for early English grammarians to borrow the vocabulary and structure of Latin for their English grammar. We frequently understand new technology by using analogies to existing technology. We still, for example, use the terms *captain, first officer*, and *purser*, borrowed from sailing vessels, to refer to those who command airplanes, and car motors are still described in terms of *horsepower*. So it seems natural for early grammarians to use the vocabulary of Latin grammar in creating their grammars of English. Scholars were already familiar with the terms, and English could gain a measure of prestige by association. Moreover, because an understanding of Latin was one goal, English grammars focused most on those places where English was similar to Latin. And in those places where it wasn't? They were either ignored or made to fit—however awkwardly sometimes—by inventing analogies to Latin (Lester, 1990).

Neither traditional grammar pedagogy nor grammar texts have changed much over the centuries. Compare, for example, a text published at the end of the nineteenth century with one published at the beginning of the twenty-first century. The former is J. C. Nesfield's *English Grammar Past and Present*, first published in 1898; it was so popular that it was in its 25th edition when the Braddock Report was released. Here is the table of contents for that first edition (as cited in Crystal, 1995):

1. Analytical outline; general definitions
2. Nouns
3. Adjectives
4. Pronouns
5. Verbs
6. Adverbs
7. Prepositions
8. Conjunctions
9. Interjections
10. Analysis of Sentences
11. The same word used as different parts of speech
12. Syntax
13. Punctuation, or the right use of stops [periods]

Compare Nesfield's table of contents to those in elementary school texts published in 2001, and it's easy to see that traditional grammar's influence is still with us. *Writer's Choice: Grammar and Composition (Grade 6)*, for example, published by Glencoe McGraw-Hill, begins with seven chapters on writing. Then comes a section on grammar with the following chapters:

8. Subjects, Predicates, and Sentences
9. Nouns
10. Verbs
11. Pronouns
12. Adjectives
13. Adverbs
14. Prepositions, Conjunctions, and Interjections
15. Subject-Verb Agreement
16. Glossary of Special Usage Problems
17. Diagramming Sentences
18. Capitalization
19. Punctuation
20. Sentence Combining

I want to be careful to note here that although I've singled out the Glencoe McGraw-Hill here, it's typical of the language arts texts I surveyed. While other texts may configure the chapters slightly differently, the texts are fundamentally similar to Nesfield's.

Textbooks aren't the only sources of grammar curricula. There are several commercially available programs as well. One popular program is The Shurley Method, perhaps one of the best examples of a traditional grammar curriculum. The Shurley Method, developed by former teachers Brenda Shurley and Ruth Kemp Wetsell, emphasizes identifying parts of speech and learning sentence structures as a foundation to writing. To understand sentence structure, students are taught to parse sentences—identify the part of speech and/or the function of each word in the sentence. In a promotional pamphlet entitled "The Shurley Method: English Made Easy," Shurley and Wetsell (n.d.) claim that their "strong grammar based approach teaches the parts of a sentence within the whole sentence so that students have a complete picture of not only how to write whole and accurate sentences, but how to connect grammar and writing" (p. 8).

To analyze sentences, students use the *Question-Answer Flow*, a concrete set of questions to ask about the words in a sentence. Here's how the following sentence would be analyzed:

```
A   Adj    SN      V    Adv   Prep A  Adj      Adj    OP
The weary traveler / slept fitfully (in the cramped airplane seat). D
```

1. Who slept fitfully in the cramped airplane seat? Traveler (subject noun)
2. What is being said about traveler? Traveler slept (verb)
3. Slept how? Fitfully (adverb)
4. In (preposition)
5. In what? Seat (object of the preposition)

6. What kind of seat? Cramped (adjective)
7. What kind of seat? Airplane (adjective)
8. The (article adjective)
9. What kind of traveler? Weary (adjective)
10. The (article adjective)
11. Subject Noun Verb - Pattern 1 (intransitive verb sentence)
12. In the cramped airplane seat (prepositional phrase)
13. Period (statement, declarative sentence)
14. Go back to the verb. Divide the complete subject from the complete predicate.

Shurley and Wetsell (n.d.) note that this approach also uses student participation (in the form of unison recitation), fun (in the form of songs to help students remember the parts of speech), and repetition to help students learn. In addition to studying the parts of speech, students learn capitalization and punctuation rules by editing sentences with errors.

Structuralist and Transformational-Generative Grammars

Why do English language arts texts today continue to be modeled on those of a century ago? Why has the traditional grammar framework had such a powerful influence? Why haven't the structural and transformational-generative grammar frameworks made more of an inroad in primary and secondary school curriculum? Why haven't linguists capitalized on the influence of the Braddock Report and introduced a more "scientific" curriculum? Many teachers, it seems, were ready to make a change. So why didn't they? Because at the time, argues Mark Lester (2001a), linguists themselves couldn't agree on the best way to describe the grammar of English. In the 1960s, the field of linguistics itself was in a state of flux. Transformational-generative grammar was emerging as a more powerful way than structuralist grammar to understand the structure of the English language. The foundation for both systems was a description of what native English speakers actually said, using rules that were organic to English. In this way, both systems shared a critique of traditional school grammar as too prescriptive and as based inaccurately on Latin grammar. Structuralism developed in the 1920s and 1930s out of the widespread nineteenth-century interest in historical research. Unlike traditional grammarians, who looked to literary masters for their models, structuralists conducted "scientific" research, collecting and transcribing the speech of native speakers. Rather than using an analogy to Latin, structuralists sought rules that seemed to emerge from their data. They focused heavily on the structure of English—hence their name—especially the order of words within sentences. In English, order determines what function each word plays in a sentence, and thus, its part of speech. For this reason, syntax and sentence structure comprise the heart of structuralist grammar.

At about the same time as the Braddock Report, linguists, led by Noam Chomsky of MIT, became increasingly critical of structuralist linguistics and its underlying assumptions about how humans learn language. The structuralists were essentially behaviorists and believed that children learned language through imitation. If that were true, Chomsky asked, why can children produce grammatical sentences they've never heard before? Furthermore, structuralist linguistics couldn't explain why native speakers agree that two sentences that aren't structurally alike are related—e.g., *Shakespeare wrote* Hamlet and Hamlet *was written by Shakespeare.*—and two structurally similar sentences aren't related at all—e.g., *John is eager to please.* and *John is easy to please.* Chomsky was interested in explaining how native speakers use their intuitions about language to generate ideas and transform them stylistically—hence the name often given to his linguistic model: transformational-generative grammar. The three grammars are summarized in Figure 2.1.

FIGURE 2.1   *Theoretical Foundation: Three Schools of Grammar Briefly Defined*

As I noted in Chapter 1, one definition of grammar is "the linguistic description of the rules of a language," what Hartwell calls Grammar 2. Different descriptions yield different results—they may focus on one thing more than another, they have more or less explanatory power, etc. Below are brief descriptions of three significant schools of English grammar in the twentieth century (Lester, 1990).

	Traditional School Grammar	*Structuralist Grammar*	*Transformational-Generative Grammar*
Description	• Developed in fifteenth to eighteenth century by British scholars. • Modeled after Latin grammar. • Based on written text of masters. • Intended to teach grammar vocabulary to study Latin. • Intended to standardize English and "fix" speakers.	• Developed in late nineteenth and early twentieth century by historical and comparative linguists. • Based on what native speakers say.	• Developed in late 1950s to the present by Noam Chomsky and linguists. • Based on structure and/or native speaker intuition. • Set of rules for simple sentences and how to transform them.

FIGURE 2.1   *Continued*

Strengths	• Based on a system and set of terms already familiar to scholars and students. • Transferred prestige of Latin to English. • Intended to help speakers achieve upward mobility.	• Descriptive, not prescriptive. • Based on scientific rigor—only on what we have objective data for. • No personal preferences. • Structure derived from English itself so better fit.	• Descriptive, not prescriptive. • Focus on universal grammar—how native speakers produce all and only grammatical sentences. • Gives native speakers a lot of credit. • Useful in teaching students style.
Weaknesses	• Latin system not well-suited to English, a Germanic language. • Tends to be prescriptive, not descriptive. • Doesn't help students improve writing and speaking when taught in isolation.	• Strong focus on structure and objective data sometimes doesn't account for what native speaker intuition knows.	• Slow to have an impact in schools. • Some say too focused on biological; not enough on cultural component of language learning.

With the field of linguistics itself in the midst of shifting paradigms, it wasn't prepared to offer the field of English language arts a grammar curriculum to take the place of traditional grammar. Moreover, neither the structuralists nor the transformational-generative grammarians had a pedagogical focus, preferring instead to concentrate on describing rather than prescribing English. Since the general public wasn't very familiar with either the Braddock Report or these new branches of "scientific" linguistics, it couldn't fill the vacuum either. So, as Lester (2001a) points out, the state of grammar pedagogy is in flux.

As a result, structuralism and transformational-generative grammar have had only a small impact on the way grammar is presented in the language arts texts I surveyed—though it has had some. Because structuralism focuses on sentence structure rather than parts of speech, current textbooks tend to pay more attention to sentences than Nesfield did. Note, for example, that the Glencoe McGraw-Hill text begins its grammar unit with a chapter on sentences and its parts. And because transformational-generative grammar is interested in how native speakers generate, embed, and transform sentences into complex syntactic structures, more and more exercises take the form of sentence combining, asking students to manipulate sentences rather than parsing or diagramming them. (You may remember doing these types of exercises yourself.) Again, note the chapter in the Glencoe McGraw-Hill text on sentence combining. However, for the most part, structuralism and transformation-generative grammar are both limited to linguistics classes on the college level.

Without a clear alternative to traditional school grammar, English language arts teachers themselves are in conflict. While all teachers will tell you that an active knowledge of formal grammar—that is, an ability to generate well-written, formal texts—is important, they're divided about how students acquire that knowledge and also about how grammar should be taught. According to a 1993 poll reported in *English Journal*, the main journal for teachers of secondary English, about 60 percent of teachers insist that students must be drilled in traditional school grammar (Warner, 1993). The remaining 40 percent believe equally strongly that there's little connection between students' study of grammar and their writing. They're convinced that linguistically derived systems of grammar better represent the English language and that grammar instruction is most productive when it's taught as part of the writing process. These teachers feel that the traditional grammar system is clearly broken and cannot be fixed, so it's time to abandon it.

Exploring Your Own Language Experience

1. Before you begin the reading for this chapter, spend five minutes or so writing in your journal about the following:
   a. Think back to your own experiences with grammar in school. How much grammar did you study? In what grades? As a separate unit? or integrated with literature and writing?
   b. How was the material presented? How were you tested on it? If you had to take statewide standardized tests that measured progress or determined whether you could graduate, did the tests ask questions about Standard English grammar? If so, how were the questions framed?
   c. If you were tracked in school, did your track study the same amount of grammar as other tracks? Why?/Why not?
   d. One reason teachers teach grammar is that they believe it helps students learn to read and write more effectively. To what extent did your study of grammar help you become a better reader and/or writer? Why?
   e. Did your study of grammar have other/additional values (instead)? If so, what? Why?

Just the Facts: Research and Theory about Grammar Instruction

Nancy G. Patterson

In "Just the Facts: Research and Theory about Grammar Instruction," Nancy G. Patterson, a Portland, Michigan, middle school teacher, provides middle school teachers with scholarly ammunition to challenge traditional grammar instruction and to promote teaching grammar in the context of writing. She cites several research studies that show that studying traditional grammar doesn't lead to improved student writing; she also offers some alternative approaches. This article first appeared in the March 2001 special theme issue on "Contextualizing Grammar" in Voices from the Middle. *Patterson serves as co-editor of the Tech Connect column in that journal.*

You have just hired into a school district, eager to practice the constructivist-based theory you learned in your foundations or methods classes. At your first meeting with other members of the English department, you are told that you will be teaching traditional grammar. You know from your college course work that this is not the best approach, but you don't know what to say to these veteran teachers.

Or, your principal or department chair sits down with the English department, and, dismayed over the latest standardized test scores, announces that you are all going back to basics. Part of that means you will all teach traditional grammar. You know that such back-to-basics rhetoric is problematic, but you are not sure how to address the issue.

Or, you are in a district language arts curriculum meeting and a high school teacher laments the fact that few of his students know what a noun is and none of them can diagram a sentence. You know that the ability to name parts and diagram sentences does not have much bearing on students' writing abilities, but you are not sure how to support your argument with this teacher.

Or, a parent tells you at parent–teacher conferences that he learned grammar in school and he wants his son to get the same lessons because English class should teach grammar. You know the issue is more complex than this, but you don't know how to speak to the issue this parent has brought up.

What do you do?

Relevant Research

There are a number of important studies that teachers should be aware of when they discuss how grammar should be taught. Perhaps the first part of the discussion should stress that, yes, grammar has a place in language arts classrooms. In fact, the conversation should never be whether or not grammar is taught. Rather, it should be about *how* grammar is taught.

Several studies offer us direction about how grammar should or shouldn't be taught. Let's look at a few of them.

Harris Study

In 1962, Roland Harris investigated grammar instruction with middle school students in London, England. Harris compared two groups of students—those who got heavy doses of traditional school grammar (what he calls "formal grammar"), and those who learned grammatical concepts within the context of language use. The second group of students learned concepts as they arose in regular language use situations such as speaking and writing. Though the "formal grammar" group studied grammar within the context of composition, the studies were not based on students' writing, and there was no mechanism in place for students to work on extended pieces of writing. Rather, their writing was short and addressed whatever grammatical concept formed the lesson at the time. According to Constance Weaver (1996), this group studied grammar through the use of traditional terminology. Students in the other group were able to produce longer pieces of writing and were shown how to think through their errors so that meaning, not terminology, became the foundation for grammar lessons. In their summary of the Harris study, Elley, Barham, Lamb, and Wyllie (1975) wrote:

> After a period of two years, five classes of high school students who had studied formal grammar performed significantly worse than a matched group of five non-grammar groups on several objective criteria of sentence complexity and the number of errors in their essays. (p. 6)

In other words, the Harris study found that the formal teaching of grammar actually had an adverse effect on students' abilities to write well.

Braddock, Lloyd-Jones, and Schoer Study

It was the Harris study, as well as others, that helped Richard Braddock, Richard Lloyd-Jones, and Lowell Schoer conclude in their meta-study, an examination of previous research studies, that the isolated teaching of school grammar did not result in the outcomes that teachers expected. The following from their 1963 report, commissioned by NCTE, *Research in Written Composition*, is frequently quoted.

> In view of the widespread agreement of research studies based upon many types of students and teachers, the conclusion can be stated in strong and unqualified terms: the teaching of formal grammar has a negligible or, because it usually displaces some instruction and practice in actual composition, even a harmful effect on the improvement of writing (pp. 37–38).

Elley, Barham, Lamb, and Wyllie Study

Another important study that teachers need to be aware of was conducted in New Zealand by W. B. Elley, a member of New Zealand's Council for Educational Research, and I. H. Barham, H. Lamb, and M. Wyllie, from Aorere College. The study was republished in the May 1975 issue of *Research in the Teaching of English*, an NCTE publication. In this study, 248 students of average ability in eight classes were studied over a three-year period of time. Students were divided into three different language arts curricular strands. One strand studied Transformational Grammar, rhetoric, and literature. Students in this strand learned to explain the rules of grammar as native speakers used the language. They learned about phrase structure and transformative rules as well as about deep structures, sentence parts, modifiers, etc. They also studied substance, structure, and style as it pertained to writing. In addition, they focused on developing a sense of key concepts in literature as well as a knowledge of form and point of view. To do this, they worked their way through a number of literature books and collections of nonfiction and drama.

Another strand dealt with rhetoric and literature, where students used about 40% of their time for free reading, another 40% for reading class sets of books, and the rest of the time for creative writing. Students received no instruction in formal or

Transformational Grammar or rules. They studied spelling and writing conventions as the need arose. They learned nothing about parts of speech or sentence analysis.

The third strand learned a heavy dose of traditional grammar. Students in that strand learned about subjects, verbs, rules of usage, parts of speech, clause structures, punctuation, etc. Students worked on exercises in textbooks, and they also read from literature anthologies as well as predetermined class sets of novels. Teachers in that strand consulted each other frequently to make sure they were focusing on the proper elements in the same way. Students in each strand were evaluated at the end of each year.

The original purpose of the Elley, et al. study was to determine how much the study of Transformational Grammar impacted student language growth. The researchers discovered that such study had a negligible impact on their growth, but it also showed that the traditional study of grammar had little or no impact on student language growth either.

Here again, then, is a study that concluded the isolated teaching of traditional grammar, meaning the identification of parts of speech and the rules of usage, had little or no impact on students' abilities to write well.

Hillocks Study

Another important meta-study, again commissioned by NCTE and this time conducted by George Hillocks (1986), concluded that there is no evidence that the teaching of grammar improves writing. His *Research on Written Composition* also concludes that isolated grammar lessons could have a negative effect on student writing. Hillocks wrote:

> The study of traditional school grammar (i.e., the definition of parts of speech, the parsing of sentences, etc.) has no effect on raising the quality of student writing. Every other focus of instruction examined in this review is stronger. Taught in certain ways, grammar and mechanics instruction has a deleterious effect on student writing. In some studies a heavy emphasis on mechanics and usage (e.g., marking every error) resulted in significant losses in overall quality. (p. 248)

Here again, we find that, even after an analysis of many studies that looked at the teaching of grammar in the language arts classroom, there is little or no evidence that isolated grammar studies improved student writing.

Shaughnessy Study

Mina Shaughnessy's 1977 book *Errors and Expectations* does not seem to relate directly to middle school writers because it focuses on adult basic writers, but her conclusions can still provide some insights for middle school teachers. Shaughnessy's work looks at the cause of error in student writing. She discovered that there were often patterns in student error, and these patterns frequently indicated misconceptions and problems with logic. Shaughnessy's research indicates that teachers can often determine the problems students have with grammar by looking at a given student's writing and discussing the writing with that student. She also points out that when students are concentrating on more sophisticated kinds of writing, they are apt to make mistakes they would not have made previously. She wrote, "It is not unusual for people acquiring a skill to get `worse' before they get better and for writers to err more as they venture more" (p. 119).

What is also interesting about Shaughnessy's study is that she makes a distinction between grammatical understanding and correctness. She points out that the goal of grammar study should be a "shift in perception which is ultimately more important than the mastery of any individual rule of grammar" (p. 129). For Shaughnessy, coming up with the right answer isn't nearly as important as the logic behind that answer. Glover and Stay, when discussing Shaughnessy's work, point out that "the development of grammatical understanding enables a student to build a paradigm through which to view the world and act in it through language, a paradigm that a student can apply in a variety of contexts. By extension, approaching grammar as a way of thinking, as a style of inquiry, and as a way of seeing the world, means approaching grammatical questions within the larger context of audience and purpose" (p. 131).

Here, then we see that grammar is a space where meaning rather than correctness becomes the focus, and that risk taking and experimentation can become fertile ground through which students can build linguistic control. The idea that grammar is meaning-based rather than rule-based may harken back to the classical view of grammar, as practiced by the Greeks.

Most theorists trace the history of grammar to the ancient Greeks who made grammar part of a trivium of rhetoric, logic, and grammar. Cheryl Glenn (1995) interprets the role of grammar in the Greek trivium as one of style more than rules of correctness. Glenn views this role of grammar, what she calls "fluid, flexible, lively, ever-changing, emotional, beautiful, stylish, graceful language performance" (p. 10) as the goal of grammar instruction.

Focus on Theory

Along with the research, there is a great deal of theory that impacts how we should approach grammar studies in the language arts classroom. One of the best articles about grammar and its role in the classroom is Patrick Hartwell's "Grammar, Grammars, and the Teaching of Grammar," published in 1985. Hartwell agrees with Braddock, citing also Janet Emig, who called the teaching of grammar a prime example of the kind of "magical thinking" that teachers engage in when they believe students will learn only what they teach and only because they teach it (p. 105). But Hartwell goes on to identify different kinds of grammar—grammars 1, 2, 3, and 4. Grammar 1 is the formal arrangement of words in patterns that convey meaning. This is the "grammar in our heads" that all of us carry around with us. It is the grammar that tells us that when we want to ask a question, we put words in a particular order so that what we say or write is clearly conveyed as a question. Grammar 2 refers to the descriptive analysis that linguists engage in. It is the formal analysis of language in action and, Hartwell warns, teaching it has no impact on an individual's use of Grammar 1. Grammar 3 refers to "linguistic etiquette," the rules of correctness that seem to occupy English teachers and their students, something Hartwell points out is not really grammar, but usage. Grammar 4 refers to School Grammar, something Hartwell warns us bears little relationship to linguists' Grammar 2.

Hartwell's distinction among the various grammars is helpful to classroom teachers. Consideration of Grammar 1, for example, can help teachers distinguish among various home dialects that students speak and realize that home dialects are valid uses of language, even though they may not be part of the language of power.

Hartwell rightly concludes that Grammar 4, School Grammar, focuses too much on memorization of rules and not enough on language to convey meaning and purpose. Hartwell suggests that we should develop a Grammar 5, a style grammar that helps students use their metalinguistic knowledge, their conscious knowledge of Grammar 1, to convey meaning and purpose. Such a grammar would help students use language as "verbal clay, to be molded and probed, shaped and reshaped, and, above all, enjoyed" (p. 126).

But students aren't the only ones who need to use their metalinguistic knowledge. Teachers must use it also, especially when they are making curricular decisions that relate to students who speak a different dialect. Geneva Smitherman's outstanding book *Talkin' and Testifyin': The Language of Black America* (1977), shows that dialects, though they may not be privileged, are as rule-bound as the dialect we refer to as Standard English. For example, Smitherman points out that it is standard in some dialects, especially those that she refers to as Black English Variation, to delete the "s" in the third person. Standard English dictates that in the sentence "The boy needs more money" the word "needs" requires an "s." In Black English Variation, that "s" is deleted. If a student writes "The boy need more money," a teacher might conclude that the student has a problem with subject/verb agreement. That conclusion, however, might not be the most appropriate one. Smitherman stresses that teachers need to "know and understand black sound" (p. 223) and by extension, the sounds of other dialects their students speak, in order to help their students move back and forth between dialects, both in written and spoken language, as they choose. Once teachers become aware of the rules that govern other dialects, they can begin to help students see that they have choices.

It is important to point out here that Smitherman is not suggesting students simply be allowed to speak and write in their own dialect, never learning how to "translate" their language into other dialects. She writes:

> . . . there is the emphasis on communicative competence. Communicative competence, quite simply, refers to the ability to communicate effectively. At this point, however, all simplicity ends. For to be able to speak or write with power is a very complex business, involving a universe of linguistic choices and alternatives. Such a speaker or writer must use language that is appropriate to the situation and the audience (p. 229).

Smitherman goes on to say that the important aspects of communication include logic, word choice, message and content, originality, and expression. These, she stresses, are the elements of power in language. And she points out that "While teachers frequently correct student language on the basis of such misguided [conceptions of correct grammar], saying something correctly, and saying it well, are two entirely different Thangs [sic]" (p. 229).

A more recent voice in the grammar discussion is Rei Noguchi's. In his book *Grammar and the Teaching of Writing*, Noguchi recommends that teachers focus their attention on the most frequent errors in student writing, particularly those that seem to upset those who hold power—academics and business personnel. Noguchi based his recommendations partly on a study conducted in 1988 by Connors and Lunsford that concluded, among other things, that five out of the top ten mistakes college students make in writing involve punctuation. The Connors and Lunsford study surveyed college instructors and asked them to identify the errors they found most frequently in student papers. The mistakes most often identified by college teachers dealt with run-on sentences, comma splices, fragments, and the boundaries between and among clauses. Noguchi recommends, then, that teachers address such issues directly, not only from the perspective of correctness, but from that of style.

The other study that Noguchi uses to support his discussion is the Hairston study, conducted in 1981 among business and professional people. The errors that bothered most of the people in the Hairston study involved subject/verb agreement, sentence fragments, and run-ons. Errors that brought about less negative feelings on the part of participants were in punctuation and word choices (its/it's, different from/different than, etc.).

The Hairston study brings up some questions regarding age and gender bias, not to mention economic class issues, but Noguchi concludes from it and the Connors and Lunsford study that classroom teachers should focus on just a few key grammatical issues that show up in student language use.

We need to be cautious when we consider those grammatical issues, though. Smitherman and Weaver, among others, remind us that language and power are very closely aligned. Weaver, reflecting on Noguchi's recommendations, writes, "I would suggest that only a few of the frequently occurring errors in the Connors-Lunsford study and only a few of the [economic] status-marking . . . errors in the Hairston study require for their elimination an understanding of grammatical concepts commonly taught. And these few kinds of errors can be understood by comprehending only a few grammatical concepts" (p. 115).

Noguchi urges teachers to adopt what he calls a "writer's grammar," one that integrates what students already know about language and what they learn about the most frequent and serious grammar and usage errors "with content and organization, two crucial areas that [traditional] grammars leave virtually untouched" (p. 120).

Conclusion

What all this indicates is that the teaching of grammar must happen within the context of larger lessons and experiences with written and spoken language. This means that English teachers must move beyond viewing grammar as a set of rules and a code of correctness, and they need to re-think the idea that a comprehensive knowledge of grammar terminology and rules somehow translates into a knowledge of linguistic structure or into an ability to write well. Instead, teachers need to move toward what Glover and Stay call "the grammar of discovery," and toward a classroom that includes grammar within the context of reading, writing, listening, and speaking. Grammar should be a means through which students learn more about themselves, their texts, and the world around them.

Works Cited

Braddock, R., Lloyd-Jones. R., & Schoer, I. (1963). *Research on written composition*. Urbana, IL: National Council of Teachers of English.

Elley, W. B., Barham, I. H., Lamb, H., & Wyllie, M. (1975). The role of grammar in a secondary English curriculum. *Research in the Teaching of English*, 10, 5–21.

Glenn, C. (1995). When grammar was a language art. In S. Hunter & R. Wallace (Eds.), *The role of grammar in writing instruction, past, present, future* (pp. 9–29). Portsmouth, NH: Boynton/Cook.

Glover, C. W., & Stay, B. L. (1995). Grammar in the writing center: Opportunities for discovery and change. In S. Hunter & R. Wallace (Eds.), *The role of grammar in writing instruction, past, present, future* (pp. 129–135). Portsmouth, NH: Boynton/Cook.

Hartwell, P. (1985). Grammar, grammars, and the teaching of grammar. *College English*, 47, 105–127.

Hillocks, G., Jr. (1986). *Research on written composition: New directions for teaching*. Urbana, IL: National Council of Teachers of English.

Noguchi, R. (1991). *Grammar and the teaching of writing: Limits and possibilities.* Urbana, IL: National Council of Teachers of English.

Shaughnessy, M. (1977). *Errors and expectations: A guide for the teacher of basic writing.* New York: Oxford University Press.

Smitherman, G. (1977). *Talkin' and testifyin': The language of black America.* Detroit, MI: Wayne State University Press.

Weaver, C. (1996). *Teaching grammar in context.* Portsmouth, NH: Boynton/Cook.

Questions for Discussion

1. What evidence does Patterson offer that traditional grammar doesn't live up to its claims to lead to improved student writing? How credible is the evidence? Why?

2. What kind of curriculum does Patterson recommend instead? Why? What research does she cite to prove this curriculum is better? How credible is this research? Why?

3. Research the Shurley Method, including examining its Website [www.shurley.com].
   a. The promotional materials claim to "teach[es] students the structure and design of their written language" (n.d., p. 8). Review what Daniels (Chapter 1) says about how students learn language. What would he say about these claims?
   b. What are the advantages and disadvantages of the method? What kind of credentials do the authors have? What kind of evidence do they offer to support the soundness of their methods? How credible is the evidence? Why?

4. To what extent is traditional grammar as Weaver defines it (see the introduction to this chapter) still taught? To what extent have structuralist and transformational-generative grammar ideas impacted curriculum? Check the following resources to find out what kind of curriculum has been officially endorsed in your state.
   a. What kind of grammar instruction is required/recommended in official state curriculum guidelines? Check with the state department of education or public instruction in your state for a copy of state standards. (The guidelines may be available on the agency's Website; your school or public library may have printed copies; or you may obtain a copy through your local school office or PTA, etc.) As part of your examination, secure the following information:
      • Publication information (title, date of publication, grade level, etc.).
      • Print out/photocopy two or three pages that represent the way grammar is discussed (and bring them to class to share with your classmates).
      • Identify what rationale, if any, is given to the students for why they should study grammar.
      • Identify what rationale, if any, is given to teachers for how and why they should teach grammar.
   b. What kind of grammar instruction appears in the latest textbooks for elementary and secondary schools? Check several commercially published texts used in your local schools. (You may have access to texts through family members, the local school or PTA, or your job; your school or public library may also have copies.) As part of your examination, secure the following information:

- Publication information (title, publisher, date of publication, grade level, [if appropriate] special section where grammar is located, etc.).
- Photocopy two or three pages that represent the way grammar is discussed (and bring them to class to share with your classmates).
- Identify what rationale, if any, is given to the students for why they should study grammar.
- Identify what rationale, if any, is given to teachers for how and why they should teach grammar.

c. What kind of grammar instruction is advocated for language minority students? If your local school district has a special program for bilingual, ESL, or language minority students; at risk students; etc., find out how the program handles the grammar curriculum. For each program you examine, secure the following information:
- A description of the program (the goals, the eligible student populations, etc.).
- Publication information (title, publisher, date of publication, grade level, [if appropriate] special section where grammar is located, etc.) for any text used.
- Photocopy two or three pages that represent the way grammar is discussed (and bring them to class to share with your classmates).
- Identify what rationale, if any, is given to the students for why they should study grammar.
- Identify what rationale, if any, is given to teachers for how and why they should teach grammar.

d. Does your state have mandated assessments of elementary and secondary students to determine their educational progress? If so, what kind of assessment? Does the assessment include knowledge of writing? knowledge of Standard English grammar? How are the questions framed (e.g., multiple choice questions about grammar errors, a grammar and mechanics portion of the writing rubric, etc.)? Find out what you can about the exam. (Descriptions of the exam may be available on your state education agency's Website; your school or public library may have printed copies; or you may obtain a copy through your local school office or PTA, etc.) What definition of grammar (i.e., Hartwell's 5 Grammars [p. 5]) does the assessment seem to be using? What evidence can you give to support your analysis?

e. Based on your examination of curriculum guidelines, texts and programs, and mandated assessments, what conclusions can you draw about the current grammar curriculum in your area?

3

Contextualizing Grammar

As we saw in Chapter 2, an important critique of traditional school grammar is that it's taught in isolation—that is, it's taught outside the context of students' reading and writing. That's why, according to the research studies, there's little connection between what students do when they complete grammar worksheets and what they do when they write essays. Everyone, it seems, agrees that contextualizing grammar is an important and necessary reform. But, as we noted in Chapter 2, reforming the grammar curriculum raises at least two important, and related, questions:

- In which context should we teach grammar?
- What grammar, or aspects of grammar, do we teach in that context?

In answer to these questions, there seem to be at least two major positions. Though not incompatible with each other, each position nonetheless identifies a somewhat different context, which in turn, results in their emphasizing different aspects of the language arts. Perhaps the most popular position locates the teaching of grammar in the writing and reading process. Constance Weaver (1996) is the name most synonymous with this position. Yet for others, those with more formal linguistic training, the appropriate context is language study. Martha Kolln (1996), Larry Andrews (1995, 1998), and Walt Wolfram (1998), for example, argue that our overall goal should be to help students become more aware of how language—either oral or written—"works."

In the Context of Language Study

Although Kolln (1996), Andrews (1995, 1998) and Wolfram (1998) each advocate their own language study or language awareness curriculum, they agree on certain key components. Kolln cites a 1994 NCTE Resolution on Language Study to identify these topics:

Language awareness includes examining how language varies in a range of social and cultural settings; examining how people's attitudes vary towards language across culture, class, gender, and generation; examining how oral and written language affects listeners and readers; examining how "correctness" in language reflects social–political–economic values; examining how the structure of language works from a descriptive perspective; and examining how first and second languages are acquired. (Kolln, 1996, p. 30)

More specifically, Wolfram (1998, p. 80) spells out some "fundamental linguistic and sociolinguistic requisites" for English language arts teachers and students:

- *An understanding of the differences between descriptive (what is) and prescriptive (what should be) traditions of grammar study*. (See Chapter 2 for a brief description of these different schools.) A descriptive perspective, Wolfram argues, leads to an appreciation of language as a unique form of human knowledge and to a respect for language variation. It also leads to an understanding of the difference between linguistic grammaticality (systematic patterns and rules) and social acceptability (socially based judgments of what's standard).
- *An understanding of the linguistic integrity of all language varieties*. This can be done, Wolfram argues, by examining the rules of various dialects. Such a study leads to an appreciation of the intricate patterns found in all dialects (Hartwell's Grammar 1 [p. 5]). It also leads to an appreciation of the scientific study of language (Hartwell's Grammar 2).
- *An understanding that language change is natural and inevitable*. Examining such changes by examining the history of English helps us realize that language change doesn't represent a decline in the use of the language. It also demonstrates one cause of variation—some speakers change while others don't. Double negatives, for example, which have been considered acceptable since Chaucer's time, have been preserved in vernacular dialects. Standard dialect speakers, on the other hand, changed their notions of the acceptability of double negatives in the eighteenth century.
- *An understanding of the different aspects of language: phonology, grammar (morphology and syntax), semantics, and pragmatics*. (See Chapter 1.)

Wolfram acknowledges that the goals of language study are more often to develop tolerant attitudes about language than to acquire a body of facts about language. But, he argues, "there are scientific, sociohistorical, and humanitarian reasons apart from any utilitarian motivation that justify the examination of language structure" (p. 81).

Kolln (1996), Andrews (1995, 1998), and Wolfram (1998) also agree in general to the advantages of language awareness programs. Such approaches:

- *Support the developing language competence of middle, junior, and high school students.* As Andrews (1998) points out, the language of adolescents is still developing.
- *Set the study of formal, written grammar in a meaningful context.*
- *Motivate vernacular-dialect-speaking students to learn Standard English conventions.* Andrews (1998) argues that:

> before students are likely to gain significant insights into how they and other speakers and writers might unconsciously or deliberately use language elements, patterns, and structures, or before they see a *reason* to pay attention to these issues, they need first of all to become more aware of language in general and how it varies, changes, and 'works' in their world. (p. 6; emphasis in the original)

- *Encourage standard-dialect-speaking students to value non-mainstream dialects and to reduce linguistic discrimination.* Wolfram (1998) argues that:

> the most effective way to develop an appreciation for the intricacies of language variation involves working through some actual linguistic patterns governing socially disfavored forms. Such an awareness affects not only the perspective of language arts instructors, but also how students feel about other students and themselves. Students who speak socially favored varieties may view their dialectally different peers as linguistically deficient. Worse yet, speakers of socially disfavored varieties may come to accept their viewpoint about their own language. Students, as well as teachers, need to understand that a dialect difference is not an inherent linguistic or cognitive difference. (pp. 91–92)

Perhaps the most developed of the language study programs is the Language Exploration and Awareness (LEA) approach advocated by Larry Andrews (1995, 1998). Through a variety of activities, the LEA approach encourages students to explore how language "works" in their world. They also study the English language from a historical and sociolinguistic perspective. This perspective helps students understand why the dialect known as Standard English, the backbone of traditional grammar study, came to have the power and prestige it has today. It also helps them understand how their home discourses—whether they're standard or vernacular dialects of English—came to be and when and where they enjoy prestige. Figure 3.1 includes examples of activities Andrews suggests to explore language.

To some extent, aspects of language study are included in the language arts textbooks I surveyed. For example, Houghton Mifflin's *English* (Rueda et al., 2001) provides an explicit rationale to students for studying grammar, framed in a discussion that contrasts informal and formal language. It explains:

> When you're talking with family or friends, you might use informal language that may not follow all the rules of standard English. All that matters, though, is that

FIGURE 3.1 *Spotlight on Curriculum: Language Exploration and Awareness*

Author(s):	Larry Andrews
Author's(s') Credentials:	Professor in the Literacy Studies Program in the Center for Curriculum and Instruction at the University of Nebraska Lincoln
Published By:	Lawrence Erlbaum Associates
Available:	*Language Exploration and Awareness: A Resource Book for Teachers*, 2nd edition.

The LEA approach takes a developmental view, recognizing that the language competence of elementary, middle, and high school students is still growing. LEA activities emphasize meaning, use authentic language found in genuine social circumstances, are student-centered and inquiry-oriented, and develop an awareness of several aspects of language. These aspects include:

- properties of communication and language
- words and lexicography
- discourse routines and social conventions
- regional, social, and historical variations in English
- meanings and general semantics
- the languages of intolerance and discrimination
- the languages of advertising
- grammar, spelling, and "good" English

Andrews provides more than 100 LEA activities suitable for upper elementary, middle school, and high school students in his book. Here are three examples:

From the chapter on words and lexicography:
EXPLORATION: Chocolate Moose

DIRECTIONS: Homonyms are words with different spellings but identical pronunciations, like "boar" and "bore" or "hall" and "haul." Fred Gwynne uses homonyms in his book, *A Chocolate Moose for Dinner*. Before enjoying a dessert of chocolate moose, what meat would you want to eat: stake?

1. Can you plan a complete menu using homonyms?
2. When you hear a homonym used in a conversation, how do you know which word the speaker is using? What does this tell you about language?

From the chapter on regional, social, and historical variations in English:
EXPLORATION: Good, Bad, or Ugly?

DIRECTIONS: Visit with a grandparent or a person old enough to be a grandparent about changes they've observed in the way language is being used today. Do they think the changes are examples of progress? Of decay? You might talk about the following:

1. What about "taboo" words? They seem to be used more casually today, in conversation, on TV. Is this acceptable?
2. What about the emphasis on gender-neutral words, like *fireperson* instead of *fireman*?

FIGURE 3.1   *Continued*

3. "Private products," for both men and women, are advertised openly. Is this a good idea?
4. What do the responses you receive tell you about language change?

From the chapter on meanings and general semantics:
EXPLORATION: Word Rainbows

DIRECTIONS: Using advertisements printed in color from catalogs, the Sunday newspaper, or circulars received in the mail, identify the *names* of as many different colors as you can that are either used in an illustration or in the description of an item.

1. Place the individual names of colors with others of its "family" of colors. (For example, "teal" and "eggshell blue" will go with "blue.")
2. How many of the more specific color names come from foods, like "apricot," "olive," "tangerine," or "apple red"? How many of the names come from nature, like "sky" or "dusk"?
3. Will the choice of color names enhance the product's image for the prospective buyer or shopper, in your judgment?
4. Is there a *logical* connection between the name selected and the objects they refer to?

Description based on *Language Exploration and Awareness: A Resource Book for Teachers*, 2nd edition. Used with permission.

everyone understands each other. Similarly, when you write journal entries, notes, or other personal writing, it doesn't matter whether every word or punctuation mark is correct. However, in class and in many life situations, formal English is often expected—when you apply for a job, for example, speak with people in a workplace, or write for an audience. This section of the book will help you develop your ability to use formal language when you need it. (p. 30)

Moreover, under its "Tools and Tips" section is a chapter on "Building Vocabulary" that includes discussions of word roots, borrowed words, word histories, and regional and cultural vocabulary.

Similarly, *Elements of Language* (Odell et al., 2001) includes a short chapter on the history of English in its "Quick Reference Handbook" section. The chapter discusses the origins and uses of English (changes in meaning, pronunciation, and spelling; borrowed words and words coined from proper names) and dialects of American English (ethnic and regional dialects; standard English; formal and informal language, such as slang and colloquialisms). The chapter makes the point that "everyone uses a dialect, and no dialect is better or worse than another" (p. 692).

Although *Writer's Choice* (Glencoe McGraw-Hill, 2001) seems to delve right into its grammar section without a rationale to students for studying it, it does provide a rationale to teachers in the form of a professional article on "Teaching Grammar and Usage" (Lester, 2001b). Lester's rationale draws on arguments from both positions. That is, he argues that grammar should be studied in the context of language study *and* of writing. Lester says, "the study of grammar in school gives students the concepts and terms necessary for *talking and thinking about the vehicle of language*. A conscious knowledge of grammatical concepts and terms is also necessary for students to compare and contrast their use of language with other people's use of language and to explore alternative ways of expressing their own ideas." He goes on to say that "in order to grasp grammar terminology, students first need *numerous examples and extensive practice sessions* to grasp the concepts underlying the terms." He also notes that "good grammar programs *constantly connect grammar to usage problems in the students' own writing*." He recommends collecting examples of errors from students' papers, discussing the errors in terms of what they are and how they can be corrected, and reinforcing the correction with exercises. (pp. T28–T29; emphasis in the original.)

In the Context of Literacy

While Kolln (1996), Andrews (1995, 1998) and Wolfram (1998) represent those who want to set the teaching of grammar in the context of language study and want to define grammar broadly as language competence (Hartwell's Grammar 1), Constance Weaver and her colleagues (2001) represent the more common position: those who advocate grammar in the context of reading and writing, and who emphasize a more narrow notion of grammar. Although they're not opposed to language study, Weaver and her colleagues nevertheless focus their energies on helping students develop a vocabulary for talking about writing (Hartwell's Grammar 5 [p. 5]). The language study and writing camps don't oppose each other but rather traditional grammar.

A writing-based grammar curriculum, as Weaver (1996) envisions it, begins by engaging students in lots of writing and reading. She recommends writing and reading every day, in all courses, using a variety of genres and levels of formality. In short, students should experience as broad a range of different types of writing and reading as they can. Within the context of these literacy events, she recommends teachers emphasize aspects of grammar that help writers revise and edit their sentences. In addition, Weaver urges us to teach only the grammar rules writers need, only when they need them, and only if students don't already know them. We should do so with inquiry-oriented activities that minimize grammar terminology.

While traditional grammar expects students to develop an extensive vocabulary of grammar terms, Weaver (1996) argues for limiting instruction to only the most essential grammatical concepts and terms:

- subject and verb (or predicate)
- independent (main) and dependent (subordinate) clause
- modifiers (restrictive, essential) and free modifiers (nonrestrictive, nonessential)

In addition, students should have strategies for correcting the following errors:

- vague pronoun reference
- possessive apostrophe errors
- unnecessary shifts in tense or person
- pronoun agreement errors
- dangling or misplaced modifiers
- ineffective fragments and comma splices
- incorrect homophones for the context

Weaver says that teachers can use grammatical terminology in mini-lessons, but they shouldn't hold students accountable for learning the terms. Writers, she notes, can use structures even if they can't name them. The reading in this chapter by Weaver, McNally, and Moerman explains more about how teachers can teach in the context of writing.

Weaver (1996) points out several differences between traditional grammar and her contextualized teaching of grammar. Figure 3.2 summarizes these differences and explains the advantages of contextualized grammar.

One criticism of contextualized grammar is that it seems scattershot, especially to teachers used to the systematic nature of the traditional grammar curriculum. In traditional grammar, students study each part of speech and kind of phrases and clauses in turn. In contextualized grammar, on the other hand, teachers address whatever comes up in students' papers. Topics from one conference to another can range from punctuating dialogue to spelling homonyms correctly to combining several short, choppy sentences. Granted, in many ways, teaching grammar in the context of writing seems more chaotic. But, research suggests it's more productive in the long run. When students focus on grammar that's immediate and relevant to what they want to say, they pay more attention to it. It becomes vital to them, and they make the effort to learn it (Calkins, 1980).

All of the current English language arts textbooks I examined contain more grammar than Weaver envisions, but in general they seem to be moving toward integrating writing and grammar. *English* (Rueda et al., 2001) actively connects writing and grammar—in both its writing and its grammar sections. *English* begins with a separate section on "Grammar, Usage, and Mechanics," after a short overview of the writing process, but the exercises in this section include not only analyzing but also revising practice. Then in "Writing Wrap-Ups" to each section, students are asked to write on their own, though the topics and genres are assigned. The writing portion of *English* is organized by genre, and each chapter cycles through the writing process, so each chapter contains a section on revising and another on editing.

Alongside *English* (Rueda et al., 2001), Glencoe McGraw-Hill's (2001) *Writer's Choice* looks especially traditional. If grammar is taught in the context of writing, it's not easily evident; in fact, nor is there much writing in the context of studying grammar. But there is some connection to literature. The grammar ex-

FIGURE 3.2   *Theoretical Foundation: Comparing Traditional and Contextualized Grammar Approaches*

Weaver (1996) argues that grammar should be taught in the context of reading and writing. She explains how a contextualized approach differs from traditional grammar approaches and argues for the advantages of this approach.

Traditional Grammar	Contextualized Grammar
Emphasizes analysis and mastery.	Emphasizes inquiry and discovery. The process approach helps students learn better.
Emphasizes learning and applying grammatical terms.	Minimizes the use of grammatical terms and maximizes the use of examples. Students are not put off by difficult vocabulary. They understand how to use structures even if they can't label them.
Emphasizes analyzing sentences.	Emphasizes production of sentences. Students learn to write by writing. They have a genuine need for learning because they're writing.
Teaches "correct" punctuation.	Teaches not only "correct" punctuation but also "effective" punctuation, as published writers use. Students explore the rhetorical effects of punctuation.
Studies only Standard English.	Explores not only Standard English (the language of wider communication), but also different ethnic and community dialects. Students learn to appreciate that different contexts require different language demands and that they need a range of different choices to be able to communicate in a variety of contexts.
Approaches grammar from the point of view of a grammarian, though the oft-stated goal is to improve writing. The focus is on the system rather than what writers need to know.	Approaches grammar from a point of view of a writer. The goal is to help students acquire a sense of rhetorical judgment and skill in editing.
Is top-down. Everyone studies the same grammar at the same pace. It doesn't matter how much grammar is intuitively obvious to a native speaker; each piece is studied in turn.	Is bottom-up. Teachers individualize instruction because not all students have the same grammar troublespots.

ercises are traditional identify-and-label exercises. In the chapter on "Subjects, Predicates, and Sentences," for example, there are numerous practice and review exercises in which students are asked to analyze various kinds of sentences and/or sentence parts. At the end of the chapter is a writing application, but it's another exercise where the ideas are already provided rather than a prompt which students generate a text from and which they express their own ideas about. However, literature plays a part here. Students are asked to study an excerpt from a novel as part of a lesson on giving writing "interest and texture" by combining simple sentences into compound ones or into sentences with compound predicates. Then they're given a sentence combining exercise. The only application to their own writing is the advice "Try to apply [the author's] writing techniques when you write and revise your work" (p. 317).

Elements of Language (Odell et al., 2001) falls in between the other two. It includes a section on publishing and proofreading, with grammar links, in its chapters on writing various genres. But the chapter on "Writing Effective Sentences," for example, contains mainly analysis exercises. The "Writing Application" at the end of this chapter asks students to write a new piece on an assigned topic, and, it's interesting to note, works students through the prewriting, writing, revising, and publishing steps in doing so.

The Status of Standard English

Regardless of which context we choose to teach grammar in, our reforms have a number of consequences. One consequence is that written Standard English no longer has the same status it enjoys under a traditional school curriculum. In traditional grammar, the rules of Standard English are the only ones considered proper, correct, or worthy of study. By implication, if not explicit statement, the rules of other dialects of English are considered "wrong" or "ungrammatical." But, as Daniels (See Chapter 1) points out in "Nine Ideas about Language," Standard English is not *linguistically* superior to the other dialects of English; we just *assign* it greater value for political reasons. Languages naturally vary across geographic regions, social classes, and historic periods because they're ever-changing phenomena. One variation is no better or worse linguistically than another. Thus, all dialects of English are worthy of study and worthy of affirmation. This is especially important to language minority students, who don't often see themselves reflected in the school curriculum because their home languages aren't Standard English. (See Chapters 6 and 9 for more discussion on dialects and vernacular dialect speakers.)

Moreover, under this new approach, the definition of "good" English changes. As Daniels points out, we all naturally, usually unconsciously, shift our style, vocabulary, and level of detail to fit the circumstances in which we are communicating—what sociolinguists call *pragmatics* (Yule, 1996). Even though we begin to develop our pragmatic sense before we begin school, it's the last of the language components we learn. We continue to develop an ever-wider range of styles that we use with an ever-wider range of speakers. We can say, then, there's some value in studying traditional grammar because we're studying the rules for the formal end of our range of styles. But we can't say that formal English is always the "right" or "correct" way to communicate. Many times, as Martin Joos (1961) points out, pragmatics requires that we use an informal, casual style (See Chapter 6). Thus, the "right" way is whatever language—whether formal or informal, written or oral, standard or nonstandard—is most appropriate to the situation.

This chapter explores productive alternatives to the isolated exercises typical of traditional grammar.

Exploring Your Own Language Experience

1. Before you begin the reading for this chapter, spend five minutes or so writing in your journal about the following:

    a. According to Daniels, "our speech patterns vary greatly during the course of our everyday routine" (p. 13). Consider your own routines and environment: what speech patterns do you use? with whom? in which situations?

    b. Linguists call for a curriculum that explores such topics as dialects, word formation processes, dictionary compilations, and social conventions, etc. To what extent did you study these aspects of language in school? Did you, for example, learn something about the history of English when you were reading early writers in your literature classes (e.g., Chaucer and Shakespeare)? Did you discuss dialects when you were reading stories in which characters spoke in dialect (e.g., *Huckleberry Finn*)? Did you study the Greek and Latin roots of words in vocabulary class?

2. Review your journal from Chapter 2. To what extent did you study grammar in the context of what you were reading and writing?

To Grammar or Not to Grammar: That Is <u>Not</u> the Question!

Constance Weaver, Carol McNally, and Sharon Moerman

> *This article first appeared in the March 2001 special theme issue on "Contextualizing Grammar" in* Voices *from the Middle. In this article, Weaver, McNally, and Moerman take individual turns arguing for writing-based grammar instruction. They believe grammar should be taught as both a means to generate detail while drafting, and to judge the effectiveness of sentences while revising.*

"Should we teach grammar, or shouldn't we?" Often presented with this apparent all-or-nothing choice, even the teachers asking the question may not have clear instructional goals for teaching grammar; they may simply think they *should* teach it. Sometimes they have other reasons, though, for thinking they ought to teach grammar: they find parents, the public, and even the politicians clamoring for grammar instruction in the hope that teaching traditional grammar from handbooks or CDs will somehow improve students writing, or at least their ability to avoid "errors."

Most often it doesn't.

Yes, some students learn the conventions of grammar, usage, and punctuation from a handbook. Or at least they appear to have learned these conventions when doing skill and drill exercises on one concept at a time, followed by related tests. But do students remember and apply these conventions in their own writing? Here, the payoff severely declines.

The problems with this common view of "why teach grammar" lie deeper than most people realize. First, we must contend with an underlying, implicit, and largely erroneous learning theory: if teachers teach something well, students will learn it and, what's more, will apply it well. What we now know from cognitive psychology is that students need guidance in developing concepts, such as the concepts of "sentence" and "not sentence." In addition, no matter how motivated the students may be to apply such concepts—for example, to avoid or eliminate run-ons and fragments in their writing—they still often need help applying these concepts in practical situations. Such help may be needed even by the students who enjoy and take pride in their schoolwork and who love analyzing data.

Much of what we teach in the name of grammar amounts to labeling parts of speech and their functions or identifying kinds of sentences, yet students need very little of this to learn the conventions of written edited English. For most students, teaching grammar as sentence analysis is another reason why the grammar doesn't transfer to student writing.

It is convenient for us to be able to refer to "nouns," "verbs," "subjects," and "predicates" when talking about things like subject-verb agreement. However, a little grammar goes a long way when it comes to helping students edit for the use of standard conventions in their writing, and the concepts can be taught as we discuss literature and the students' own writing.

Yet another major problem with the demand for teaching grammar is exemplified in the tendency to limit the concern about "grammar" to just the issue of conventions, or what is commonly called "correctness." Even teachers often fail to realize that they can do a great deal to help students write more effectively by attending to grammatical options, such as reducing a sentence with supporting details to an appositive, a participial phrase, or an absolute. When we help students see how to *add* details using such phrases, we are actually helping them to generate content. Other grammatical issues we can attend to are modifier placement, sentence variety, and sentence structure. The choice and placement of these grammatical options join with word use and other features to create a distinctive style and voice in a piece of writing. Thus, guiding students in sentence expansion and revision is critical to helping them become more *effective*, not just more *correct*, as writers. See, for example, Harry Noden's *Image Grammar* (1999).

Both our personal teaching experiences and the findings of research studies support the conclusion that most students do not benefit from grammar study in isolation from writing, if indeed our purpose in teaching grammar is to help students improve their writing (e.g., Hillocks and Smith, 1991). In short, teaching traditional grammar in isolation is not a very practical act.

What we *have* found practical, though, is drawing upon literature for models of effective sentences and paragraphs, while incorporating only the most useful grammatical concepts (and even less terminology) into our teaching of writing. This enables us to help students improve sentences as they learn to recognize skilled use of detail, style, voice, and, of course, the conventions of edited American English. When we have students do activities—let's say brief writings to practice using a particular grammatical construction—it is typically as a prelude to writing another piece where we simply encourage students to experiment with the grammatical options they've been learning. If we think of writing as a recursive process, then teaching grammatical options and syntactic effectiveness is most appropriate as a prelude to writing and during revision, while teaching writing conventions is most helpful during the editing phase. Revising for greater grammatical effectiveness and editing for conventions can be spurred by mini-lessons, but ultimately, we have found individual conferences to be absolutely indispensable.

Teachers who are familiar with NCTE's resolutions on the teaching of grammar will see that the teaching of grammar in and for writing is in line with those resolutions, while isolated teaching of grammar is not. Teaching grammar in context is also in line with the NCTE standards for the English language arts, particularly standard 6 (NCTE, 1996):

> Students apply knowledge of language structure, language conventions (e.g., spelling and punctuation), media techniques, figurative language, and genre to create, critique, and discuss print and nonprint texts. (p. 36)

There is nothing in the NCTE standards about teaching grammar—or anything else—as an isolated subject. Rather, the language arts are seen as a unit, permeating inquiry and learning throughout the curriculum.

It should not be surprising, then, that our teaching experiences as well as our professional reading have convinced us that teaching a limited number of grammatical concepts in the context of their use is far better than isolated grammar study in getting students to appreciate and use grammatical options and conventions more effectively. Or as Rei Noguchi (1991) puts it, "Less is more" (p. 121).

Connie's section of this article begins by alluding to minilessons and writing practice, after which she focuses on "grammar emerging" as viewed through writings of seventh-grade students. Such examples encourage us to rethink how we can best promote detail and grammatical variety in students' writing. In the following section, Carol discusses some activities that are helping her students to appreciate and use longer, more interesting sentences, and to draw upon a wider repertoire of syntactic options. This is followed by a section on revising sentences in a paragraph. Finally, Sharon discusses the importance of keeping the issue of writing conventions in perspective, while nevertheless helping students learn to edit their own writing.

For us, the question is *not* a simple dichotomy, "To grammar or not to grammar?" Rather, the question is, "What aspects of grammar can we teach to enhance and improve students' writing, and when and how can we best teach them?" "In the context of writing" is our short answer, but we keep learning more ways as we keep taking risks as teachers.

Connie: Prewriting and "Grammar Emerging"

Decades ago, I was deeply affected, as a writer and as a teacher, by a little book called *Notes Toward a New Rhetoric* (1967). In this book, Francis Christensen pointed out that "Grammar maps out the possible; rhetoric narrows the possible down to the desirable or effective" (p. 39). With respect to sentence combining (which had not yet seen its heyday), Christensen wrote: "We need a rhetoric of the sentence that will do more than combine the ideas of primer sentences. We need one that will generate ideas" (p. 26).

Through Christensen's generous examples from both professional and student writing, I became convinced that focusing on certain grammatical forms was the best way to help students generate details and images. Christensen's research on the kinds of constructions commonly used by adult published writers but seldom used by twelfth graders led me to focus on two of these three constructions, namely participial phrases and absolutes. After having my freshman writing students practice these two constructions by doing sentence-combining exercises (yes, sentence-combining, not sentence-generating), I used to read them all but the ending of Ray Bradbury's "The Foghorn," after which I asked them to write their own endings, being sure to include participial phrases and absolutes that would carry narrative and descriptive details.

Here is an example of the kinds of sentences my students produced as part of their narrative conclusion, with the requisite constructions italicized:

participial phrase →	The monster lunged forward, *leaving a trail of slime,*
absolute →	*his eyes fixed on the red, white, red, white of the revolving light,*
absolute →	*his mournful voice echoing the sound of the foghorn.*

A participial phrase begins (usually) with a participle, either a present participle ending in -*ing*, or a past participle, such as *broken, frightened, sung* (as in the opening phrase of this sentence: *Frightened* by the foghorn, the monster lunged forward). An absolute is a phrase that usually can be restored to full sentencehood by adding *am, is, are, was, were,* as in the examples above. By focusing on participial and absolute phrases that provide detail, zooming in like the zoom lens on a camera, my students found themselves able to infuse images and sensory detail into their narratives, and the use of detail even seemed to carry over into their expository and persuasive writing. In short, their writing improved greatly.

Today, I use sentence-imitating and sentence-generating activities that result in real pieces of writing. I have learned how grammar and detail can emerge through good preparation for writing, including viewing art and reading and discussing good literature.

Grammar Emerging through Prewriting Activities

We can learn valuable lessons from Sarah, a seventh-grade teacher (Woltjer, 1998; Weaver 1996b).

Sarah had previously encouraged her seventh graders to use adjectives and adverbs in their writing, but found that often her students' "descriptive" poems or paragraphs included little description and no details to make the pieces come alive. When it was suggested that she guide her students in writing a "five senses" poem about fall,

Sarah decided to experiment with two different ways of encouraging students to use adjectives and adverbs. First, she asked the students to write about fall but gave them little direction, except for mentioning "Be sure to use those adjectives and adverbs for detail!" The students turned in their writings at the end of class.

About two weeks later, Sarah guided the students in writing their second fall poems, the "sense" poems. She explains:

> The Monday before, I had each student bring in one or two leaves, so by Wednesday we had a large basket of them. Before writing on Wednesday, we did prewriting exercises together as a class. My students loved it! We threw the basket of leaves in the air and watched them fall in different directions. Then the students took turns placing their leaves on the hot air register and watched as their leaf got blown up toward the ceiling. After this, they went around the classroom sharing a favorite fall memory or Thanksgiving tradition. Finally, with that introduction, I explained the writing assignment as using the five senses, and they began writing. Those that had trouble with the first fall writing assignment now had previous knowledge and ideas from the prewriting activities on the five senses to provide organization. The difference in their writings was amazing!

Figure 1 shows the "before and after" poems from two students. One important thing to notice is that many of the descriptive words in the "after" poems aren't necessarily adjectives or adverbs; they are nouns ("razor blades") or verbs ("mulched"), as in the sensory poem from Tom. Another important point is that while the "before" poems

---

FIGURE 1   *"Before" and "after" poems from Sarah's seventh graders*

Tom's poems

BEFORE
It is fall you rake the leaves crustily over a pile "o" mud.
It is nearly ear shattering when you rake the flames on the ground. How chilling it be, no one knows. It (fall) is so unpredictable.

AFTER
Smells like destruction when burned.
Clogging your lungs.
Tastes like the dirt of the earth, *destroying your taste buds.*
See the leaves on the trees fall effortlessly to the ground,
Where they will be raked, mulched, and burned.
Touch them—they feel like razor blades, when you jump on them.
Hear them? You can't!
But if you can't hear them, do they really fall?

Amy's poems

BEFORE
Fall is the leaves changing colors; they can be green, yellow or red.
Fall is the cold and the freezing at night.
Fall is when your backyard is covered with leaves.

AFTER
I can smell the apple pie *baking in the oven.*
I can smell the *burning* leaves in the neighbor's yards.
I hear the leaves *crackling under my feet as I trudge through the yard.*
I hear children *yelling as they jump in a pile of leaves.*
I see blended colors on the leaves like someone painted them.
I touch the leaves and I feel the veins.
I touch the leaves and sometimes they break in my hands.
I taste the turkey as the grease runs down my throat.
I taste the pumpkin pie and now I know it is fall!

used some adjectives and/or adverbs, the "after" poems used a much greater variety of constructions that function adjectivally (to modify nouns) or adverbially (to modify verbs or whole clauses). Examples are the participle and participial phrases in Tom's and Amy's "after" poems.

What is to be learned from Sarah's experience? Several things, I think (Weaver 1996b):

1. Various kinds of prewriting experiences can greatly enhance the quality of students' writing. This is something Sarah already knew and typically practiced.
2. A variety of adjectival and adverbial constructions will probably emerge when students are guided in focusing on the details of experience, rather than on grammar.
3. Asking students to focus on "adjectives" and "adverbs" might actually limit students' use of the more sophisticated structures they would use naturally.

The last two lessons were important ones Sarah learned—and important, I think, for many of us to learn, as teachers. (For a fuller version of Sarah's story, in her own words, see Woltjer, 1998).

Grammar can help us generate ideas; however, the reverse occurs as well. Not only can grammar generate ideas, but ideas can generate grammar. The two are mutually reinforcing.

Sarah's experiences, as well as my own, have confirmed for me that the use of sophisticated grammatical constructions in writing does not necessarily have to be taught. It can be generated through a focus on ideas for writing, and through the examples offered by quality literature. For other students, though, the explicit use of imitation and sentence generation may produce a breakthrough in writing, as Carol describes in the next section.

Carol: Learning Grammar with The Giver

Specific grammatical constructions evident in the current literature students read are potential springboards for teaching stylistic writing options that students can integrate into their writings and revisions. When read in the context of a great book, grammatical constructions used by professional authors model syntactic options that can be used by student writers.

Drawing upon research, Connie Weaver states that sentence combining helps students "expand their syntactic repertoire in order to write more syntactically sophisticated and rhetorically effective sentences" (1996, p. 142). Indeed, one of the most prevalent tendencies of middle school writers is to include a high frequency of short, choppy sentences—all of like construction—in their writing.

Just to show my seventh grade students what could be done to revise a piece of writing containing short, choppy sentences, I took a passage from Chapter 9 of *The Giver*, beautifully written by Lois Lowry, and put it through a regression process that turned it into a piece of writing that any middle school student might have written:

> His training had not yet begun. He left the auditorium. He felt apartness. He made his way through the crowd. He was holding the folder she had given him. He was looking for his family unit. He was also looking for Asher. People moved aside for him. They watched him. He thought he could hear whispers.

I had the students read through this altered rendition of Lowry's writing and asked them to discuss what they thought of it. As I predicted, the students thought it was too choppy, and even questioned that it was actually from the book they were currently reading, since it differed so drastically from Lowry's style. I assured them that it was actually from the chapter we would be reading later that same day, but told them I had changed Lowry's writing to reflect what I often saw in their own writing.

As a group, we discussed how the first two sentences might be combined into one, longer, more interesting sentence. Then, I invited the students to rewrite the altered passage, revising the paragraph toward what they imagined they would find in Lowry's actual text.

> Joe wrote:
> Training had not yet began for Jonas's assignment. Leaving the auditorium Jonas felt apartness. Making his way through the crowd was tough because of the number of people. Trying to find Asher, and his family unit, Jonas thought he heard whispers.

> Ann wrote:
> His training had not begun yet, but he left the auditorium feeling apartness. He made his way through the crowd, as he was holding the folder she had given him. He was looking for his family unit. But he was also looking for Asher. People were moving aside for him. The crowd was watching him. He thought he could hear whispering.

> Brian wrote:
> Training had not yet begun for Jonas. Leaving the auditorium Jonas felt apartness. Holding the folder the chief elder gave him he made his way through the crowd. Jonas was looking for his family unit and Asher. Watching him, the people moved aside for him. Thinking he could hear whispers.

Compare the writings of these students to Lowry's actual passage where she describes Jonas leaving the Ceremony of Twelve:

> But his training had not yet begun and already, upon leaving the Auditorium, he felt the apartness. Holding the folder she had given him, he made his way through the throng, looking for his family unit and for Asher. People moved aside for him. They watched him. He thought he could hear whispers. (p. 62)

The students were a bit dismayed that the last three sentences were actually as choppy in Lowry's text as in my chopped up version. We discussed why Lowry chose to do this, and the class realized that the choppiness of construction mirrored the apartness that Jonas was beginning to feel immediately following the Ceremony of Twelve. It was Lowry's stylistic choice to use simple sentence construction to parallel Jonas's growing feeling of isolation.

I must state here that this class had previously studied the effects of beginning sentences with participial phrases via Noden's *Image Grammar* and his concept of "brush strokes." So, in addition to combining sentences, many students also integrated this previously learned stylistic grammar choice to enhance their re-creations of Lowry's passage.

Noden directly compares an artist's development of a painting with the writer's development of a piece of writing:

> Just as the painter combines a wide repertoire of brush stroke techniques to create an image, the writer chooses from a repertoire of sentence structures. Although professionals use an array of complex structures, students can begin to learn the art of image grammar by employing five basic brush strokes: (1) the participle, (2) the absolute, (3) the appositive, (4) adjectives shifted out of order, and (5) action verbs. (p. 4)

The text of *The Giver* provides many examples of each of Noden's "brush strokes." In another minilesson, I retyped the following sentences from Chapters 16 and 18 for the students to examine:

"Warmth," Jonas replied, "and happiness." And—let me think. *Family*. That it was a celebration of some sort, a holiday. (p. 117)

The Old of the community did not ever leave their special place, the House of the Old, where they were so well cared for and respected. (p. 117)

Jonas thought of his favorite female, Fiona, and shivered. (p. 132)

I asked the students to carefully consider the construction of these sentences. I had to ask them to look beyond the comma before they really started to catch on to the fact that the word or phrase after the comma actually just renamed the noun before it. The students were grasping the idea of the appositive, even though they didn't know its name!

I modeled writing sentences with appositives for them by asking them to give me several words or phrases that described Jonas and using those nouns or noun phrases as appositives in writing my sentences about Jonas.

Next, I invited them to try the same approach in writing about the Giver:

David wrote:
The old receiver of memory has now moved on to become the Giver. The Giver, Jonas's instructor, holds the memories of what it was like before sameness was among them and their society.

Christina wrote:
Giving memories to Jonas, the Giver shares the pain and the joy. The Giver, the old receiver of memory, is giving Jonas painful memories as well as joyful memories.

Mindi wrote:
The Giver, an old man weighed down by positive and negative memories, is kind but to the point. He is shut away from everyone, chosen when he became a Twelve to be different and endure the pains of some awful memories.

Notice these descriptions not only use appositives correctly, two of them also make use of participial phrases and none are short, choppy sentences by any means.

The goal is to see students incorporating these grammatical constructions into all of their writing and, consciously or unconsciously, to become more sophisticated writers. And this is beginning to happen. I was delighted when I read these most recent journal entries from the following students who were writing in response to Chapter 19 of *The Giver*:

Charlene wrote:
How could this place seem so peaceful and wonderful? Why would they kill little children and elderly people? I hate this community! This is such a bad thing and people actively kill other people. I would never be able to live with that, knowing that the life of someone has been taken away from them and that they actually killed other people. I though it was a utopia. A utopia should not have people killing other people. It's just not right to do that!

Mindi wrote:
Oh wow! How could they just kill a baby, so innocent, so unknowing? How could Rosemary kill herself? I understand, I guess, that the community doesn't feel emotions,

but Rosemary could feel. She knew what would happen. Why does the Receiver let that happen? So is there really an elsewhere or is Elsewhere really death? I think this community needs help!

If I had started these lessons by telling my students we were going to be studying grammar, or more specifically, participial phrases and appositives, and doing sentence combining, my guess is their attitude would have precluded the positive results that I see more and more often in their everyday writing. Indeed, exercises on these aspects of grammar from an English book would have been just that—exercises—the results of which would most likely not have transferred to real student writing at all!

My experiences with teaching grammar in the context of literature are similar to an experience Sharon recently had with one of her students in an editing conference. In both cases, students were engaged in improving their writing, not just learning grammar for the sake of knowing the proper terminology or in order to pass a grammar test. Students were learning grammar incidentally as they focused on improving their writing.

Connie: Revision of Sentences and Paragraphs

Most of us English language arts teachers have not actually had much guidance in revising sentences to create more effective paragraphs. We have had our sentences "corrected" if they were actually fragments or run-ons or victims of a comma splice. We may even have had an exercise or two in moving elements within sentences. But few of us have received help expanding or combining sentences within our own writing in order to add detail, to reduce whole sentences conveying details to subordinate constructions, to make our sentences flow, or to use form to reflect content. Therefore, we tend to teach as we were taught, limiting ourselves mostly to the "correcting" of sentences. But we need to do better in order to help students write better than we were taught to write. We need to have students combine, move, revise, and expand sentences for greater effectiveness.

I'll use myself as an example. After six years of repeated grammar study in junior high and high school, I could use not only subordinate clauses but also appositives and participial phrases that occurred at the beginning of a sentence or immediately after the subject. But my narrative and descriptive writing was stiff. Stylistically, it sounded like ineffective expository writing with unnatural sentence structures and insufficient detail. As I mentioned earlier, it wasn't until I read the Christensen book, *Notes Toward a New Rhetoric* (1967), that I learned to write more effective sentences with more concrete details. After examining published adult writing, Christensen concluded that the constructions most lacking in high school students' writing were appositives, participial phrases, and absolute constructions. Equally or more important for me as a writer, Christensen pointed out that these and other constructions, when serving as nonessential "free modifiers," most often occurred in the final position in a sentence. Next most frequent was initial position, before the subject. Least frequent were exactly what my teachers unfortunately had emphasized, modifiers right after the subject. (Note to teachers worrying about my use of "be" verbs in these last two sentences: I chose to include the clarifying material last in the sentences, for emphasis.)

Years later, in trying to illustrate for my students what I had learned about using subordinate detail and the judicious placement of modifiers, I wrote a short piece about my experience whitewater rafting in Costa Rica. Here is how a certain excerpt read in my first draft, with few details, and these details occurring in complete sentences instead of being subordinate to a main subject-verb unit:

So on the third day of our trip, I shouldn't have been surprised that the flooding Pacuare rose while we slept beside it for the night. Nor should I have been surprised, I suppose, that we were now "going swimming" for the second time.

But this time was worse than the first. The wall of water momentarily crushed me. I surfaced quickly. I was grateful that this time I had not come up under the raft. Thank God! But then another wave engulfed me. It drove me deeper into the blackness. I dared not open my eyes.

Keeping in mind what I had learned from Frances Christensen about using participial phrases and absolutes, and about placing most of them in final position, I then expanded my draft to produce the following, with the absolute and the participial phrases italicized:

So on the third day of our trip, I shouldn't have been surprised that the flooding Pacuare rose while we slept beside it for the night, *its muddy waters picking up speed as it swelled its banks* [absolute]. Nor should I have been surprised, I suppose, that we were now "going swimming" for the second time.

But this time was worse than the first. The wall of water momentarily crushed me, *pushing me toward the bottom of the river* [participial phrase]. I surfaced quickly, grateful that this time, I had not come up under the raft. Thank God! But then another wave engulfed me, *driving me deeper this time, much deeper, into blackness* [participial phrase]. I dared not open my eyes. (Weaver, 1996a, p. 119)

While revising, I kept in mind that I wanted to do four things: to add participial phrases and absolutes if or as appropriate, in order to convey details; to reduce most sentences focusing on details to these or other subordinate constructions; to include most of these "free modifying" constructions at the ends of sentences; and especially to create a narrative sense of movement with the participial phrases in final position. I think I have accomplished all four goals in this short excerpt.

Over the years, I have learned to address these goals mostly as I write my first draft, instead of having to go back later to deal with sentence and paragraph structure in a separate revision cycle. I have also learned to experiment with choices in grammar and punctuation that support, mirror, and convey content (see Romano, 1998). But most important, I have learned to focus on using certain grammatical constructions—namely participial phrases, absolutes, and their placement—and that attempt, in turn, has nudged me into adding details that convey images or ideas (Christensen, 1967, p. 26).

In *Image Grammar* (1999), Harry Noden demonstrates how to help writers appreciate and achieve such goals as I attempted with the whitewater rafting piece—and many more. For example, he discusses a revision scenario described in Olsen's *Envisioning Writing* (1992). The teacher asked the students to write a brief character sketch. One of the sixth-grade students wrote the following:

The Big Guy

James weighs 240 pounds and use to be the champ. He beat Mohamad Ali for the crown. He's 38 know and he had drugs and pot. He's been in jail for 5 years and that ended his carrear. He's had a though time finding a job. His face is scared. He wares a ripped T shirt with knee pants. He's trying to make a come back in the boxing world.

It's tempting to wield the red pen and go straight for the jugular of the Error Beast (Weaver, 1982). Instead, however, the teacher had students draw the character they were describing, then revise the writing to include details from the drawing. Here is this student's final edited version:

> The Big Guy
>
> The lonely man stood in a ring holding tight to the ropes. His head was bald. His chest was hairy and sweaty. His legs looked like they were planted to the ground like stumps. His muscles were relaxed in the dark ring. His mouth looked mean and tough the way it was formed. He was solid looking. His boxing gloves had blood stains on them. His still body structure glowed in the darkness. He braced himself against the ropes. His white pants had red stripes, the hair on his chin prickled out like thorns.

In terms of detail, this paragraph is *much* better than the original. Nevertheless, I was struck by the monotonous nature of the sentences, almost all of which begin with "his." The details all had equal grammatical status, since they all were presented in independent clauses rather than subordinate grammatical constructions. To my ear, this had created a boring, clumpety-clump rhythm within the paragraph.

What, I asked myself, would I do to help the writer make the sentence structures themselves more interesting, and how could I develop one or more minilessons using this piece of writing? What details would I subordinate? Indeed, what details would I group together before even trying to combine sentences and thereby subordinate some details? In the revised paragraph, I marked sentences whose details I would combine. Here, one combinable pair of sentences is indicated with italics, while a group of three is indicated with boldface:

> The lonely man stood in a ring holding tight to the ropes. *His head was bald. His chest was hairy and sweaty.* **His legs looked like they were planted to the ground like stumps.** His muscles were relaxed in the dark ring. **His mouth looked mean and tough the way it was formed. He was solid looking.** His boxing gloves had blood stains on them. His still body structure glowed in the darkness. He braced himself against the ropes. His white pants had red stripes, *the hair on his chin prickled out like thorns.*

Next, of course, came the problem of ordering. I decided to restructure one sentence and to group together sentences that might go together in terms of content, with some details to be subordinated in a next draft:

> The lonely man stood in a ring holding tight to the ropes.
>
> His head was bald.
> The hair on his chin was prickling out like thorns.
> His chest was hairy and sweaty.
>
> His muscles were relaxed in the dark ring.
>
> He was solid looking.
> His legs were planted to the ground like stumps.
> His mouth was formed mean and tough.
>
> His boxing gloves had stains on them.
> His still body glowed in the darkness.
>
> He braced himself against the ropes.

Doubtless my reordering was influenced by the fact that I already had some idea how I wanted to restructure the sentences. One version of a final draft could read as follows:

The Big Guy

The lonely man stood in a ring holding tight to the ropes. His head was bald, the hair on his chin prickling out like thorns, his chest hairy and sweaty. His muscles were relaxed in the dark ring, but he was solid looking, his legs planted to the ground like stumps, his mouth formed mean and tough. His boxing gloves had blood stains on them and his still body glowed in the darkness as he braced himself against the ropes.

In this particular revision, I created four new absolute constructions: *the hair on his chin prickling out like thorns, his chest hairy and sweaty, his legs planted to the ground like stumps, his mouth formed mean and tough.* Perhaps this was overkill, but at least I had grouped and subordinated details to make the sentences more interesting and the passage more flowing. The student writer had already added details after drawing a picture of the big guy, but still needed help with recombining, reordering, and revising sentences. For ideas on recombining and revising sentences, look for any of the several books Don Killgallon has published on sentence composing, including not only a theory booklet but a book for high school, one for middle school, and one for elementary.

It's unfortunate when we teachers ignore the possibilities for revision in a piece like this student's original, but instead see only a need for wielding the "red pen," defacing the student's work, and often demoralizing the student as a writer. It is unfortunate when we assign writing and then simply grade it, making the writing assignment merely an opportunity for testing. Much better to help students like the writer of "The Big Guy" become more proficient in writing by making the writing situation an opportunity for genuine teaching.

As teachers, we need to help students learn various revision strategies at the sentence and paragraph level. Occasional minilessons like those I developed with "The Big Guy" may help substantially, but they will still need to be followed by assistance in individual conferences or small groups. Incidentally, I have used this particular example in workshops with teachers who never group or combine the sentences in quite the same way as I have done! There is much opportunity here for experimentation and learning—both teachers' learning and students' learning. We need to take risks as teachers in order to encourage our students to take risks as writers.

And we need to hold off with the infamous "red pen," instead *guiding* students not only in sentence and paragraph revision but in editing, as Sharon demonstrates in the next section.

Sharon: Putting Conventions into Perspective and Helping Students Edit

Recently in a graduate class I read aloud the following essay written by one of my eighth-grade students.

My Grandfather's Death
by Chasity

I still remember my mom in the living room with her brothers as my grandfather took his last breath. I was only seven and I was the only kid there. I knew my grandfather was sick for awhile and that he may die soon, but I never thought that it would change my life that much.

My mom was the saddest. She was a daddy's girl, and as she rested her head on his arm, I couldn't even imagine what might be going through her head. As she walked in the kitchen, you could see the sadness and misery on her face.

The next day was very hard for her and the family. When we went to the funeral home everyone was hugging and kissing each other. I wanted to go up there and see him, but that being the first time I had ever seen a dead body, I was a little scared to, so I made my cousin Ashley go with me. He didn't look dead to me, he just looked like he always did except he was wearing a light blue dress shirt and he had a very peculiar smile. It was weird.

When "Amazing Grace" played, my mom burst out in tears with about seven other people that I saw. So I put my hand on hers thinking it would help, but she cried more. I couldn't even look at her.

When we went to the cemetery, my mom was staring at him going down, crying, but her eyes were glowing. I could tell she was thinking about what his last breath was: "I'll tell Mom you said hi." I knew she was happy he went where he wanted to be—with his wife.

My grandfather and I were very close. I sometimes think of me on his lap with hot cocoa watching Scooby-Doo. Sometimes I think he's still here with me, holding my hand, walking me through life.

When I finished reading this piece, I looked around the room at the tear-filled eyes. I was not surprised—I had the same reaction when I read it. Then I asked them, "Would you FAIL this piece?" They looked at me as though I had just arrived from outer space. Then I put Chasity's piece—exactly as she had written it when she turned it in—on the overhead (see excerpt, Figure 2). "*Now* what do you say?" I asked them.

This time they were silent for a different reason.

If scored against a typical rubric, Chasity's essay would have earned the lowest score—1—for conventions, because the surface errors in this piece severely interfered with understanding. But what about content and ideas? Organization? Style? Just as clearly, Chasity would score well in those areas. Would it be fair for Chasity to fail based on the number of convention errors?

I have to admit, when I first looked at Chasity's piece I was perplexed, and it took several attempts before I could decipher what she was trying to say. But once I realized the depth of her feelings and her ability to articulate them, I was completely taken aback. Chasity is one of those students we call "resistant" and "reluctant." She doesn't hand in a lot of work, and what she does hand in isn't always up to par. I couldn't help thinking it was no wonder; she must be a discouraged student—and a discouraged writer. But this! This piece had style and voice. It had depth and feeling. Clearly she had created pictures in my mind, and she had evoked an emotional response. For the first time, Chasity had handed in a completed piece of writing. I wanted to support her, assure her that this really was a good piece of writing, and that we could work on editing the piece together. I knew beyond a shadow of a doubt that if I handed Chasity's story back to her full of correction marks, she would likely shut down again. She had taken a risk, and I did not want to discourage her.

This was our first serious piece of writing of the year. We had already spent some time revisiting the writing process and had practiced prewriting, drafting, revising, and editing. Before getting started on this writing assignment, we did some minilessons on the introductions and conclusions, and we talked about what it means to stay focused and organized. We read some personal narratives and discussed what was good, what we liked, and what we didn't like. I instructed them to make me laugh, make me cry, but make me do *something* when I read their papers. "Put me there! Make pictures in my head as I read your papers!" I told them dramatically. "Put a WOW at the end!" I gave them the rubric I planned to use and asked them to score their own writing before turning it in for me to score.

My grandpa's death   GA
                                                          Chasity

I still rember my mom in the
living room. Whith her bothers
as my grandfather took his last
breath. I was only seven and I
was the only kid there. I new
my grandfather was sick for a
wile. and that he may die soon.
aut I neven that it would change
my life. That much, my mom
was the. sadest she was a daddy's
girls. as she rested here head on
his arm. I I don't even enagen
what mate be going thowher
head. as she walked in the kitchen
you could see the sadiness and misery
on her face.
        The next day was very
for her and the family. when
we went to the funial home.
every one was hging and kissing
each other. I wanted to go up
there and see him but that
beening the first I ever seen a
dead body I was a litlle scared to.
so I made my cousin Ashley

FIGURE 2   *Excerpt of Chasity's essay*

Chasity had, indeed, created pictures in my head. I could vividly see her mother, a daddy's girl, resting her head on her dying father's arm. I could feel Chasity's pain and confusion as she tried to console her inconsolable mother, only to see her cry more. But what about the misspellings, the misplaced periods and commas, the lack of quotation marks . . . ?

Like so many of my colleagues, I strive to be the best English teacher I can possibly be, so I persistently ask myself, "What is best for my students?" Research consistently shows teaching grammar in isolation does not work: most students do not remember it, and they seldom transfer it to their writing. As Weaver noted in *Grammar for Teachers* (1979): "There seems to be little value in marking students' papers with 'corrections,' little value in teaching the conventions of mechanics apart from actual writing, and even less value in teaching grammar in order to instill these conventions" (p. 64).

The grammar debate rages not only in English teacher journals, listservs, and classrooms, but also in my own head. Where does teaching grammar fit in? Should I teach grammar in isolation (skill and drill) and have students identify parts of speech on worksheet after worksheet? Based on current research, my experiences as a teacher, my participation in Third Coast Writing Project, and improvement in my students' writing, I think not.

Research over the last two decades gives us no reason to challenge these conclusions. So I ask myself, "Why should I waste valuable classroom time fighting what has already been proven a losing battle?" The answer to this question was even more apparent with Chasity's piece about her grandfather. If Chasity had focused on conventions instead of content, I am not even sure she would have tried writing the piece. I recalled Weaver's advice in *Teaching Grammar in Context* (1996a):

> To avoid stunting students' growth as writers, we need to guide our students in the writing process, including the phases of revising and editing their sentences and words. It would also be helpful to avoid correcting the kinds of construction that published writers use with impunity and indeed with good effect. And we need to respond positively to the new kinds of errors that reflect syntactic risk and growth. Time enough to help students correct these errors when they have gotten their ideas down on paper, experimenting with language in the process. In short, the Error Beast is to be welcomed and tamed, not slain. (p. 101)

I talked to Chasity before school the morning after I read her essay. I told her that she had done a terrific job of putting me there with her, of making pictures in my mind and evoking an emotional response. She seemed genuinely pleased. I explained that I was concerned about her editing, and asked her if she would conference with me individually so that we could edit it together. Thankfully, she agreed.

In an article titled "Developing Correctness in Student Writing: Alternatives to the Error Hunt," Lois Matz Rosen states:

> Although numerous research studies show that there is little or no transfer of learning from isolated drills to actual writing experiences and that the time-intensive practice of the teacher's "error hunt" does not produce more mechanically perfect papers, this 100-year-old tradition still persists. (p. 139)

Later in the same chapter, Rosen goes on to say

> Research has never been able to show that circling all the errors—the error hunt approach to marking—makes a significant difference in writing quality; instead it discourages the student whose paper is full of mistakes and focuses students on errors instead of ideas. Students are more likely to grow as writers when the teacher's primary purpose in reading student papers is to respond to content. (p. 149)

With Weaver's and Rosen's advice fresh in my mind, Chasity and I sat down together. I asked her to read the piece to me *exactly* as she wrote it. She read it, and as I suspected she would, she read it as she *intended* it to be read. We talked about conveying meaning, and how important it was for the reader to understand the significance of her grandfather's death. Suddenly, conventions and correct spellings had *relevance*. She cared about correctly placing periods and commas. She agonized over her words and sentences. She corrected as she read, and as we conferenced, she began to feel her way through her corrections. She was actually engaged in the editing process! She knew what she wanted to say, she just needed some help making the conventions correct. It was the first step in encouraging her to write more, read more, participate in class more. In other words, it was a step toward success. For me, it was confirmation that "taming the Error Beast" truly was better than trying to slay it.

I have come to realize that I simply must allow my eighth graders time to grow as writers, teach them to say what they mean first, encourage them to effectively communicate their thoughts and ideas. Writing is a process. It's ongoing and alive. Just like my kids.

Conclusion

In recent decades, as English language arts teachers have learned to teach writing instead of merely assigning it, it has become increasingly obvious that engaging and guiding students in the writing process instead of having them perform countless grammar exercises is a more effective way to teach writing. The research clearly shows that most students do not transfer "skill and drill" into vivid, imaginative writing, or even into focused and interesting informational or persuasive writing that contains specific and precise vocabulary.

We need to analyze what makes our students' writing effective. Is it the organization? The specific, even vivid details? What is it they do well? In all cases we have cited here, it was not the ability of any of the students to regurgitate grammar terminology or label the parts of sentences that made their writing more powerful. It was their ability to create images, evoke a response from the reader, and use the craft of writing to create better writing. We have found, too, that students who understand the importance of vivid detail in creative writing find it easier to grasp the importance of specific detail in informational and persuasive writing.

Through minilessons, writer's workshop, and conferencing, we teachers can help students determine a purpose and audience for their writing, work with them to develop ideas, and guide them in organizing and reorganizing their piece of writing, as necessary. Our role as writing teachers does not stop here, however, nor should we leap from this point to wielding the red pen in a bloody and usually futile attack on the "Error Beast."

Instead, as we've tried to demonstrate in this article, we teachers need also to help students add effective detail through constructions like appositives, participial phrases, absolutes. We need to help them manipulate elements within sentences, and sentences within paragraphs. Furthermore, we need to help students learn to edit for the conventions of writing. This is not a one-time process, because noticing and revising our departures from convention is not an easy task, even for most adults. Furthermore, learners make new kinds of errors as they try new things in their writing (Weaver, 1996a). We need to be students' advocates rather than their adversaries, appreciating their risk taking and guiding them as writers instead of just grading their writing. We need to be mentors and master craftspersons who assess their writing only after helping them improve it, which in turn helps them write more effectively the next time.

One way to gain more time for mentoring is to eliminate isolated study of grammar from the curriculum, replacing it with minilessons and hands-on guidance in developing more effective sentences and paragraphs, followed by assistance in learning to edit.

Perhaps we will need to assign fewer writing projects in order to spend time helping students polish some pieces of writing, but the results are well worth it in students' self-esteem, willingness to write, and increasing ability to demonstrate more aspects of good writing with less direction and guidance. In this respect, too, we have found that less is more.

Many students of language, especially linguists, argue for restoring grammar to the curriculum. But when we examine their arguments, we discover that they, too, do *not* usually mean that we should return to teaching traditional grammar from a grammar handbook. Typically, they mean that we should explore some of the interesting phenomena about language structure—interesting, but often not directly related to improving our writing. They mean that we should study language more broadly, including dialects, language history, and the origins and meanings of words and word parts. They mean that we should study theories of how language develops, universals in language development, and how language is acquired in a child's early years. They mean that we should study how people use language to exercise power and control over others. Some of them also mean that we should teach grammar in the hope of improving students' writing—though they're not agreed as to which grammar. They mean all of these and more—but *not* that we should teach traditional schoolbook grammar.

We agree that language study is important and can be made interesting, meaningful, and useful to students. We agree that language study should be included in the English language arts curriculum. But this is not "teaching grammar," as conceptualized by many teachers and most administrators, parents, and the public. We agree that "grammar" should be taught, too, but only as it aids writing, or in an elective course. Thus we strongly proclaim, "To grammar or not to grammar: That is *not* the question!" It's a question of why, when, what, and how to teach selected aspects of grammar, in order to strengthen students' writing.

References

Bradbury, R. (1990). The foghorn. In *The golden apples of the sun* (pp. 1–9). New York: Avon. (Original work published 1952, Curtis.)

Christensen, F. (1967). *Notes toward a new rhetoric: Six essays for teachers.* New York: Harper & Row.

Hillocks, G., Jr., & Smith, M. W. (1991). Grammar and usage. In J. Flood, J. M. Jensen, D. Lapp, & J. R. Squire (Eds.), *Handbook of research on teaching the English language arts* (pp. 591–603). New York: Macmillan.

Lowry, L. (1993). *The giver.* Evanston, IL: McDougal Littell Literature Connections.

National Council of Teachers of English and International Reading Association. (1996). *Standards for the English language arts.* Urbana, IL: Author.

Noden, H. (1999). *Image grammar: Using grammatical structures to teach writing.* Portsmouth, NH: Boynton/Cook.

Noguchi, R. R. (1991). *Grammar and the teaching of writing: Limits and possibilities.* Urbana, IL: National Council of Teachers of English.

Olson, J. (1992). *Envisioning writing: Toward an integration of drawing and writing.* Portsmouth, NH: Heinemann.

Rosen, L. (1998). Developing correctness in student writing: Alternatives to the error hunt. In C. Weaver (Ed.), *Lessons to share: On teaching grammar in context* (pp. 137–155). Portsmouth, NH: Boynton/Cook.

Weaver, C. (1979). *Grammar for teachers: Perspectives and definitions.* Urbana, IL: National Council of Teachers of English.

Weaver, C. (1982). Welcoming errors as signs of growth. *Language Arts, 59*, 438–444. Reprinted in Weaver, 1996a.

Weaver, C. (1996a). *Teaching grammar in context*. Portsmouth, NH: Boynton/Cook.

Weaver, C. (1996b). Teaching grammar in the context of writing. *English Journal, 85*, 15–24.

Woltjer, S. (1998). Facilitating the use of description—and grammar. In C. Weaver (Ed.), *Lessons to share: Teaching grammar in the context of writing* (pp. 95–99). Portsmouth, NH: Boynton/Cook.

Questions for Discussion

1. Why do all of the major authors cited—Andrews, Kolln, Wolfram, and Weaver—believe language and grammar instruction is valuable? What kind of grammar do they advocate? Why? How is their grammar different from traditional grammar?

2. Research Andrews' Language Exploration and Awareness Program. What are the advantages and disadvantages of the method? What kind of credentials does the author have? What kind of evidence does the author offer to support the soundness of his methods? How credible is the evidence? Why?

3. To what extent is grammar taught in the context of writing? Return to the resources you looked at in Chapter 2. Do the official curriculum guidelines of your state recommend teaching grammar in the context of reading and writing? To what extent do the textbooks you examined integrate grammar with the other language arts? To what extent do special programs for language minority students connect grammar to reading and writing? To what extent is knowledge of Standard English grammar measured in the context of writing? (Again, print out/photocopy relevant pages to bring to class to share with your classmates.) Based on your research, what conclusions can you draw about the extent to which grammar is contextualized in your area?

4. To what extent is language study, as the NCTE Resolution on Language Study defines it, explored? Return to the resources you looked at in Chapter 2. Do the official curriculum guidelines of your state recommend/require language study? To what extent do the textbooks you examined explore the history and the dialects of English as well as other language study topics? To what extent do special programs for language minority students explore the history and the dialects of English as well as other language study topics? (Again, print out/photocopy relevant pages to bring to class to share with your classmates.) Based on your research, what conclusions can you draw about the extent to which language study is encouraged in your area?

Part II

Responding to Student Writing

One aspect of language we continue to develop throughout our lives is our sense of rhetorical judgment. These are judgments we make about which words to use in which order to meet our readers' expectations and achieve our purpose(s) (Kolln, 1999). We continue to learn more about the linguistic and rhetorical demands of various situations as we continue to experience an ever wider range of written genres and an ever wider range of interlocutors (people we communicate with).

With an increasing expertise in making rhetorical and stylistic judgments, students have tools not only for generating ideas and drafting texts but also for revising and editing them. They can decide what content, organization, and stylistic choices will best achieve their purpose(s) for writing and meet their readers' expectations. They can also evaluate their texts to see where there are gaps between what's needed and what they've written.

The two chapters in this section explore how teachers can help students develop their sense of rhetorical judgment. They address the following questions:

- How can teachers facilitate students' development as writers? How can they use conferences and textual comments to help students better understand reader expectations and the effects of stylistic alternatives?
- Why do students make "errors" (mainly grammatical errors) when they write? How can teachers help them "see" the differences between what they've written and what's appropriate for the context?

4

Evaluating Student Writing

Of course, writers must have some knowledge of basic English vocabulary and sentence structure to even create a text in English. Without this knowledge, they wouldn't be able to encode their ideas in English. But they must also use their knowledge of rhetoric to write. Experienced writers know that they must generate relevant background information, supporting details, and illustrative examples so their readers understand and are persuaded by their ideas. They know they need to shape these ideas into attention-grabbing introductions, logically organized bodies, and into conclusions that bring a sense of closure. Thinking both about what they want to say and about what the reader needs helps writers come up with ideas—either as they draft or as they revise.

Similarly, a knowledge of style (Hartwell's Grammar 5 [p. 5]) can also help writers generate ideas—again, either as they draft or as they revise. In the reading for Chapter 2, Constance Weaver (2001) writes about a white water rafting trip she took in Costa Rica. She generated a first round of narration and details—details that gave an overview of the story. But then, as part of the revision process, she went back to generate more descriptive details. She used her awareness of participial phrases and absolutes to come up with additional details to enliven her prose.

Weaver's story makes it clear that it's difficult to separate the writing process neatly into prewriting (sometimes called generating and shaping), writing (drafting), and rewriting (revising and editing) stages, because one stage recurs so quickly to another. Thus, strategies for revising can become strategies for generating ideas, when writers are comfortable enough to use their rhetorical knowledge spontaneously as they draft. If they don't feel comfortable, then they can draw on it as they revise and edit.

Language Learning Strategies

Writers develop their rhetorical knowledge and sense of judgment implicitly through reading and other language experiences (Hartwell's Grammar 1 [p. 5]) and explicitly through instruction (Hartwell's 3, 4, and 5). They use strategies similar to those pre-school children use to learn to talk. As Daniels (1983 [See Chapter 1]) points out, children learn language mainly by forming hypotheses about how it works and testing those hypotheses. They use the language(s) they hear around them as data to inductively formulate what they think are the rules for forming and pronouncing words, organizing words into sentences, and for communicating effectively with various people. They try out these rules, and if their interlocutors (the people they're communicating with) respond favorably (or at least, don't respond negatively), then they figure they've gotten the rules right—at least in that context.

Likewise, children learning to write must first notice salient features in the texts they read to help them develop hypotheses about what good writing is, and in which contexts (Long & Robinson, 1998; Ray, 1999; Siegel, 1999). Take, for example, the rhetorical dilemma of how to orient a reader in the opening paragraphs of a text. The first step in answering that question is for writers to pay attention to introductions as they read. How did other writers structure their introductory material? What did they use to grab their readers' attention, introduce the topic, provide background information, etc?

Second, writers must hypothesize about how to write texts of various genres. According to Collins (1998), we form mental pictures about what texts look like, about what characteristics readers expect them to have, and about how we create them. These hypotheses, these mental pictures, guide our actions. Without an ability to visualize a text, we're hard-pressed to write one. To test this claim, imagine that I asked you to write a business letter. Did an image of one immediately spring to mind? Do you know what to do to write one? Do you know what parts such a letter should have, what tone? You could probably answer these questions easily, because most of us have had some experience with business letters—we've written them and we've received them. Now imagine that I asked you to write a mortgage contract. Did an image come to mind? Do you know what to write? For most of us, that image is somewhat vague. Perhaps you've never seen a mortgage—most people see only a handful of such documents in their whole lifetime.

Third, writers must also develop an ability to monitor and adjust their own language (J. Williams, 1995). In order to judge whether our hypotheses are correct and whether we've successfully encoded our mental picture in language, we have to be able to identify if and where there's a gap between what we've produced and what's expected or needed. These questions have to be asked at both the global and local levels. Does our drafted introduction look like we think it should? Does it serve the needs of our readers? Have we used appropriate grammatical forms?

This strategy requires us to distance ourselves from our text enough to see it critically, to see it as our readers would. The goal in making this critical judgment is to create what writing researcher Linda Flower (1979) calls *reader-based prose*. This kind of text both expresses a writer's ideas and meets a reader's needs. This kind of prose typically starts out as *writer-based prose*, as a record of the writer's thoughts only the writer can easily understand. Good writers work to transform—to organize and develop—this string of ideas into a text that's meaningful to a reader as well.

Writing Instruction that Develops Rhetorical Judgment

These are three key strategies young writers use to develop their sense of rhetorical judgment. For the most part, this process is invisible; students usually aren't aware of what they're learning about texts as they read. This process also seems to be true for older writers developing their first language abilities and for learners learning their second language—at least to some extent. Psycholinguists aren't sure to what extent adolescents and adults (especially second language learners) have access (or complete access) to the same language learning mechanisms young children have. It may be that older learners and second language learners rely on more generalized learning strategies than on specific language learning strategies believed by some to be hardwired into the brain (Ellis, Basturkmen, & Loewen, 2001). Thus, it's likely that adolescents and adults would benefit from some explicit instruction in writing (Hartwell's Grammars 3, 4, and 5) to help them develop their rhetorical judgment.

Teachers can talk about texts with students in ways that tap into the key language learning strategies children use. Some approaches teachers can use include the following:

- Teaching students how to identify salient features in model texts and how to develop hypotheses about them.
- Modeling for students how to read their texts to find any gaps between what readers need and what they've written in revising workshops.
- Encouraging students to pay careful attention to teacher and peer comments.

Identifying Salient Features in Model Texts

Studying models and imitating master authors is a pedagogy with a long tradition—it was used, for example, in medieval schools to teach students to write well in Latin. It's also a versatile technique because it can be used to study a variety of features—from the structure of essays, to rhetorical purposes, to sentence punctuation. For example, I ask my basic writing students to write an analytic essay, using the following prompt: Tell about a time you made a difficult decision, and using information from the readings, explain why it was so difficult to make. I teach them how to write the essay in part by asking them to read several successful essays written by previous students. By examining carefully the structure of the essays, my students learn what essential elements must be included in their own drafts—i.e., an introduction that mentions both the event to be analyzed (a time they made a difficult decision) and the tool of analysis (information from the readings on what makes decisions hard to make); one or more paragraphs telling the story of the decision; a paragraph analyzing the decision in terms of the reading; a conclusion; and a Works Cited list. At first the assignment looks daunting, but once they see how others have done it, they relax. As one student said, "Is that all? Well, I can do that." With a model to help them visualize a finished text, the task is manageable.

In addition to this look at global organization, we can go back to the essays to look for more specific features, such as how the authors used the source reading, how they introduced it into their own text, and how they cited it. We can also look at surface features. For example, one time I asked them to look at the fragment in the following passage a student wrote:

> Jo from *Little Women* is my favorite character. She's like me. Always writing.

We looked at what effect the fragment had—that is, how a reader might interpret it. Some students were bothered by it. They didn't like the violation of standard conventions and, if they had been the writer, wouldn't have taken the risk of a deliberate fragment. So we looked at other possible ways to punctuate the passage:

> She's like me, always writing.
> She's like me—always writing.

My students liked the dash because it called more attention to the *always writing* phrase than the comma did. With a dash, the writer could achieve a rhetorical effect similar to the one achieved by the fragment without risking alienating readers. Sometimes, comparing one choice with several alternatives helps students see what kind of rhetorical effects various linguistic choices have.

My students and I can have these discussions about rhetoric because I've taught them how to identify salient features in model texts and develop hypotheses about them. In this, I've found Katie Wood Ray's (1999, p. 120) five-step process helpful:

- *Notice* something about the craft of the text.
- *Talk* about it and *make a theory* about why a writer might use this craft.
- Give the craft a *name*.
- Think of *other texts* you know. Have you seen this craft before?
- Try and *envision* using this crafting in your own writing.

Ray's process is summarized in Figure 4.1.

FIGURE 4.1 *Teaching Tip: Teaching Students to Learn from Models*

Regardless of whether students learn implicitly or through explicit instruction, one key strategy they use is to notice salient features in the language around them. I've found that students learn more from models if I teach them a specific strategy for observing, theorizing, and practicing the features they see in the exemplary texts. It's based on Katie Wood Ray's (1999) five-part strategy for reading to understand the craft of writing. It's what Frank Smith (1988) calls *reading like a writer* and Frank O'Hare (1979–1980) calls *reading-for-writing*. I use this technique to look at both how texts are structured and what rhetorical effect particular grammatical choices have.

1. *Notice* **something about the craft of the text.** I give students a text that uses the features I want them to learn. After we read and discuss the content, I ask them to focus on the feature in question. Say, for example, we look at how authors refute points. We notice for example that it involves a three-step process: summarize the opposition's point, signal a switch in point-of-view with a transition like *but* or *however*, and explain why the point is problematic.
2. *Talk* **about it and** *make a theory* **about why a writer might use this craft. This is what O'Hare calls the "Why Game."** Why is it important to summarize the opposition's point? Why use a transition? Will any transition work? Why must it be something like *but* or *however*? Are there other strategies for refuting? It's important for students to understand what role these various parts play in the reading process. When students know why each step is important, they're more likely to include it in their own writing.
3. **Give the craft a** *name*. We might use the technical terms here—refutation, transition, etc.—or a more informal name—the "yeah, but what about . . ." move. Here's where I'm likely to introduce grammar terms (Hartwell's Grammar 5 [p. 5]) as a way to talk about a writing strategy.
4. **Think of** *other texts* **you know. Have you seen this craft before?** We look at this feature in other texts for two important reasons. First, it enables students to see it at work in other contexts. This usually enriches their theory of how the technique works. Second, it helps them see that these techniques are not "owned" by any one writer, but are available to all writers, including them.
5. *Revise* **your writing to add this feature.** Studying the structure of published texts is a waste of time if students cannot see themselves using the same techniques in their own writing. So I give them time to try out the technique in their own writing.

In teaching students to learn to write from models, lessons in writing craft inevitably bring in discussions of grammar, especially in terms of naming these techniques. In discussing the rhetorical effect of various structures, students see first-hand how grammar can be vital to expressing their ideas effectively. Like Andrews' (1995, 1998) LEA approach, students study authentic texts and how they work in the world. As a result, students theorize about writing and develop ideas about writing that are more rhetorically and linguistically sound than the traditional rules of grammar.

Finding Gaps in Texts

Another approach teachers can use to help students develop rhetorical judgment is to hold regular revising workshops. In these workshops students learn how to read their texts to find any gaps between what they've written and what readers need and how they can fill the gaps by using a variety of strategies. For example, in addition to reading several successful analytic essays, my basic writers read several that aren't successful because they have gaps of some kind. We talk about what's strong about the essays and what needs work. Then we talk about ways that writers can improve the texts.

Because basic writers tend to not have many revision strategies in their repertoire, it's important that I model some strategies successful writers use. I want to help them develop a broad mental picture of writing and the writing process that can guide my students to successful action. Skilled writers have a range of strategies available to them for solving writing problems. They know a number of genres they can use to express their ideas. They know a number of ways to generate and to revise ideas. They have a good control of stylistic features. My basic writers, on the other hand, usually need help in imagining other possibilities, which a more experienced writer can give them. Nancie Atwell (1998) says:

> The longer I write and confer with young writers, the deeper the pool of experi-
> ence from which I can draw potential options for my kids. I tell and show what I
> know because this is my responsibility to the students in my care: to find out
> where they are and where they need to go next, and to demonstrate all the ways
> I know to arrive at the new place. (p. 222)

So in my basic writing class, we talk about a number of strategies they can use to monitor their text, to revise it, and if they need to, to generate additional details. Some of the strategies are described in Figure 4.2.

The final step of our revision workshop is for my students to return to their own texts and the texts of their peers to make similar judgments.

Evaluating Student Writing

But perhaps the most successful way for students to learn about the effectiveness of their texts—and by implication, the soundness of their hypotheses about writing—is to receive thoughtful feedback from classmates, teachers, and others. Teachers can help students by modeling the kinds of questions writers need to ask themselves about their own texts. Thus, when teachers evaluate student writing they should make visible how they read in general and how they're reading this text in particular. Skilled writers anticipate the needs of their readers and generate passages that fulfill those needs. Student writers, on the other hand, usually have a much harder time imagining their readers' responses as they're drafting or revising. So, as Nancy Sommers (1982, p. 148) points out in her classic study of responding to student writing, "We comment on student writing to dramatize the presence of a reader."

Thoughtful evaluators concentrate first on global concerns, such as organization and development, because global changes are likely to make the biggest impact on the reading of the text. When we read, we typically read for the overall meaning of a text. We don't actually read the words on the page. Rather, we use what we know about the topic and the text thus far to predict what the next phrase is likely to be. We glance at it long enough to confirm our predictions, adjust our sense of the text thus far, and move on to predict the next phrase. We need to read quickly because our cognitive abilities to process information are limited; if we take too long, we lose the gist of the text. Gaps in organization and development slow down our processing, and thus impede our ability to create meaning. Once the global concerns are taken care of, then teachers can help writers with surface structures (see Chapter 5).

According to Cooper and Odell (1999), the best way to develop skill in representing your reading process to students is to pay attention to your reactions to the text. Where does it make you frown in confusion? Where does it startle you with new information you didn't anticipate? Where are you relieved to see an example? Where does it make you smile at its grace? I might say/write to a student, either in a conference or a marginal comment, something like the following: "When I first read this sentence, I was expecting . . . ." Articulating your process of reading serves as a model for students of the critical readers they need to be of their own drafts.

However, pointing out where the text is difficult to read is only part of our task as evaluators. We should also use our comments as an opportunity to teach the craft of writing. If we assume that students go as far as their current repertoire will take them, then, for example, pointing out that a passage is awkward is of little help. What they need is advice about how to get beyond the awkwardness. Peers often don't know—or feel comfortable—enough about writing to offer advice, but as experts, teachers can. Thus, whether in conferences or in end comments, our responses should:

- *Take what students have to say seriously, respecting their purposes for writing.* In the reading for this chapter, Straub recommends we approach our comments as if we're engaging in a conversation with the author, exploring together what the writer has to say. As Atwell (1998, p. 230) says, "When what I know of writing and the writer will help a student learn something or meet his or her intentions, the conference becomes an occasion for student and teacher to collaborate on the writing." Likewise, Sommers (1982) reminds, we must be careful not to appropriate the text to our purposes.
- *Make specific, action-oriented suggestions.* The most significant finding in Sommers' classic 1982 study of how teachers respond to student writing is that the majority of teacher comments were too vague to be helpful. The

FIGURE 4.2 *Teaching Tip: Teaching Revision*

Perhaps the best book on teaching revision, especially to upper elementary and middle school students, is Barry Lane's (1993) *After The End: Teaching and Learning Creative Revision*. Lane is particularly good at connecting concrete names and images to abstract revising strategies so that students can remember them and envision using them. Several of the strategies below are adapted from his book; others are adapted from Neman (1995) and Schaffer (1996).

Zoom in ↓ to find a focus.	Reread your draft. Which sentence is the best, most concrete sentence (or passage) in the draft? Copy this sentence (or passage) onto a new page and begin writing again. Continue this process until you figure out a concrete thesis statement that says what you want to say. *Note: It's likely your best sentence (or passage) will come in the middle or near the end of your draft after you've had a chance to "warm up."*
Stretch a rubber band ↓ to add tension and complexity to your thesis.	Reread your thesis. Does it make an arguable claim? Does it go against common, popular, or traditional belief? Does it include or imply the opposition's point of view? Revise your thesis to include at least two viewpoints. *Note: To add complexity to your claim and to create an interesting tension in your paper, use a version of one of the following phrases to write your thesis:* • *It's commonly thought that . . . , but in actuality, . . .* • *It might seem that . . . , but really . . .* • *Although (or even though) critics think that . . . , I believe . . .*
Ride the roller coaster ↓ to write paragraphs with general and specific details.	Study each paragraph. Do you have a general sentence about the topic of the paragraph? If not, study the details and try to summarize them into a generalization. Is the general topic developed with at least one sentence of more specific details? If not, add more specific details. Does the topic need an example? If so, add an example.
Hold a question conference ↓ to generate new content.	Ask your writing partner to read your draft. Where does your partner want to know more information? Ask your partner to write down at least five questions for you to answer to fill in the missing information. *Note: In order to help you generate new content, your writing partner should ask questions that begin with these question words: who, what, when, where, why, and how. Yes-no questions often don't work in this situation.* Use the Spider Leg technique to read the questions, write out the answers, and insert the new details into your text at the appropriate spots.

FIGURE 4.2   *Continued*

Deflate a balloon ↓ to cut out and/or summarize details.	Cut out dialog or details that are irrelevant or unimportant to your main point or that bog down the story or argument. **OR** Summarize ideas that are not very important to your main point in one or two sentences.
Explode a moment ↓ to add details.	Identify an important moment in your story or an important idea in your argument and develop it by adding more specific details about it.
Take a snapshot and/or a thoughtshot ↓ to generate descriptive details.	Identify places in your story or argument where more **physical** description is needed—in other words, identify places where you need to stop the flow of your story or argument to give a verbal picture of someone or something. In a story, snapshots describe a scene, a character or an action. In an argument, snapshots give necessary background information or provide an example. AND/OR Identify places in your story or argument where more **mental** description is needed—in other words, identify places where you need to stop the flow of the story or the argument to report thoughts or feelings. In a story, "thoughtshots" explain how the characters feel and why. In an argument, a thoughtshot makes a concession, points out a qualifier, etc. (adds nuance and complexity to the argument). *Note: Snapshots and thoughtshots vary in length—from a few words, to a single sentence, to a paragraph or more.*
Make a chess move ↓ to move passages around.	Make an outline of your draft. For each paragraph of your draft, briefly identify what that paragraph *says* (its content) and what it *does* (its purpose). Then analyze your outline. Have you used the most "logical" organization for your topic (e.g., chronological for stories, least → important reasons for argument)? If not, move passages around. Do you repeat your topic in separate paragraphs? If so, combine them or move one paragraph so it follows the other. Does one paragraph have two or more topics? If so, break it up into several paragraphs.

These revision strategies teach students about organization and development. If writers can internalize these lessons, they can use them spontaneously as they're drafting. Thus, revising strategies can also become prewriting strategies.

comments seemed rubber stamped, general enough to apply to any text without much trouble. As a result, students didn't know what to do to revise their papers.

- *Give students a sense of priority.* Straub (2000) recommends teachers focus on only one or two points in their commentary, choosing points that will make the biggest impact on the quality of the papers. These are likely to be more global suggestions about content and organization. Likewise, Sommers (1982) argues for evaluating higher order concerns before lower order ones.

In short, then, when teachers evaluate student writing they must do more than simply mark the grammatical errors—though there may be a point in the process when editing advice is needed. They must use their conferences and marginal comments to help students develop themselves as writers. According to Straub (2000), guiding students successfully through the writing process should result not only in a particular piece of revised and polished writing, but should also help students understand writing in a larger context. Yes, we may want students to make changes in their text. But, according to Sarah Warshauer Freedman (1985), we also want them to make changes in the procedures they use to produce their writing (e.g., to read their own texts more critically, to plan more before they begin drafting, to zoom in on their thesis more sharply, etc.). And, we want them to have a deeper understanding of writing in general and how it works in the world. It's only when students generalize about their experiences in ways that make those experiences applicable in new contexts does learning—and improvement—occur.

In order to create a kind of environment that focuses on developing rhetorical judgment, teachers should emphasize evaluating writing over grading it. Figure 4.3 explains the key differences between these two terms, which are often used synonymously, but which seem to me to be quite different in attitude.

This chapter explores how teachers can help students develop their rhetorical judgment, in part by modeling for them how to evaluate their texts.

Exploring Your Own Language Experience

1. Before you begin the reading, spend five minutes or so writing in your journal about the following:

   What kind of responses did your teachers give your writing? Which were helpful? Which were not? How did you respond to these comments (emotionally, intellectually, etc.)? Based on these experiences, what might you keep in mind about responding to student papers in your own classroom?

FIGURE 4.3 *Teaching Tip: Distinguishing Between Evaluating and Grading*

In order to create the kind of environment that encourages students to work hard to learn to write, Cooper and Odell (1999) argue that it's essential to make a distinction between evaluating writing and grading it. Though these terms are often used synonymously, Cooper and Odell (l999) point out these differences.

Evaluating	*Grading*
• Is judging a piece of writing to see if it's effective.	• Is assigning a letter, number, or ranking to a piece of writing.
• Should be done by writers themselves, their peers, and teachers.	• Done by teachers.
• Done at every stage of the writing process.	• Should be done only at the end of the writing process.
• Helps writers move successfully through the writing process.	• Often has the psychological effect of shutting down the writing process.

Students learn more from evaluation than they do from grading. Because evaluation happens at various stages of the writing process, when students are most engaged in it, they're more willing to attend to suggestions from others. Because, in contrast, grading happens at the end of the process, when students feel "finished" with it, students tend to ignore grades and comments. This distinction suggests that teachers put off grading as long as possible, and concentrate on the writing process, so that they can get a greater return on the energy they put into commenting on papers.

Guidelines for Responding to Student Writing

Richard Straub

This chapter is taken from The Practice of Response: Strategies for Commenting on Student Writing *(2000, Hampton Press). In this text, written primarily for pre-service teachers, Richard Straub tries to make sense of what many teachers say is their most difficult task: responding well to student writing. Straub analyzes and evaluates the strategies that experienced teachers use to respond to student writing. In this reading, he offers a number of suggestions to help young teachers create their own philosophy and style of responding.*

Offering advice about responding to student writing is like offering advice about playing chess. You can learn how each piece moves, a number of gambits, and some general strategies. But the game has to be played—and learned—on the board, amid a hundred shifting factors. The moves you make depend on the board in front of you, the ground you want to hold or seize. It's only after you've played a while—only after you've gotten an idea of all the choices and the way contingency must be reckoned with at every turn—that you're in a position to really learn the game. Learning how to respond is a bit like learning to use your pawns wisely or knowing when to put your queen into play. You try to follow certain principles. You look for certain keys. You watch for certain warnings. In this chapter, I'd like to offer a fairly detailed set of strategies for responding with the aim of helping new and experienced teachers get some bearings on how they might best respond to their students' writing. I'll offer advice not only about making comments themselves but about situating comments within the larger work of the writing classroom.

Teacher response, I am assuming here, is integral to effective writing instruction—as important as any other activity or responsibility we take up as writing teachers. The comments we make instantiate what we really value in student writing. They offer an opportunity to make the key concepts of the class more meaningful to students. And they enable us to give substance to the claims we make about their roles as writers, our roles as teachers, and the work of writing. If we claim to be facilitators in the classroom, our comments should be noticeably encouraging and helpful. If we claim to give students practice in making their own choices and developing their authority as writers, our comments should allow them room to decide which comments they take up and which they pass up in revision. If we claim to emphasize the content and thought of writing, our comments should deal mostly with the author's ideas.

Running through all of the advice below is the belief that careful, thoughtful commentary can make a real difference in the immediate and long-term development of student writers. Never mind claims that teacher commentary doesn't make a difference. Never mind the easy skepticism that students don't even read the comments; all they're interested in is the grade. Give students sincere, well-designed comments, comments that give them thoughtful feedback about what they have to say (not just how they say it or whether it's correct) and how they might work on their writing, in a classroom that is charged with a belief that students can learn to write better, and they will read the comments, appreciate them, and get something out of them—if not on the next draft, then on the next paper or the one after that, or perhaps when they write again next semester.

Bringing the Class into Your Responses

1. Response begins with the course description. It begins with the assignment and the work in class. It begins with your values and expectations. It begins with what the students write. You read the writing, but you read the writing both as a reader and with the reader in mind. You read with an eye to the assignment, to the work you've done in class and the work you hope to accomplish. You read with an eye to the writer in the text and the student behind the writing. Before you even pick up the pen or open a file, much about how you'll respond has already been determined. So it makes sense as you invent the class, day by day, in the assignments, the lessons, the class discussions, and the things you say about writing, that you also consider how these choices will ultimately come to bear on the way you read and respond to what your students write—and how your responses, in turn, might help you shape your instruction.

2. Before you start to read a set of papers (optimally even as you put together the assignment and talk with students about the writing they are to do), consider the aims of the writing. Try to get a sense of what you are looking to accomplish with

this writing right now, in the short term, and over time, in the long term. What do you want to accomplish through your reading and your comments? What is the one thing, above all others, you'd like these comments to do? How does what you are looking for here go with what you have been working on or what you intend to work on in the class? Decide what your main focus will be—and what you will generally *not* deal with in these papers.

3. Decide how long you'll take with each paper—and how many you'd like to have finished in an hour or two. Do all you can to stick to the plan. You may not be able to keep up, but you've got a goal in mind.

4. Once you start actually looking at the papers, you have two choices: reviewing the paper first, before you make any responses, or responding as you read the first time through. Both options have their strengths and drawbacks. The first method: Read the paper over once quickly and select the focuses of your response. Put a line next to key passages and jot down a list of your concerns as you go. Then, after you've gone through the paper, decide your major points, work up a general strategy, and compose your response. This might seem at first to take more time, but it probably ends up being more efficient because it allows you to focus better when you comment on the paper. The second method: Just comment as you read the first time through the paper, and cast your comments in terms of a reader's moment-by-moment responses. Whenever something strikes you as worthy of a comment (based, if you're smart, on priorities you've established), you write it down. This method is more risky: it can take a lot of time, it can lead to some erasing and recanting, and it can easily lead to commentary that ranges far and wide and fails to provide adequate direction to the writer. But it does provide an opportunity to provide fuller responses to specific passages (and, when it's well done, perhaps greater guidance and stronger control).

Viewing Response as an Exchange

5. Look to engage students in an inquiry into their subject, by treating what they have to say seriously and encouraging them, in turn, to take their own ideas seriously. Turn your comments into a conversation with students, a real dialogue that encourages them to read the comments and respond to your responses. Write out your comments, especially your most important comments, in full statements. Short, cryptic comments, abbreviations, and a lot of editorial symbols may too readily be taken as the hasty marks of an editor or critic . . . or the pouncing corrections of a teacher. Fuller comments help create an exchange between reader and writer, teacher and student. They dramatize how you are reading and making sense of the text, and they construct you as someone who is intent on helping them improve their writing.

6. Write your comments as much as you can in nontechnical terms, tying the comment to specific concerns in the writing and using the language of the student's text. The goal here, again, is to enact an exchange. The more you address the content of the writing, tie your talk to the student's language, and refer to specific issues and passages in the writing, the more likely you'll engage the student and bring her into a discussion.

7. Try to link your comments to the key terms of the larger classroom conversation. It's important to establish a vocabulary for talking about writing—one that may very well go beyond the language that students bring into the course. Yet, at the same time, keep this talk grounded in your students' own writing.

8. Add follow-up comments that explain, elaborate, or illustrate your primary comments. Comments that explain other comments will be construed as help.

Responding as Selecting

9. Focus your commentary on no more than two or three concerns in a set of comments, making sure that your comments reflect your priorities and advance the goals of the course. Students do best when they can work on a couple areas of writing at a time.

10. There's no need to address every instance of a problem—or, for that matter, every success. Select key instances and build your response on them. Leave the rest for the student to identify and work out on her own.

11. Don't overwhelm the writer with comments. Look to address 5 to 10 passages per paper. Look to write somewhere between 12 to 25 comments (i.e., statements) per paper, including marginal and end comments. It's not the number of comments that distinguish informed teachers' responses from uninformed teachers'; it's what you do in the comments you provide. Instead of being comprehensive, try to cover less ground and be more effective with what you do take up.

12. Be respectful of the student's space: be careful about crossing through sentences or writing indiscriminately between the lines of the text. You expect students to be neat and orderly; try to be so yourself.

13. Look for ways to limit what you take up and try to accomplish in a given set of comments. Not every paper that you read needs to be commented on extensively—or, for that matter, commented on to the same extent. Write more comments on papers that seem more open to fruitful revision. Write more comments for students who need more help or students you want to challenge to do even better work.

Focusing on First Things First

14. Emphasize matters of content, focus, organization, and purpose. Work on these concerns until the writing achieves some reasonable level of maturity. If you're working on early drafts or even immature final drafts, feel free to deal exclusively with matters of content. There is no sense in getting into shaping and refining a paper that has nothing yet to say.

15. Address local matters in detail only after the writing is doing more or less what it sets out to do in content, focus, and organization. Unless you have good reason, don't emphasize matters of correctness either too early in the drafting of a paper or too early in the course. Asking students to serve several masters can lead only to their serving none of them very well.

16. Employ minimal marking for errors: punctuation, grammar, spelling, and other local conventions. Instead of marking and explaining every error, just put a tick mark in the margin next to the line where the error occurs. Leave it up to the student to locate and correct the error. Have students meet with you if they have trouble, or check their work after they've had a chance to make corrections. (Another option: when you return the papers with your comments, have a 15-minute workshop in which students find and correct the errors you've minimally marked in the margins.)

17. Keep an eye always on the next work to be done: the next draft, the next paper, the next issue of writing that the class or this student writer will take up. Make comments that are geared toward improvement, not simply the assessment of a finished text.

18. Experiment with ways of focusing your comments on certain issues at certain times in the course. Sequence your comments across the semester, taking up issues that are most important to you at the start of the course and adding other areas as you go. On early papers, for example, present only positive comments or restrict yourself to commenting only on the content and development of student writing. On some papers, or some drafts, just deal with the voice and tone of the writing. On final drafts late in the semester, abandon work on developing the content and focus exclusively on sentence structure or the pacing within paragraphs.

Shaping Your Comments to the Larger Context of Writing

19. Read the student's text in terms of its (stated or assigned) rhetorical context. Does the writer construct a persona that is appropriate to the occasion? How well does the writing address the intended audience? Does it achieve the purposes it sets out to achieve?

20. Tie your talk on the page to the work you've been doing in class, and your immediate and long-terms goals. Use the key terms of the class in your responses—again, to give them local habitation and a name.

21. Decide how closely you are going to hold students to following the exact demands of the assignment—or how much room you are going to allow them to develop their own topics and their own purposes in their own ways.

22. Shape your comments according to the needs of the individual student. It's not the paper in front of us, after all, that we're teaching. Work on what the student would do best to work on.

Creating a Give-and-Take Relationship with Students

23. Learn the uses of both directive and facilitative forms of commentary. Without criticism and calls for changes there'd be less direction in your responses. Without comments that play back the text, ask questions, provide reader responses, and offer explanations, there'd be less help and encouragement in your commentary.

24. Look to take advantage of the many uses of praise: to recognize a job well done, to teach a principle, to underscore successful strategies, and to encourage students to continue working on their writing. Use praise in one area or in one passage to build confidence in tackling others. Write at least as many praise comments as criticisms. Be supportive and encouraging. Yet also be demanding. Look to move the student, wherever she is now in her development as a writer, forward.

25. Frame your comments in forms that modulate the control you exert over students' writing. Instead of relying on commands, shape your calls for changes in the form of advice. Instead of using only direct criticism, present some of your criticisms as qualified evaluations or reader responses, forms that highlight the subjective or contingent nature of commentary. Ask questions—and real, open questions, not simply questions that disguise some criticism or command. Too many directive comments can close down interaction and take away the authority a writer needs to develop as an author, a writer with something to say. Students do best when they are involved in an exchange, not in a battle of wills. More than a critic pointing out problems or an editor dictating changes to be made, look to create yourself in the role of a reader, a guide, a helpful teacher, a challenging mentor, or some kind of coach.

26. Try to make at least occasional use of comments that simply play back your reading of the student's text, without overtly evaluating, questioning, or advising the student about the writing. Comments that provide your interpretations will let the

writer know how his writing is being understood. They will also let her know you are reading the writing first of all for its meaning.

27. Fit your comments to your own strengths and style as a teacher, and along the way look to add to your strengths as a responder. No one way of responding will work, or work the same way, for every student. It is necessary, then, to develop a repertoire of responding strategies, to meet the demands of different students and different settings.

Using Marginal Comments or End Comments

28. There's no necessary difference between putting comments in the margins or in a separate response, in end notes and letters. Marginal comments allow for greater immediacy and specificity. They allow you to deal directly with specific issues in relation to specific passages. They also lend a ready concreteness to your responses. End comments encourage you to provide a fuller context for your comments and carry on a fuller discussion about them. They also give you a chance to lend some perspective to the various issues you raise in the margins. In end comments, generally speaking, start with some piece of praise or a general overview of what you see the student doing in the writing. Direct the student's attention to your key concerns. Elaborate and explain your comments and tie them back to the student's text. Look to make your end comments somehow complement your marginal comments. The end note may highlight and elaborate the key marginal comments. It may focus on one key area that is addressed in the margins. It may take up areas that are not treated in the marginal comments but that you now want to focus on. The over-riding idea here, as in response in general, is to find ways to involve students in an exchange about their writing, with the aim of leading them to work further on developing themselves as writers.

Integrating Responses into the Class

29. As teachers, we show what we value by spending time on it in class. If all we do after we've spent hours making comments is hand the papers back in a rush at the end of a class, while students are packing their books away, we make the statement that the comments are not important, that they are not to be taken seriously. We allow the comments to be seen as a matter of course: students write papers and hand them in, the teacher comments on the papers and hands them back, we all move on to the next paper, checking another thing off the list of things to do. Develop a different habit. Whenever you're about to hand papers with your comments back to students, take time to talk about the responses you've made. Indicate any important patterns you've seen in their papers, note the key concerns of your responses, and discuss the purposes behind your comments. Let students know what they are to do with the comments now that they are in their hands.

30. Make response a two-way street—or, better yet, a free-flowing highway. When the students hand in their papers, encourage them, in a separate note attached to their writing, to direct your attention to special concerns they have about the writing. Read the paper in light of these concerns, or use them in discussing your own responses to the paper. At different times in the course, have students react to your responses, identifying any questions or confusions they might have and pointing out those they find the most and least useful.

31. Concentrate most of your work with response in the first half of the course. Gradually have students take on greater responsibility for responding to one an-

other's papers. The more students see you modeling your own ways of reading, evaluating, and responding to writing, the more adept they will be when it comes time for them to respond to one another's writing. The more you put into your responses early on in the course, the more you will be able to establish a firm foundation for your work to come, and the more you can rely on students to provide feedback to one another's writing later on.

32. Make self-evaluation a part of the course: Have students periodically evaluate their own strengths, progress, and areas for improvement as writers. Such work will lead them to develop a keener sense of what you are looking for, and what they might look for, in their writing.

These, then, are some principles to follow, some guidelines to help you find your way. Ultimately, of course, if responding is indeed like playing chess, you finally have to develop a feel for it on your own. Discover your own strengths. Find your own best strategies. Develop your own style. The best comments, finally, do not focus on one area or another. They do not provide just a little criticism or a lot of help. They are not directive or facilitative. The best comments take on what is most important in this paper, for this student, at this time. They encourage students to look back on their choices and consider their options. They pursue. They apply pressure. They offer incentive. They teach. And they challenge the student to make the next move.

Questions for Discussion

1. Straub infers that teachers have many purposes—some more obvious than others—in responding to student work. What are these purposes? How do they help students understand how writing works?

2. Why is it important to make a distinction between evaluating and grading in responding to student writing?

3. Return to the textbooks and state curriculum guidelines you examined in Chapter 2. To what extent do they include strategies for developing writers' sense of rhetorical judgment? How do they treat it? If your state has mandated assessments to measure educational progress, is writing ability assessed? If so, how?

4. Read the draft journal entry by Alex (p. 218).
    a. Imagine that Alex is your student. What comments will you give him—either in conference or in writing—about his journal entry? What do you think is strong about it? What advice will you give him about its content, organization, and tone? In your response, use the various forms Straub says a teacher's comments might take: advice, questions, readerly "play back," and praise.
    b. Perhaps you mentioned in your comments to Alex that he could develop his entry with more details. Suggest one or two revising strategies from Figure 4.2 that Alex can use to develop his story.

5. Read the outline and final draft of the in-class essays by Angie (p. 221).
    a. Imagine that Angie is your student. What comments will you give her—either in conference or in writing—about her essay? What do you think is strong

about it? What advice will you give her about its content, organization, and tone? In your response, use the various forms Straub says a teacher's comments might take: advice, questions, readerly "play back," and praise.

b. Angie's outline and her use of the five-paragraph essay organizational structure locked her into repeating many details. Is this repetition effective? Why/why not? If not, suggest one or two strategies from Figure 4.2 that Angie can use to create a less repetitive story.

6. Read the pre-writing and final draft of the in-class essay by Jennifer (p. 222).

a. Imagine that Jennifer is your student. What comments will you give her— either in conference or in writing—about her essay? What do you think is strong about it? What advice will you give her about its content, organization, and tone? In your response, use the various forms Straub says a teacher's comments might take: advice, questions, readerly "play back," and praise.

b. What difference(s) do you notice between Jennifer's Pre-Writing and Final Draft? What hypotheses, what strategies does Jennifer seem to have about revising? What suggestions can you make to encourage her to try out one or two of the revising strategies in Figure 4.2?

5

Understanding "Error"

As I noted in Chapter 4, it's essential that writers develop their rhetorical judgment, especially their ability to see the gap between what they've written and what is expected (J. Williams, 1995). Writers must be able to see these gaps not only in the organization and development of their ideas, but also in the grammatical features of their texts. These grammatical gaps are often called errors.

General readers typically measure the quality of writing by the number of errors they see in it—the fewer, the better. Many people, when they become too distracted by a text with errors to read it, assume that the writer was too hasty, too careless, too insensitive, or too uneducated to produce the kind of text they expected (Beason, 2001). Any of these conclusions—whether accurate or not— exacts what Larry Andrews (1998) calls a "social tax," which the writer must pay in terms of lost credibility and rapport. Most English language arts teachers feel obligated to respond to the grammar in student texts in order to help students avoid this social tax (Rosen, 1998).

The general public puts such great stock in correct grammar in part because they see it as a concrete feature of writing—either it follows the rules or it doesn't. Like traditional grammarians, the public usually believes that errors are violations of standard (usually written) grammar, and that students wouldn't violate these rules—wouldn't make errors—if they simply studied the rules and practiced them repeatedly (Town, 1996). Kroll and Schafer (1978) call this a *product* approach to error.

However, research has shown us that the relationship between grammar and writing well is more complex than traditional grammarians suggest (see Chapter 2). Likewise, the explanation about what constitutes errors, why students make them, and how students can identify errors on their own is more complex than it seems on the surface. For a richer, more productive understanding of error, we need to turn to language study and composition pedagogy. These fields provide some alternative ways to think about why students make errors and how we can help writers avoid them.

One such alternative is what Kroll and Schafer (1978) call the *process* approach to learners' errors. In the process approach, teachers look at student errors, not simply as failures, but as "windows into the mind[,] . . . as the product of intelligent cognitive strategies and therefore as potentially useful indicators of what processes the student is using" to learn language (pp. 243–244). Teachers analyze and investigate errors to better understand the strategies that prompted the errors so they know how to help students develop more conventional strategies. Three important principles of the process approach include the following:

- There is a distinction between competence errors and performance errors.
- Errors are an inevitable part of learning to write.
- Errors depend on the context and on the reader.

Competence Errors and Performance Errors

The first principle is that we should make a distinction between competence errors—rules of language that students don't know or know only partially—and performance errors—rules that students know but make incidental mistakes with. This is a distinction that Rei R. Noguchi (1991) and other transformational-generative grammarians make. They say that native speakers are competent—that is, they have a general innate knowledge of the spoken rules of their home language—but they sometimes in specific cases make mistakes, perhaps because they're tired or under stress. They may, for example, write *story* when they mean *store*.

But language development (Hartwell's Grammar 1 [p. 5]) is an ongoing process, and students may not yet have mastered completely and competently all of the features unique to writing, specifically to writing academic Standard English. So sometimes, students have a hypothesis about a particular feature that's logical but incorrect (Shaughnessy, 1977). For example, one semester, I had a student named Carol, who seemed to have a lot of trouble with sentence fragments and run-on sentences. After reading several of her drafts, I finally noticed that she always used semicolons with the subordinating connector *although* and commas with the adverbial connector *however*. Once I discovered this particular pattern, I realized that she needed help in distinguishing which kind of punctuation went with which kind of conjunction. I'd been talking to her needlessly about identifying sentence boundaries—which she already knew how to do—and hadn't gotten at the cause of the problem. After we talked about how to punctuate subordinating clauses and sentences connected with adverbial connectors, Carol's sentence errors cleared up immediately. This confusion about punctuation seemed to be a competence error because it was a mistake that Carol made over and over again. Her hypotheses about how to use semicolons and commas didn't match standard conventions. But it was in examining the pattern of the mistakes that her hypothesis was revealed. And once I understood her hypothesis, I knew how to address her punctuation errors and help her master them. This is the value of error-analysis, a key component of the process approach to learners' errors (Kroll & Schafer, 1978).

Error analysis is based on the assumption that even though students make errors, they know a great deal about language. This assumption is important to

Noguchi (1991) and the transformational-generative grammarians. He recommends the following strategies to help students correct their errors: he says teachers should:

- *Acknowledge that students already know a lot and create lessons that bring a student's unconscious knowledge to conscious awareness to help them edit.* In this case, when I made visible Carol's understanding of punctuating sentences with various kinds of connectors, it was possible for Carol to correct her unconventional hypothesis and, in turn, her sentence punctuation errors.
- *Not focus so much on the errors that they're unable to see how much of the writing is grammatical.* Much of Carol's writing was clear and well organized. Most of her sentences were punctuated correctly. I needed to remember these things when I felt frustrated by Carol's errors, especially at first when it didn't seem that Carol was making any progress in mastering sentence boundaries.
- *Analyze the errors, look for patterns, and try to figure out what students are thinking,* as Kroll and Schafer (1978) also suggest. This is what I did when I finally noticed that Carol's confusion was about punctuation and not sentence boundaries.
- *Distinguish between performance errors and competence errors.* Our lessons will be more productive when we focus on competence errors—on places where students are genuinely confused. Students generally recognize and correct performance errors when they're revising. Indeed, when students gain control over the content of their writing, they usually gain control over the grammar as well (Atwell, 1998). That's one reason it's important to evaluate content first and grammar later.

The Inevitability of Errors

A second principle of the process approach is that we should recognize that errors are an inevitable part of learning (to write) (Shaughnessy, 1977). For basic writing theorist Mina Shaughnessy, students make errors because learning to write academic English is like learning a new dialect—in fact, for language minority students it *is* learning a new dialect, because academic English is based on Standard English. Students can transfer much of their knowledge of the language from speaking to writing, but some features of writing must be learned specifically for a new medium. These features, such as spelling, punctuation, formal vocabulary, and complex syntax, are what give students the most trouble.

Indeed, violations of these conventions comprise much of the list of the 20 most frequent errors in college student writing, as identified in a 1988 study by Robert J. Connors and Andrea A. Lunsford. These rhetoricians identified the errors in 3000 compositions from college students across the nation. They excluded spelling mistakes from their error list because this kind of mistake was so common that it skewed their statistics. Nine of the 20 on their list involve punctuation, while another six involve preciseness in language. Four involve issues of formality. Their list suggests that students who master these errors will significantly master the conventions of writing. Connors and Lunsford's list of errors appears in Figure 5.1.

Like Noguchi (1991) and Kroll and Schafer (1978), Shaughnessy recommends that teachers analyze errors in students' writing, look for patterns, and try to figure out the hypotheses students are using. She has these additional recommendations:

- *Help students understand the differences between written and spoken language* (see Chapter 6).
- *Give students lots of practice in writing without penalizing them.* Give students both informal, writing-to-learn kinds of assignments in addition to formal, revised/edited assignments. Also incorporate peer review and peer editing sessions into the writing process.
- *Ask students to keep a list of personal grammar troublespots.*

The Contextual Nature of Errors

The third principle of the process approach is that we should acknowledge that what constitutes an error depends on the context and on the reader (Andrews, 1998; J. M. Williams, 1981). Just as beauty is in the eye of the beholder, so are errors in the minds of readers. According to Andrews, students make errors when they use language that's inappropriate for the context, that doesn't suit the writer's purpose, or that distracts the reader. For Andrews, errors are measured against a potential to please or irritate an audience rather than an ideal, standard version of the language. Errors are what readers find distracting, what makes them levy a social tax on the writer.

This social tax—this negative impact on the writer's ethos—was the subject of a recent study by Larry Beason (2001). He surveyed 14 business people to learn their response to five kinds of errors—misspellings, fused sentences, sentence fragments, word-ending errors, and unnecessary quotation marks. One theme that emerged from follow-up interviews was that although some errors distracted readers more than others, respondents found all errors bothersome. They said errors reflected poorly on writers as writers and as business people. They felt writers who were careless in their writing would be careless in conducting business as well. Beason argues that teachers must impress upon student writers that errors matter because they influence how readers view writers.

The results of Beason's study are similar to that of a 1981 study by Maxine Hairston. She sent a questionnaire with 65 sentences, each containing a grammatical error, to professionals, asking them to read the sentences quickly and decide whether the errors bothered them a little, a lot, or not at all. She didn't say specifically how or why she chose the errors under study, but she was interested in workplace writing and in advice she should give advanced composition students. In particular, she asked her respondents, "If you encountered the sentence in a report or business letter, *would it lower your estimate of the writer, and how much?*" (p. 795; emphasis mine). In other words, she asked whether the respon-

FIGURE 5.1 *Theoretical Foundation: Frequency of Errors in College Student Writing*

Connors and Lunsford (1988) analyzed the grammatical and mechanical errors in 3000 graded college essays from around the country. They and their research staff not only identified the errors, but also tabulated which errors were most frequently marked by the instructors who graded the papers. The most common errors were spelling errors—by a factor of 300 percent. Because this kind of error was so frequent, it skewed the rest of the data, so Connors and Lunsford eliminated it from their list. The new list of 20 most frequent errors appears in the first three columns of the chart. Many of the errors are unique to writing. Half of the errors are errors in punctuation. Another error—*its/it's*—represents a special kind of spelling error. Other errors—*vague pronoun reference*, for example—may represent errors in the level of formality and explicitness needed for writing a text that must stand alone (see Chapter 6).

The fourth column ranks each error in terms of how frequently it was marked. Even though some errors appeared less often than others, teachers were more likely to mark them. For example, *wrong word* represented only 7.8 percent of the errors, but it was the most common error marked. Other frequently marked errors included possessive apostrophe errors, sentence fragments, and subject-verb agreement errors. This ranking suggests that teachers are bothered by some errors more than others.

Error or Error Pattern	Percent of Total Errors	Rank by Number of Errors Marked by Teacher
1 No comma after introductory element	11.5	2
2 Vague pronoun reference	9.8	4
3 No comma in compound sentence	8.6	7
4 Wrong word	7.8	1
5 No comma in nonrestrictive element	6.5	10
6 Wrong or missing inflected endings	5.9	5
7 Wrong or missing prepositions	5.5	8
8 Comma splice	5.5	6
9 Possessive apostrophe error	5.1	3
10 Tense shift	5.1	12
11 Unnecessary shift in person	4.7	14
12 Sentence fragment	4.2	9
13 Wrong tense or verb form	3.3	13
14 Subject-verb agreement	3.2	11
15 Lack of comma in series	2.7	19
16 Pronoun agreement error	2.6	15
17 Unnecessary comma with restrictive element	2.4	17
18 Run-on or fused sentence	2.4	16
19 Dangling or misplaced modifier	2.0	20
20 Its/it's error	1.0	18

dents would levy a social tax, and if so, how much. Based on the results, she determined five levels of seriousness. She suggests we should focus first on helping students master those features that are most distracting to readers so that writers can maintain their audience's goodwill.

To help students appreciate the importance of context when they make their linguistic choices, Andrews (1998) recommends that teachers:

- Develop students' awareness of appropriate language in many contexts.
- Give students opportunities to practice using language in many contexts.
- Focus on those violations that exact the most social tax or that happen most often.

Helping Students Become Independent Self-Editors

These three principles can help teachers take a process approach to learners' errors. When teachers investigate students' errors—that is, when they try to understand the students' thought processes behind the errors—they can use that knowledge to develop productive approaches for helping students eliminate errors. First, they can use that knowledge to develop a list of priorities, to decide which errors students should work on first. Second, teachers can use their knowledge to help students revise their unconventional understanding of academic English. The pedagogical goal is for students to take responsibility for their errors and become independent self-editors.

According to Rosen's (1998) reading for this chapter, teachers should set priorities, rather than try to address every error in a student's writing. Rosen reports on her study of how teachers mark grammar errors. One strategy was to mark every error, but Rosen concludes it wasn't a productive approach. Although parents seemed pleased with this system, students didn't pay attention to the marks, and in the end, it didn't lead to fewer errors in their writing. A more productive strategy is to prioritize errors—to identify the one or two most frequent and most relevant errors to address. Atwell (1998) notes that students can deal with only one or two errors at a time. Moreover, J. M. Williams (1981) notes, even experienced writers don't follow every rule in the handbooks. One such scheme for prioritizing errors can be found in Figure 5.2.

A second pedagogical goal is to help students take responsibility for themselves for following the conventions of written English. Ideally, students would have such control over these conventions that they could use them easily as they draft. Short of that, however, students should be able to identify—during the revising and editing stages of the writing process—places in their text where there's a gap between what they've written and what is expected and know how to "fix" the gaps. We should, for example, help students notice when they've failed to use Standard English conventions. In other words, we should help them master new language skills so fully that these features become an integral part of their intuitive grammar (Hartwell's Grammar 1 [p. 5]) and also help them develop their

FIGURE 5.2   *Teaching Tip: Prioritizing Errors*

In "The Phenomenology of Error," Joseph M. Williams (1981) makes the case for prioritizing errors when reading student papers. He notes that even though handbooks contain many rules, in practice, experienced writers regularly obey some (e.g., subject-verb agreement) and not others (e.g., avoiding split infinitives). Similarly, experienced readers are routinely bothered by some errors (e.g., double negatives) and not by others (e.g., the use of *whose* in relative clauses even though the antecedent is non-human, as in *an idea whose time has come*). He argues that when teachers read student writing, they should do the same. They should focus on those errors that experienced writers regularly obey and that experienced readers find bothersome when violated. Williams leaves it up to individual teachers to establish their priority list. Here is the list that I use with my basic writing students; it's based on Connors and Lunsford (1988) and Hairston (1981).

Errors I'd Like My Basic Writing Students to Master

Errors that May Impede Meaning	*Errors that are Comprehensible but Distracting*
Spelling • Non-homonym misspelling • Wrong word for context (*form* vs. *from*)	• Homonym confusion • Vernacular spelling (*thru*) • Uncapitalized proper nouns
Punctuation-Sentence Boundaries • Fused sentences • Sentence fragments	• Comma splices • Run-on sentences
Punctuation-Other • Restrictive/Nonrestrictive comma confusion • No commas after introductory subordinating clauses	• No commas after nonsubordinating introductory elements • Possessive apostrophe errors • Unnecessary commas
Level of Formality/Text Can Stand Alone • Word whose meaning is illogical for context • Vague pronoun reference • Dangling or misplaced modifiers	• Unnecessary shifts in person • Unnecessary shifts in tense • Subject-verb disagreement when subject is distant from verb • Nonparallelism in a list • Nonstandard or missing prepositions
Interference from Vernacular Dialects • Non-standard or unmarked verb tense • Unmarked elements (*two cat, John hat*)	• Non-standard verb forms (*I seen*) • Subject-verb disagreement • Using object pronouns as subjects: *Me and him were the last to leave* • Double negatives

---

(continued)

FIGURE 5.2   *Continued*

In compiling my list of priorities, I:

- Focused on errors in features unique to writing, such as punctuation, homonym spelling, and maintaining a consistent level of formality.
- Distinguished between errors that may impede meaning and those that are comprehensible but nonetheless distracting. I want to impress upon my basic writing students that writing is above all communicating to a reader, so it's important for them to read their text critically for any gaps between what they've written and what a reader needs to understand the text.
- Noted that some "errors" result because the writer is using the grammar of vernacular dialect of English when readers expect the grammar of Standard English. I want my basic writers to understand that the grammar of their home dialect isn't wrong, but it isn't appropriate in all situations (just as Standard English isn't). The goal is to help them become linguistically flexible so they can use the appropriate grammar in the appropriate situation.

(See Chapter 10 for tips on prioritizing the errors for English Language Learners.)

language monitors (Hartwell's Grammars 3 and 4), so they can edit their errors. Among the strategies Rosen (1998) advocates is teaching students more effective strategies for proofreading.

However, the current English language arts textbooks I examined are mixed in their presentation of proofreading strategies. For example, the Glencoe McGraw-Hill *Writer's Choice* text (2001) has a chapter called "Troubleshooter" to "help [students] correct common errors" in their writing; it identifies problems and offers suggestions, but it doesn't provide practice (p. 249). *Elements of Language* (Odell et al., 2001), on the other hand, takes students through the writing process, including a step on proofreading. Moreover, a number of "grammar links" feature exercises in which students are asked to revise sentences. Likewise, each of the grammar units in *English* (Rueda et al., 2001) contains a section called "Revising Strategies," in which students learn and practice an editing strategy.

There is, however, a grammar curriculum that focuses explicitly on proofreading strategies: a set of popular grammar exercises called Daily Oral Language (DOL) and Daily Oral Language Plus. These exercises, created by teachers Neil J. Vail and Joseph F. Papenfuss (1989), "develop vital grammar, spelling, and punctuation skills in just 5 to 10 minutes a day," according to promotional materials for the new edition of the Daily Oral Language teacher's manual published by Great Source Education Group. Each day, teachers write one or two sentences on the board or an overhead and ask students to identify and correct the errors they find. Students can correct the errors without necessarily using traditional grammar terms. The ensuing discussion almost always involves reviewing relevant rules students already know or teaching mini-lessons on new rules. Figure 5.3 describes this program more fully.

Some critics argue that DOL exercises are as decontextualized as traditional grammar, and to some extent they're right. DOL is a prepackaged commercial

FIGURE 5.3 *Spotlight on Curriculum: Daily Oral Language*

Author(s):	Neil J. Vail and Joseph F. Papenfuss
Author's(s') Credentials:	Teachers
Published By:	Great Source Education Group
Available:	181 Ballardvale Street
	Wilmington MA 01887
	1-800-289-4490
	www.greatsource.com

Daily Oral Language is just one of the "Dailies" programs published by the Great Source Education Group. Other "Dailies" include Daily Oral Language Plus, Daily Sentence Composing, Daily Phonics, Daily Vocabulary, Daily Spelling, Daily Analogies, Daily Geography, Daily Mathematics, and Daily Science Workout. All follow the same 5- to 10-minute lesson format.

Daily Oral Language

Designed for students from grades 1 through 12, each lesson includes two sentences with several grammatical, mechanical, or usage errors.

This example comes from Week 28 of the Grade 7 set:

To be corrected:	My raleigh ten speed bike needs many new parts given to me by my grandparents.
Correct:	My Raleigh ten-speed bike, given to me by my grandparents, needs many new parts.

The skills covered in this exercise are capitalizing proper adjectives, hyphenating compound adjectives (number + unit of measure), correctly placing misplaced modifiers, and adding commas to nonrestrictive clauses.

Daily Oral Language Plus

This program adds a weekly paragraph to proofread to the daily sentence-length exercises. It has lessons from grades 1 through 8.

This example comes from Week 28 of the Grade 7 set:

To be corrected:	During the 1930s, some people wanted to look like the stars of hollywood films. Some women wanted gourgeous, wavy hair and some men wanted gray flannel suits. Padded shoulders were very popular, and hemlines was long. A long, double-breasted overkoat with a belt were just the thing for a fashionable man, and every fashionable woman wore an hat.
Correct:	During the 1930s, some people wanted to look like the stars of Hollywood films. Some women wanted gorgeous, wavy hair, and some men wanted gray flannel suits. Padded shoulders were very popular, and hemlines were long. A long, double-breasted overcoat with a belt was just the thing for a fashionable man, and every fashionable woman wore a hat.

(continued)

FIGURE 5.3   *Continued*

The seven corrections in this paragraph include capitalizing the name of a place, spelling *gorgeous* and *overcoat* correctly, adding a comma before a coordinating conjunction, making the subjects and verbs agree in two places, and using the article *a* before a noun beginning with a consonant sound.

Description based on promotional materials from Great Source Education Group. Used with permission. (See Chapter 8 for a description of Daily Sentence Composing.)

program that does indeed ask students to critique sentences removed from their own writing. Nevertheless, there are two important advantages to this program over the traditional grammar curriculum:

- *Students are studying grammar from the point of view of a writer.* This provides a context for helping students make judgments about what's grammatically inappropriate in the sentence. It also emphasizes those features most problematic to writing, such as punctuation. It's assumed that features common to both oral and written language won't cause native speaking students much trouble, so there's little need to study these features explicitly.
- *Students are identifying errors—even if they can't label them with traditional grammar terms.* They're drawing on their native speaker's intuition (Hartwell's Grammar 1 [p. 5]).

One way to overcome the criticism of decontextualization is to use passages from students' papers rather than commercially prepared sentences in daily proofreading practice. In my basic writing classes, we practice proofreading passages from their papers in mini-lessons at the beginning of class every day. I use passages from my own students' work because it brings a sense of relevance and urgency to the discussion. They recognize their own words and pay close attention to the suggestions being made. I also like to use passages of two to six sentences (rather than isolated single sentences as the commercially prepared exercises do) because I believe that writing is about extending ideas across sentence boundaries, and because students might not see certain kinds of errors, such as errors in coherence, if they focus on single sentences.

Before I begin daily proofreading exercises, I do an extended lesson on how to proofread. Madraso (1993) points out that many teachers admonish their students to proofread, but don't teach them how. A key component of successful proofreading is to use the correct reading strategy. In typical reading (which I call critical reading for the sake of convenience), we don't really look at each word; rather we predict what's likely to come next and then glance at the text long enough to confirm our predictions. So we don't really "see" what's there. In proofreading, however, we have to slow our reading down enough to actually "see" what's there. I suggest a number of ways students can slow down their reading. I also suggest ways to take advantage of word processing functions, such as FIND/SEARCH, to aid in proofreading. Figure 5.4 explains the lesson I use to introduce proofreading to my basic writers.

FIGURE 5.4   *Teaching Tip: Teaching Proofreading*

Rosen (1998) and Madraso (1993) suggest we teach students how to proofread more effectively. They can learn to do so if they understand more about the nature of proofreading. One element they must understand is that proofreading requires us to do a different kind of reading from the critical reading we normally do. Another element is that proofreading requires us to make several different kinds of judgments (Hull, 1987). In addition to the grammatical errors most people think of when they think of proofreading, editors look for semantic errors (errors in meaning because of missing or incorrectly used words) and syntactic errors (errors as a result of awkward or incorrect sentence structure). These elements are part of the lesson I use to introduce my basic writers to successful proofreading strategies. Here are the steps I follow:

1. Discuss why proofreading is hard.
2. Explain what errors to look for when proofreading and how to correct them.
3. Identify several strategies for proofreading.
4. Practice proofreading using passages from students' own papers.

Why Proofreading is Hard
Proofreading is hard because we often don't use the right strategies. Although proofreading is reading—inside the word *proofreading* is the smaller word *reading*—we have to read in a different way than when we read critically. So we have to learn to switch gears and use the strategies of proofreading.

Critical Reading	*Proofreading*
• When we read critically, we don't really look at each word. Instead, we use our knowledge of the topic and of English grammar to predict what's likely to come. Then we glance at the text long enough to confirm it's what we predicted.	• When we proofread, we have to look at each word to judge whether it's: • the best word choice, • a clearly expressed phrase, • spelled and/or punctuated correctly, • grammatically correct, • etc.
• When we read critically, we project sounds onto the words. This sound helps us connect written words to concepts we already know.	• When we proofread, we have to distinguish spoken words from written ones. We have to distinguish between: • what's acceptable in informal speaking and what's acceptable in formal writing, • the way words sound and the way they're spelled, • places where we pause when we speak and places where we punctuate, • etc.

Proofreading is hard because different kinds of language are appropriate in different situations. We must shift levels of formality, vocabulary, details, etc. depending on our audience and the

(continued)

FIGURE 5.4   *Continued*

situation. Sometimes we don't recognize what is and isn't appropriate in a situation, especially if it's new to us, and so overlook some things that are inappropriate.

One way to illustrate the difference between critical reading and proofreading is to read the following triangles. It generally takes students several tries before they read the phrases accurately. They're predicting what's likely to be there, rather than looking at the text itself.

To help students understand how we project sound onto words, I ask them to read several texts and to describe the "speaker" in each. I choose texts in which the speakers have clear voices that are different from each other.

What Errors to Look for in Proofreading
When you're proofreading, you should look for three different kinds of errors:

Semantic errors—places where the meaning isn't clear.
- Identify by reading slowly enough to recognize that words are missing.
- Also identify by reading critically enough to recognize unclear or inaccurate pronouns, transitions, etc.
- Correct by rewording the sentence or by changing the punctuation.

Examples of semantic errors:
- Words accidentally left out, especially negative words.
- Unclear or ambiguous pronouns.
- Missing or wrong transitions.
- Sentence punctuation errors.
- Missing or wrongly placed commas or apostrophes.

Syntactic errors—places where something doesn't seem right because of the order of the words.
- Identify by reading your paper aloud and paying attention to places where you stumble or have to repeat the phrase because something doesn't read right.
- Correct by trying out different ways to phrase the sentence until it "sounds" right.

Examples of syntactic errors:
- Unclear or awkward phrases.
- Awkward or unnecessary shifts to passive voice.
- Places where the elements aren't parallel.
- Fused sentences.

FIGURE 5.4   *Continued*

Grammatical errors—places where something violates the conventions of formal, written language. • Identify by testing your writing against the rules of formal, written English. • Correct by applying these same rules.	*Examples of grammatical errors:* • Subject-verb or noun-pronoun agreement. • Verb formation. • Misspellings not caught by the spellchecker.

Some Strategies to Use to Proofread More Effectively

Here are some suggestions for becoming a better proofreader:

1. Slow down your reading enough to focus on each word by:
   • Reading your paper aloud or listening while someone else reads exactly what's on your paper.
   • Following along with a pencil as you read silently.
   • Running a blank sheet of paper slowly down the composition so you're forced to read one line at a time.
   • Reading one sentence at a time from the bottom up. This takes each sentence out of context, so you can focus on errors and not meaning.

2. Learn to use the "sound" of words to identify errors by:
   • Paying attention to places where you stumble as a reader. This generally indicates errors in meaning and word order.
   • Associating certain words and phrases with "alarm bells." When you hear the sound of homonyms, such as *there*, you should stop and check to see if the spelling is right for the context. Other words that should send off alarm bells are connecting words like *because*. Check to make sure you don't have a sentence fragment.

3. Learn to use built-in word processing features to help you identify errors by:
   • Running the spell check function before you print your paper.
   • Running the grammar-check function to alert you to features such as homonyms.
   • Using the **SEARCH** function to find all cases of "alarm bells" words, such as *because*. Each time the cursor stops on *because*, read the sentence to make sure it's not a fragment.

4. Keep a personal list of proofreading troublespots and work especially hard to master them. List the three biggest problems at the top of your paper and read for those first.

5. Check a handbook if you have questions.

6. Find a friend to help you proofread your paper. Proofreading is very detailed work. Some people can see details easily while others have a hard time. You should make a genuine effort to improve your own skills at proofreading, but if you're just not good at it, then you should find a proofreader you can trust to help you.

(continued)

FIGURE 5.4   *Continued*

Practice with Passages from Students' Texts

In commercially available proofreading curricula, each exercise is usually one sentence long. Students quickly learn to expect errors, so they don't get the chance to develop their sense of judgment. In proofreading their own papers, on the other hand, students have to read extended texts and make judgments about when sentences are correct and when they're not. Therefore, asking students to proofread passages of 2 to 6 sentences from their papers gives them more realistic practice. The extended passages are not only long enough material to give students a better context for understanding the content, but they almost always include sentences in which there are no errors. Students learn to trust when their writing is correct and when they need to make changes.

I want students to learn to "see" their errors on their own. Many of these errors will disappear when students revise. When they have more control over their content, they'll inevitably have more control over their grammar and mechanics. Nevertheless, some errors will remain because students don't "see" them or because they genuinely don't know they're errors. I help students "see" the former by minimally marking their papers. I help students with the latter through direct instruction or explicit correction—in individual marginal comments, small group editing conferences, or whole-group mini-lessons. Figure 5.5 explains the system I use to mark students' papers.

This chapter explores strategies that teachers can use to better understand errors that students make in their writing and to help students become more independent self-editors.

FIGURE 5.5   *Teaching Tip: Minimally Marking Student Papers*

Research suggests that students improve their editing success if they receive some kind of feedback from the teacher and it turns out that feedback need only be minimal to make an impact (Haswell, 1983; Ferris & Roberts, 2001). Haswell (1983) argues for making only minimal marks on students' papers—he puts a checkmark in the margin for each error he sees in a line of text. He expects students to correct as many errors as they can find before they receive a grade for their paper. He notes that his system of minimal marking is beneficial because it:

- emphasizes student performance and encourages revision—students need to return to their text before they get a grade on it.
- encourages students to take more responsibility for correcting their own errors. Haswell doesn't identify the errors, only gives students clues about where to look. Students must figure out for themselves what the errors are and how to correct them. According to Ferris and Roberts, this encourages students to rehearse the grammatical rules they know and learn them more deeply.
- is a more productive use of teachers' time. Many teachers get frustrated when they spend hours writing in corrections on students' papers, but students continue to make the same mistakes again and again. Minimal marking not only saves teachers the time of making corrections, but encourages students to become more independent self-editors and to master more of their errors over time.

Haswell doesn't say specifically who his students are, but presumably they're mainstream, native speaking students. But even students who are in the process of learning English can successfully

FIGURE 5.5 *Continued*

correct errors in the papers with only minimal marking. In a study of the editing abilities of 72 intermediate-level ESL students, Ferris and Roberts found that students needed some kind of help in locating their errors, but feedback didn't need to be any more explicit than putting a check mark in the margins or underlining a word. In their study, students who didn't get any feedback at all could find and correct only about 18 percent of their own errors. With minimal marking, the success rate jumped to 60 percent. Ferris and Roberts conclude that:

- When editing their papers, students can benefit from feedback about where their errors are.
- The feedback doesn't need to be particularly explicit for students to catch a majority (i.e., 60 percent) of their own errors.
- For the remaining 40 percent of errors that ESL students can't catch on their own, teachers should write in the correction for the student (see Figure 10.4).

However, they also note that in interviews with ESL students, the students preferred that their teachers not only underline the words with errors, but also give them clues about what kind of error it is, such as writing *tense* under a verb tense error. Ferris and Roberts point out that for students in their study, the codes didn't improve students' ability to correct errors to a statistically significant degree—it just made them feel more comfortable.

Knowing that students can benefit from minimal marking, but prefer to have coded clues, I use a modified version of Haswell's minimal marking system. When students are ready to focus on the surface errors in their papers, I:

- *Underline* words I want students to notice when they're editing their papers (e.g., words containing subject-verb agreement or possessive apostrophe errors). These are errors I think they can easily correct on their own once they can "see" the errors.
- *Underline and label* those words containing errors I think students can correct on their own if they have a clue (e.g., verb tense).
- *Underline and write in a suggestion* those words containing errors important enough to mark, but which students aren't likely to correct on their own (e.g., nonparallelism). Sometimes, I put a question mark at the end of my suggestions. This usually indicates something more stylistic than grammatical in nature (e.g., wordiness); the question mark means students retain the final right to choose to accept these suggestions.

Exploring Your Own Language Experience

1. Before you begin the reading, spend five minutes or so writing in your journal about the following:

   a. What is an error in writing? How do you know when you come across one in your writing? someone else's writing?

   b. How did teachers deal with errors in your writing? How useful were these procedures in helping you master that error?

   c. How confident do you feel that you can recognize—and then correct—the "errors" in your own writing? When/where/how did you learn this skill? What did your teachers do to help you learn to proofread/edit?

Developing Correctness in Student Writing:
Alternatives to the Error Hunt

Lois Matz Rosen

> *In this article, Rosen gives teachers a number of ways to help students take responsibility for finding and correcting their errors. Rosen first published her article in the March 1987 issue of* English Journal *and then later updated it to be published in a book entitled* Lessons to Share on Teaching Grammar in Context *(1998, Heinemann). The book was compiled by Constance Weaver as a companion to her book* Teaching Grammar in Context. *The* Lessons *book is intended to show teachers how they can enact Weaver's ideas on teaching grammar in the context of writing in a classroom.*

Introduction
"Developing Correctness in Student Writing" was first published in *English Journal* in March 1987. When Connie Weaver asked for permission to reprint it in her volume, I felt a need to update it, adding recent research and methods.

My recent search into the articles and books of the past decade revealed several new developments in the area of teaching "correctness" in writing. First, research studies have proliferated, trying to document the relationship between students' writing, revising, and proofreading skills and the use of computers with word processors and spelling and grammar checkers. The mixed impact of computers on students' mechanical/grammatical skills is discussed in the revised article below.

Second, at the time I researched and wrote the original version—the mid-1980s—the movement toward teaching writing as a process and mechanical/grammatical skills as part of that process appeared to be better accepted in elementary classrooms than in secondary classrooms. As a result, most of the techniques I presented in 1987 came from writing teachers and theorists who worked at the elementary level. One of the first things I realized in updating this article was that attention to teaching mechanics and grammar within the process of writing and revising was now given prominent attention at the secondary level. Many of the strategies I outlined in 1987 are now actively used in classrooms K–12, while secondary teachers have added their own approaches to correctness, described in the following revision.

Finally, an unexpected controversy was introduced with publication of Lisa Delpit's articles questioning the efficacy of the process approach for students who speak a non-mainstream dialect (1986, 1988). This, too, merits consideration, given the ever-growing linguistic, racial, and ethnic diversity that now characterizes so many English language arts classrooms throughout the United States.

Although no new research either proving or disproving these approaches to mechanical and grammatical correctness in writing has been done in recent years, as more and more teachers adopt writing process strategies into their classes, teaching correctness in the context of the students' own writing becomes more widespread. The updated article below confronts this lack of recent substantive research, making recommendations for the future.

Developing Correctness in Student Writing, 1987–1997

> I don't understand why good students leave out possessives when I've taught it, reinforced it, quizzed it . . . . Yet even after all this, there are those errors in the title, in the very first sentence!

Do I read a paper and ignore all punctuation? What good is that for them?

I put 5X on their papers and they have to write it over five times. It's so stupid, obviously. But I can't reinforce this by doing nothing.

We spend hours at night with papers. It's not fun after a while and it gets to you . . . . I'm not sure the students get as much from it as the time I spend on it.

These comments by high-school English teachers discussing the process of marking student papers reflect the dissatisfaction and frustration of many teachers over the problem of dealing with errors in student writing—the obvious mistakes in spelling, punctuation, capitalization, grammar, and usage that often pepper student papers and refuse to disappear despite the teacher's most diligent attention. Traditionally, teachers have worked to eradicate error in two ways: by teaching mechanical and grammatical correctness through drill exercises in grammar/usage texts, and by pointing out all errors when marking student papers, perhaps also expecting students to make corrections when papers are returned. Although numerous research studies show that there is little or no transfer of learning from isolated drills to actual writing experiences and that the time-intensive practice of the teacher's "error hunt" does not produce more mechanically perfect papers, this 100-year-old tradition still persists. (See Braddock et al., 1963; Haynes, 1978; Rosen, 1983, for discussion of research in this area.) The presence of grammar/usage texts in almost any language arts classroom attests to this approach to correctness, as do the results of several recent studies into teachers' marking procedures.

The Error Hunt

Harris (1977) found that 66 percent of the corrections and annotations the high-school teachers in her study made on student papers were on mechanics and usage. Searle and Dillon's study (1980) of the commenting done by nine teachers in grades four through six revealed that teachers in their study tried to correct all errors in spelling, usage, and punctuation, which led to a heavy emphasis on what the researchers characterized as "Form-Correction Response" (p. 239). Applebee's 1981 study, *Writing in the Secondary School: English and the Content Areas*, reflects the same pattern:

> The major vehicle for writing instruction, in all subject areas, was the teacher's comments and corrections of completed work. Errors in writing mechanics were the most common focus of these responses; comments concerned with the ideas the student was expressing were the least frequently reported. (pp. 90–91)

A study I completed in 1983 of patterns in responses by the high school English teachers quoted at the opening of this article showed similar results. Almost 50 percent of their combined responses (defined as any type of written feedback to the student including underlinings, symbols, phrases, corrections, suggestions, and comments) on their students' papers focused on mechanical and grammatical errors. Each of the six teachers in my study had a specific approach to dealing with errors on student papers.

One teacher admitted that she tried to find and mark 100 percent of the mistakes "because parents like it." This technique, coupled with her strong belief that students needed lots of feedback on their ideas, led to papers that averaged eight responses per page and often resulted in a returned paper so full of marks and remarks that it seems likely a student would have difficulty figuring out what was worth attending to. Another teacher concentrated on two or three types of errors for each writing assignment, told the students when making the assignment which ones she would look for, and then tried to find 100 percent of these errors on each paper. This technique cut down on the time she spent marking papers, but she was not encouraged by any rapid improvement in correctness. A third teacher put a minus (–) sign in the margin beside each line that had an error in it in the belief that this was less punitive to students than pointing out the actual mistake. Because she worked with basic writers whose skills in this area were low, 90 percent of her responses on student papers were these minus signs. When papers were returned, a full class period was spent with students identifying and correcting their errors. Combine her marking emphasis with class time on error correction, and one can see the strong focus on correctness that this method produced: a silent message to these basic writers about the importance of avoiding error when one writes.

Symbols to ease the marking burden were used by all the teachers in my study: the standard "awks" and "frags," but idiosyncratic ones as well, such as one teacher's "T E" for a "target error" that had to be "terminated" by the end of the year. Only one of the teachers in my study told me he preferred to dismiss the problem as one that would take care of itself. "I mark the errors that bother me when I see them; it's not much of a problem," he said. The other teachers, however, seemed to support the statement quoted earlier: "I just can't reinforce this by doing nothing."

The problem writing teachers face when dealing with mechanical/grammatical error in student writing is a more complex one than simply deciding whether or not to ignore it. The visual signposts, the surface features and grammatical structures of English that readers expect, are certainly an important part of any written communication. Numerous surface errors *do* distract the reader, and we are all aware that society places great value on correctness as an indication of writing ability. Nevertheless, anyone who has read through a perfectly correct but perfectly empty student paper can verify the primary importance of *what* the student says regardless of how correctly it is stated. The dilemma, then, becomes one of balance and proportion in the writing program. Namely, *how does a teacher focus on content in student writing and still ensure that progress is also being made toward mastery of the mechanical and grammatical structures of written English?*

Recent research and theory in writing instruction suggests that this dilemma can be resolved by abandoning the traditional approach to error outlined above and working with other methods that are proving to be highly effective in helping students at all levels develop competence in the mechanical/grammatical aspects of writing. Before I discuss these new approaches to correctness, let me first present several key assumptions about the nature of the composing process and the way it is learned that provide the underlying rationale for the methods that follow.

Underlying Assumptions

Writing is a complex process, recursive rather than linear in nature, involving thinking, planning, discovering what to say, drafting, and redrafting. Writers who worry about mechanics while they are composing are not concentrating fully on what they have to say because it is difficult to do two things well at the same time, especially if neither task is yet completely under the writer's control. Therefore, any attention to correctness should be saved for *postwriting*—the final proofreading and polishing stages of a finished piece. Students should be told this, and teachers should not contradict this message by commenting on errors in early drafts, journals, or free writing unless they seriously interfere with meaning.

Learning to use the correct mechanical and grammatical forms of written language is a developmental process and as such is slow, unique to each child, and does not progress in an even uphill pattern. Weaver (1982) argues that "semantic and syntactic growth are normally accompanied by errors in language use" (p. 443). She demonstrates by tracing changing patterns in the kinds of sentence fragments students make from first through sixth grade. As the young writers in her study worked to express increasingly more complex ideas and to use more sophisticated sentence constructions, the kinds of fragments predominant in early grades disappeared, only to be replaced by others. First-graders, for example, produced numerous fragments that were explanatory clauses beginning with *because:*

> I want a car, *because* I'm old enouf.

By sixth grade, types of fragments had blossomed to include a wide variety of subordinate clauses:

> Finally one day *when the machine spanked a kid, Billy.* Billy turned around and hit the machine.
>
> I would like to have a raffle. *So we can have some money for a special pro. in our room like roller-skating, skying* [skiing] *ice skating*

When students struggle to learn new skills such as using dialogue or writing a persuasive essay, they need time to master the unfamiliar aspects of mechanics and grammar that accompany them. To quote Weaver, "growth and error go hand in hand" (p. 443), which suggests that writing teachers must have a certain tolerance for error, accepting it as a normal part of writing growth.

The mechanical and grammatical skills of writing are learned when a writer needs to use them for real purposes to produce writing that communicates a message he or she wants someone else to receive. A piece of writing should not be seen as a test of the student's ability, or lack of it, to produce perfect prose, but rather as a chance for a developing writer to use all his or her present language capabilities to their fullest extent in producing a genuine written communication.

Responsibility for the correctness of any given piece of writing should fall mainly on the student, not the teacher. Students learn to become accurate and self-sufficient writers by searching for, finding, and correcting their own mistakes. They may fail to achieve perfection; they may miss many errors, in fact, but in the end they learn much more from identifying and correcting whatever errors they can find on their own papers and those of their peers than from the teacher's painstaking proofreading which may identify errors they don't understand or, worse yet, focus their attention on correctness instead of content. Copyediting is one of the skills a competent writer must learn, and it is never too early to start teaching independence in this area.

Students learn to write by writing, and they learn to control the mechanical and grammatical elements of written English by writing, revising, and proofreading their own work—with some help or direction from the teacher when necessary. They do not learn to write correctly by studying about writing or doing isolated workbook exercises unrelated to their own writing. In *The Art of Teaching Writing,* Calkins (1986) urges teachers to trust the "incidental learning" that takes place when students are actively and frequently engaged in writing (p. 199). They begin to read like writers and to view the world with a writer's eyes, not only for language and ideas but for the surface features of writing as well.

Methods

The following approach to correctness, culled from the work of such master-teachers as Donald Graves, Lucy Calkins, Ronald Cramer, Mina Shaughnessy, or experimented with in my own work with developing writers, views correctness within a larger framework that puts composing at the center of writing instruction. It also changes the teacher's role from drill sergeant/error hunter to coach/helper. If there is a common theme running through the methods below, it is that *revision is the key* to helping students master the mechanical and grammatical aspects of writing. When students view early drafts of their work as fluid, rather than fixed, they are free to concentrate on what they wish to say. Aspects of correctness can then be saved for final drafts with specific points of grammar and mechanics taught when necessary as students compose and revise their own writing. The techniques described below encourage students to work independently on correctness, show them how to become competent proofreaders, and at the same time suggest ways for a teacher to deal with the mechanical problems that appear on student papers. Although several of these methods were originally designed for elementary students, they are equally effective with secondary level and college students.

Let Students Write. The most important technique a teacher can use to guide students toward mechanically and grammatically correct writing is also the simplest: let them write. Let them write daily if possible and provide opportunities for them to experiment with all kinds of whole discourse from journals, letters, and personal essays to poems, short stories, and analytical prose. Mina Shaughnessy's (1977) work with adult basic writers at the City University of New York led her to observe that the single most important characteristic of these students was their lack of writing experience. She writes, "the basic writing student is . . . likely to have written 350 words a semester. It would not be unusual for him to have written nothing at all" (p. 14).

Let Students Read. A classroom environment rich with reading materials supports writing development, with frequent exposure to the language of written discourse and the patterns of Standard English. Students who grew up in households where "I seen" and "He has went" are acceptable forms of speech need to hear, see, and read standard forms of written English in the literature and nonfiction of the classroom. In the act of reading, even with the student's major emphasis on meaning-making, the mechanics of punctuation, spelling, capitalization, as well as standard forms of grammar and usage are visually present. Over time, these become absorbed as part of the student's linguistic knowledge. In a landmark study by Connors and Lunsford (1988) analyzing types and frequency of errors on college students' freshman composition papers, the researchers found such a preponderance of spelling errors they omitted spelling from their analysis. Combining spelling errors with other visual components of language, such as homophones, and comparing their analysis to similar studies done earlier in this century, they concluded that the error patterns in today's college freshmen "seem to suggest declining familiarity with the visual look of a written page" (p. 406). Our students are products of the media generation, not accustomed to spending sizable portions of their time reading. Consequently, one of the most important ways to help students develop their mechanical and grammatical writing skills is by immersing them in a rich and continuous classroom reading environment.

Provide Time for All Stages of the Writing Process. A third fundamental method for increasing correctness is showing students that writing consists of several overlapping steps: prewriting and planning, writing and revising, editing and proofreading. Or, as Kirby and Liner (1981) put it so aptly for students, "getting started, getting it down, getting it right, checking it out" (p. 8). Teaching effective strategies for each of these stages increases students' confidence as writers and allows them to concentrate their full attention on correctness at the stage of writing when it matters most.

Use Editing Workshops. A fourth basic method for working with correctness is the use of editing workshops—classroom time regularly set aside for final editing and polishing of papers that have already been revised for content. Delegating specific classroom time for this task is valuable in two ways: First, it gives students a definite message about both the importance of correctness and the appropriate time in the writing process to focus on it. Second, many strategies for effective proofreading and mastery of mechanical/grammatical skills can be incorporated into this workshop time while still keeping the classroom focus on the students' own writing. Four different activities teachers and students can engage in during an editing workshop are recommended throughout the literature on teaching the composing process.

Modeling. Many students, even at the college level, don't know how to proofread effectively. When directed to "check your paper for errors," they quickly scan over their work, perhaps adding a comma here or there or changing a spelling that suddenly looks odd. In *Children's Writing and Language Growth*, Cramer (1978) recommends modeling the editing process by obtaining permission from one student writer in the class to make a transparency of his or her paper for editing by the whole class on the overhead projector. Once the class has had a chance to read the paper projected on the screen, the teacher opens discussion by focusing on the content of the paper. "What do you like about this paper?" or "What has the writer done well?" are good questions to ask at this point. Then the teacher directs the discussion to proofreading by asking, "Can anyone find something that needs to be changed?"—a neutral question, suggesting error correction is a natural part of this stage in the writing process. As students identify and correct individual errors, the teacher corrects each on the transparency, giving a brief explanation of the reason for the correction, and also starts a list on the chalkboard of kinds of errors identified: spelling, capital letters, run-on sentences, etc. The teacher can point out errors the students don't identify and use this as an opportunity to discuss the error, or can stop when the class has corrected all the errors it can identify. The final step is for the students to apply this process to their own papers, using the list on the board as a guide for the kinds of errors to look for.

If this write/model/apply process is followed regularly, students receive numerous short lessons on grammar and mechanics plus the constant opportunity to apply these lessons to their own papers. The middle school teachers I work with in the Flint, Michigan, Community Schools have been using this modeling strategy with their classes with good success. Students get involved, arguing points of grammar with each other and voluntarily checking the dictionary. One teacher tells of the gradual inching up of student chairs to the overhead projector as they group-edit and the enthusiasm with which students approach their own writing after the modeling session.

Individual Editing Conferences. While students are actively involved in editing their own writing, the teacher can give individual help with proofreading by holding miniconferences. In *Writing: Teachers and Children at Work*, Graves (1983) describes brief conferences focusing on proofreading held with the writer when the paper is essentially completed and moving toward a final draft. The teacher quickly scans the paper, looking for recurrent errors, and tells the writer what kinds of proofreading activities are needed. This can be done in two- or three-minute conferences at the teacher's desk, or the teacher can move up and down the aisles, leaning over shoulders, and concentrating more attention on students whose writing would benefit from more help with mechanics. The dialogue might go something like this: "OK, John, looks like you're ready for a final proofreading and polishing. First I'd like you to circle all the words you think might be misspelled and look them up in the dictionary. Then work on complete sentences. There are several places in your paper where you've got two sentences strung together." The teacher might ask John to work with him in identifying the first few run-ons and correcting them before telling John to do the same throughout the rest of his paper and then let the teacher see it again. There could be a brief lesson on possessives for one student, another on *its*, *it's* for someone else. Never lingering for more than a few minutes with each writer, the teacher identifies an area for proofreading, illustrates what he or she means, and gets the writer started working independently. The eavesdroppers on either side of the aisles often learn as much as the student being worked with. "Can I help you with anything?" works well as an opening question from the teacher for it permits an immediate and accurate response to a student's need. Nancie Atwell (1987), in her classic text on teaching writing, *In the Middle*, describes longer conferences she holds with students periodically to teach the individual skills in mechanics and usage that each student needs.

Peer Proofreading. Another valuable way to work toward correctness during editing workshop time is to have students work together when proofreading. Students always say it is much easier to correct someone else's work than it is to identify errors in their own, and this technique depends on that perception. If writing is not seen as a *test* of an individual student's writing ability but as a process that is growing and developing, this method permits for learning by both writer and editor. Proofreading thus becomes a collaborative learning experience. When I do this with my own students, both basic writers and average freshmen, I usually put students in pairs after each has had a chance to proofread his or her own paper. The only rule I impose is that no corrections are to be made on the writer's paper without the knowledge and consent of the author. This means both writers must confer over any error on either paper and both must agree on the correction. I also ask that the editor initial all corrections he or she finds, which gives me some sense of the mechanical skills both the writer and the proofreader bring to the paper. If the two writers can't agree on an error, I am called over to make a decision, giving me a chance to teach a minilesson as I resolve the problem. Students enjoy being editors for each other, and I find that it takes a great deal of pressure off each writer to correct the work on his or her own. Peer proofreading can also be handled in groups of three or four students, who are instructed to pass their papers around the group, each student correcting any errors found. It helps if the groups are structured so that each one has a student good at spelling and mechanics.

Minilessons. Brief ten-minute lessons on common mechanical problems can have immediate value when they are taught as part of a writing workshop. A short lecture at the beginning of a proofreading session can then be applied immediately to the students' own papers, reinforcing the new information through personal use rather than through a textbook exercise. Students can share problem sentences during these short sessions, ask specific questions from their own writing, and get help from the shared knowledge of the entire class. Teaching these skills and having students apply them while writing is in process produces much better results than teaching them from grammar/usage texts as isolated skills. By giving minilessons during writing workshop time throughout the school term or year, a teacher could easily review almost all the kinds of mechanical errors students make and never need to rely on a textbook or drill exercises to reinforce the learning. If several students in a class share the same mechanical/grammatical problem, grouping these students for a minilesson and then permitting them to work together to correct this error on their own papers can be highly effective.

Help Students Self-Edit. Several correction strategies are aimed at enhancing students' abilities to self-edit. Among the most useful are the following.

Editing Checklists. These are lists of common errors that students can use as a guide when proofreading their own papers. Simple lists for young children can ask questions about spelling and capital letters, while older writers can be instructed to check their writing for a dozen or more surface features such as run-ons and fragments, subject-verb agreement, and possessives.

Proofreading Strategies. Show students some methods to improve their own proofreading:

- run a blank sheet of paper slowly down the composition so you are forced to read one line at a time
- read one sentence at a time from the bottom up to take each sentence out of context and thus focus on errors, not meaning
- circle all suspected spelling errors before consulting a dictionary
- list three your most frequent errors at the top of the paper, then read the paper three times, each time focusing on one of these errors
- read aloud to yourself or a friend, or read into a tape recorder and play it back
- have someone else—a classmate, parent, or the teacher—read the paper aloud to you, exactly as it appears on the page

An Editing Corner. Something as simple as an editing corner heaped with handbooks, dictionaries, and a thesaurus can also help students become responsible for their own mechanical/grammatical correctness. The walls around the editing corner can be decorated with a chart on how to proofread, a list of spelling demons, rules of punctuation or capitalization, and examples of dialogue punctuated properly. One-page handouts with explanations and examples of common errors and ways to correct them can be filed in this corner along with displays of student writing taken through several drafts, including final proofreading. Students should be allowed free access to these materials as they write. They should be encouraged to use the corner to solve mechanical problems themselves.

Make Students Responsible for Developing and Monitoring Their Own Editing/Proofreading Skills. The ultimate goal of any approach to correctness is to have students become competent self-editors, recognizing and knowing how to correct any deviations from standard usage in their own writing. Keeping records of their own errors is one way of encouraging students to assume this responsibility. Some teachers just have students keep a sheet in their writing folder on which they record errors pointed out by the teacher or peers with the idea that they'll work to eliminate these errors in future papers. Madraso (1993) has students keep a three-column "Proofreading Journal," with the first column for the error, the second column for the solution, and the third column for a strategy for spotting the error in the future. Andrasick (1993) uses a system for helping students recognize and learn how to correct their own individual error patterns. When reading student papers, she first responds to content, then goes back and indicates errors using a standard set of proofreading symbols. When students get their paper back, they transfer the list of errors for that paper to a 3 × 5 card, correct them on the paper with help from the teacher, peers, or a handbook, and then make a note on the card of the mechanical/grammatical error they will work on for the next paper. Each student has an ongoing card filed in the class "Goof Box" with this information listed for all their papers. After using this process for several papers, Andrasick asks students to review their "Goof Box" card and write a reflection, noting patterns of change—errors now eliminated and new ones that need attention. She also has them write about and share with each other the strategies they use to identify, learn about, and correct their own errors. With this system, students become consciously aware of their own editing skills, developing a sense of control over proofreading and error correction, and assuming responsibility for their own self-editing competence.

Abandon the Error Hunt. Another cluster of correctness strategies centers on marking techniques for the teacher, ones that differ significantly from the traditional "red-pencillitis" approach and are always preceded by classroom use of editing workshops and self-editing strategies.

Benign Neglect. Students involved for the first time in the process approach to writing, those newly engaged in journal-writing, prewriting exercises, multiple drafts, revision, and proofreading, can benefit from a period of teacher inattention to correctness when marking final drafts of papers. If students' previous writing instruction focused heavily on form and correctness, they need time to recenter their attention on what they have to say as writers and to learn the various composing strategies that will make writing more pleasurable for both the writer and the reader of his or her paper. If students are generating a great deal of writing and are frequently engaged in editing workshop strategies, the teacher can safely focus written comments on content. This benign neglect gives students a chance to internalize writing and proofreading skills and to demonstrate what they do know before the teacher begins to identify and work on areas of weakness.

Selectivity. Rather than engage in intensive error correction when responding to student writing, teachers are encouraged by recent writing researchers and theorists to adopt a more moderate approach to error and to look for patterns in the errors an individual student makes. Research has never been able to show that circling all the errors—the error hunt approach to marking—makes a significant difference in writing quality; instead it discourages the student whose paper is full of mistakes and focuses students on errors instead of ideas. Students are more likely to grow as writers when the teacher's primary purpose in reading student papers is to respond to content. However, if attention to content and correctness are combined when marking papers, it is more helpful to select one or two *kinds* of errors the individual student is making than to point out every error in the paper. The teacher can identify a selected error, show an example or two on the student's paper, and either explain the correct form or direct the student to a handbook for further explanation.

Error Analysis. A third method for working with student error when responding to student writing, one that can be especially fruitful for the teacher, is to approach it from an analytic perspective. The composition teacher as error analyst looks for patterns in the errors of an individual student, tries to discover how the student arrived at the mistake by analyzing the error (i.e., is it lack of knowledge about a certain grammatical point? a mislearned rule? a careless error? overgeneralization of a particular rule? the influence of oral language?) and plans strategies accordingly. Kroll and Schafer (1978), Bartholomae (1980), and Shaughnessy (1977) have demonstrated the efficacy of error analysis in helping teachers better understand the source of student error as an aid to planning more effective ways of dealing with it.

Publish Student Writing. The final basic strategy recommended for working toward correctness is publishing. All writers, professionals as well as students, need a reason for laboring over a draft until it is perfect: The urge to see oneself in print can be a powerful drive toward revision and proofreading. Watch what happens when a class publication is handed out. Each writer is likely to flip immediately to his or her own work for a minute of personal pleasure before browsing through the rest of the book. Writing teachers need to take advantage of this human need to be heard, to leave a physical imprint on the world, by offering numerous opportunities for sharing and publishing: bulletin boards in the class and the hall, "paper of the week" on the door, individual books, dittoed class books, a classroom anthology of one piece from each writer that sits on public display in the library, writing as gifts for parents, pen pals, contests to enter, and a class newspaper.

Computers and Correctness

As the use of computers for writing has grown, so has the proliferation of studies examining the effects of computers on writers' processes and final products. Research results are mixed: While most researchers agree that students develop more positive attitudes toward writing and do more revision with computers, the effect on the quality of the papers themselves is contradictory. Numerous studies show computers have no effect on the overall quality of the papers; however, most of these studies were limited to a ten- or twelve-week period of study, perhaps too brief for computer use to impact writing improvement, especially since learning to use the computer often takes up instructional time at first. A 1992 study of eighth-graders who were already experienced computer users had more promising results. The researchers found that "papers written on computer were rated significantly higher" (p. 249) than handwritten papers in all four qualities assessed, including mechanics (Owston, Murphy, & Wideman, 1992). Concerned about the influence of spelling on the higher ratings assigned word-processed texts, the researchers assessed a random sample of papers from both categories, finding no difference in mean spelling errors between the computer-written papers and the handwritten ones, indicating that spelling did not bias the ratings. This study offers evidence that computers might provide yet another strategy for improving students' mechanical/grammatical skills.

At the present time, it makes sense to involve students in writing on computers as much as possible for ease of revision and the use of such writing aids as a spell checker, thesaurus, or grammar checker. Just remind students that the beautifully typed paper emerging from the printer still needs the same attention to mechanical and grammatical correctness that any piece of writing requires before it is ready for evaluation or publication.

Correctness in the Linguistically Diverse Classroom

Advocates for writing process instruction have been criticized for neglecting form and correctness in favor of fluency by those who don't fully understand the ways in which writing process instruction includes attention to all aspects of writing development. But criticism has also come from teachers of minority students. Delpit (1986,1988) and Reyes (1992) have been critical of writing process instruction for speakers of non-mainstream dialects, such as blacks and ESL students, arguing that this method does not give these students explicit instruction in the standard literacy skills they need for access to higher education and the workplace. At first this position seems in direct conflict with the methods advocated throughout this article, and the danger is in misunderstanding their position as calling for a return to isolated instruction in grammar and mechanics. Yet both educators agree that skills must be taught within a context that encourages full development of linguistic skills and "critical and creative thinking" (Delpit, 1986, p. 384). It is my contention that, in the hands of a skilled teacher who fully understands ways to integrate skills instruction into a rich writing and reading workshop environment, writing process instruction would include whatever direct instruction was necessary for students to develop standard literacy skills. Minilessons in skills followed by direct application to students' own writing, extended minilessons that also include some practice exercises in the skill being taught (Weaver, 1996), individual conferences with the teacher to work at the specific skills each student needs, and an emphasis on preparing writing for publication, all give nonmainstream students the direct instruction necessary for developing standard English skills. Yet these strategies also provide a climate supportive of students' individual growth as thinkers and writers. Speakers of nonmainstream dialects and ESL students may indeed need more instruction in the mechanical and grammatical skills of Standard English than white middle-class students, but skills instruction for all students is best taught within the context of the writing process and in a classroom that stresses writing as a meaning-making and communicative activity.

Research Indications

As these methods for working toward correctness show, over the past two decades writing teachers and theorists have developed a body of techniques that can be termed a process-oriented approach to correctness, methods that help students master the mechanical/grammatical aspects of writing without making correctness the central focus of the composition program. Relatively few studies document the effectiveness of this approach. Mainly the literature on how to teach writing deals with the process as a whole and shows its effectiveness in improving the quality of student writing in all dimensions, including surface level correctness. However, two studies suggest specifically that working with correctness within the writing process is more effective than the traditional skills approach.

Calkins (1980), in "When Children Want to Punctuate: Basic Skills Belong in Context," reports on a 1980 study of teaching punctuation in the third grade. In one classroom the teacher taught language mechanics through daily drills and workbook exercises; her children rarely wrote. In another classroom the children wrote an hour a day three times a week with no formal instruction in punctuation. At the end of the year, the "writers" not only could define and explain many more marks of punctuation than the children who had been drilled in this (8.65 kinds as opposed to 3.85 kinds) but also were actively using these punctuation marks for real purposes in their own writing. Calkins notes that "When children need punctuation in order to be seen and heard, they become vacuum cleaners, sucking up odd bits from books, their classmates' papers, billboards, and magazines. They find punctuation everywhere, and make it their own" (p. 573).

The second piece of research documenting the fact that developing writers *do* learn mechanical and grammatical skills through the process of writing is a 1984 study by DiStefano and Killion with fourth-, fifth-, and sixth-grade students. Students in the experimental group were taught by teachers trained in the process model of writing, while the control group students were exposed to a skills approach. Using pre- and postwriting samples in September and May, the researchers showed that students in the process model group did significantly better than those in the skills group in organization, spelling, usage, and sentence structure, with the latter three items ones that are usually associated with a skills approach. The students in the skills group did not do better than the process group on any of the three grade levels. The researchers conclude "that the writing process model takes into account skills such as spelling and usage as well as organization of ideas" (p. 207).

Despite the growth of the process approach to writing in the past ten years and its concomitant methodology for teaching mechanical/grammatical correctness within the context of writing, we do not have a body of recent research substantiating the efficacy of this approach. Teachers using these methods report student success along all dimensions of writing (for example, see Atwell, 1987). The need for research into this aspect of writing is crucial if we are to better understand how to help our students develop the full repertoire of writing skills they need for success in mainstream society. Research data will also help teachers promote these newer writing approaches with parents, administrators, and the public.

I suggest case studies of successful writing classrooms at all educational levels, with a particular focus on students' development of mechanical/grammatical skills, and longitudinal case studies of writing development in students from school districts that have adopted process approaches K–12. We must examine the interaction of teaching methodology, cognitive and linguistic development, and writing skill development as it occurs in rich reading/writing environments. In addition, we need comparative studies of mechanical/grammatical skill development in a variety of classroom contexts and with a variety of methodologies, attempting to better understand which approaches are most successful in helping students become more correct writers.

I also recommend that teachers continue to do informal research in their own classrooms, trying the correctness strategies described in this article, using the results to inform their own teaching practices, and sharing this information with fellow teachers. Formal and informal studies such as these would give educators the information needed to adopt strategies firmly grounded in research as well as in the best practice reported by successful writing teachers.

Conclusions

Writing instruction has long been dominated by an emphasis on correctness. Increasingly, however, as our knowledge of the writing process and the way it is learned grows, we are coming to understand that correctness develops naturally when students are continuously engaged in composing and revising activities that are meaningful to them. When young writers need a better understanding of mechanical and grammatical matters to ensure more effective communication of their ideas, they learn what they need to know to prepare final drafts for readers. The methods described above are designed to support this learning of the mechanical and grammatical elements of written language while still keeping writers focused on the content of their writing.

In compiling these techniques, I do not suggest that teachers either ignore mechanical and grammatical correctness in writing or replace grammar exercises and intensive marking with a heavy emphasis on editing workshops. Rather, I present these methods so that teachers will see them as evidence that skills *can* be learned in the context of writing and will, therefore, free students from the correctness focus in composition and permit them to find themselves as writers.

References

Andrasick, K. (1993). Independent repatterning: Developing self-editing competence. *English Journal, 82* (February): 28–31.

Applebee, A. (1981). *Writing in the secondary school: English and the content areas.* Urbana, IL: National Council of Teachers of English.

Atwell, N. (1987). *In the middle.* Portsmouth, NH: Boynton/Cook.

Bartholomae, D. (1980). The study of error. *College Composition and Communication, 31* (October): 253–269.

Braddock, R., Lloyd-Jones, R., & Schoer, L. (1963). *Research in written composition.* Urbana, IL: National Council of Teachers of English.

Calkins, L. (1980). When children want to punctuate: Basic skills belong in context. *Language Arts, 57* (May): 567–573.

Calkins, L. (1986). *The art of teaching writing.* Portsmouth, NH: Heinemann.

Connors, R., & Lunsford, A. (1988). Frequency of formal errors in current college writing, or Ma and Pa Kettle do research. *College Composition and Communication, 39* (4): 395–409.

Cramer, R. (1978). *Children's writing and language growth.* Columbus, OH: Charles E. Merrill.

Delpit, L. (1986). Skills and other dilemmas of a progressive black educator. *Harvard Educational Review, 56* (4): 379–385.

Delpit, L. (1988). The silenced dialogue: Power and pedagogy in educating other people's children. *Harvard Educational Review, 58* (3): 280–298.

DiStefano, P., & Killion, J. (1984). Assessing writing skills through a process approach. *English Education, 16* (December): 203–207.

Graves, D. (1983). *Writing: Teachers and children at work.* Portsmouth, NH: Heinemann.

Harris, W. (1977). Teacher response to student writing: A study of the response patterns of high school English teachers to determine the basis for teacher judgment of student writing. *Research in the Teaching of English, 11* (Fall): 175–185.

Haynes, E. (1978). Using research in preparing to teach writing. *English Journal, 67* (January): 82–88.

Kirby, D., & Liner, T. (1981). *Inside out: Developmental strategies for teaching writing.* Portsmouth, NH: Boynton/Cook.

Kroll, B., & Schafer, J. (1978). Error–analysis and the teaching of composition. *College Composition and Communication, 29* (October): 242–248.

Madraso, J. (1993). Proofreading: The skill we've neglected to teach. *English Journal, 82* (February): 32–41.

Owston, R., Murphy, S., & Wideman, H. (1992). The effects of word processing on students' writing quality and revision strategies. *Research in the Teaching of English, 26* (October): 249–276.

Reyes, M. (1992). Challenging venerable assumptions. *Harvard Educational Review, 62* (Winter): 427–446.

Rosen, L. (1983). *Responding to student writing: Case studies of six high school English teachers*, Ph.D. dissertation, Michigan State University.

Rosen, L. (1987). Developing correctness in student writing: Alternatives to the error hunt. *English Journal, 76*, 62–69.

Searle, D., & Dillon, D. (1980). The message of marking: Teacher written response to student writing at intermediate grade levels. *Research in the Teaching of English, 14* (October): 233–242.

Shaughnessy, M. (1977). *Errors and expectations.* New York: Oxford University Press.

Weaver, C. (1982). Welcoming errors as signs of growth. *Language Arts, 59*, 438–444.

Weaver, C. (1996). *Teaching grammar in context.* Portsmouth, NH: Boynton/Cook.

Questions for Discussion

1. Why does a definition of error depend on context?

2. Imagine that you were being interviewed by Rosen for her study of how/why teachers grade papers. What role do you think teachers should play in helping students produce "error-free" writing? How does this role compare to the role(s) suggested by Straub?

3. Research the Daily Oral Language program. What are the advantages and disadvantages of the method? What kind of credentials do the authors have? What kind of evidence do they offer to support the soundness of their methods? How credible is the evidence? Why?

4. Return to the textbooks and state curriculum guidelines you examined in Chapter 2. To what extent do they teach students to edit or proofread their work? How do they treat it?

5. Read the in-class essay by Yasmin (p. 220).
   a. Imagine that Yasmin is your student. What comments will you give her—either in conference or in writing—to encourage her to revise her in-class essay? What do you think is strong about her paper? What advice will you give her about its content, organization, and tone?
   b. Does Yasmin seem to have good control of the surface conventions of writing, such as grammar, spelling, and punctuation? Why/why not? Do you notice any striking "errors" when you read her essay for the first time? If so, identify one or two surface errors to comment on in an editing conference with her. What advice will you give her about correcting these errors?

6. Read the first draft of the definition essay by Louray (p. 222).
   a. Imagine that Louray is your student. What comments will you give her—either in conference or in writing—about her definition? What do you think is strong about her paper? What advice will you give her about its content, organization, and tone?

   b. Now compare the first draft with the later draft. What difference(s) did you notice in the two drafts in terms of content? In terms of surface errors? Did Louray respond to the global changes (in content, organization, development, etc.) you suggested to her in the question above? Did she identify and correct some of her surface errors on her own? For Louray, which errors seem to be performance errors and which seem to be competence errors?

   c. Rosen argues that teachers should analyze students' errors in order to gain an insight into what hypotheses students have about writing. Identify one or two error(s) that still remain in Louray's later draft. What rule(s) does she seem to be using that causes this(these) error(s). What will you say to help her understand her errors?

7. Read the essay by Amy (p. 226).

   a. Imagine that Amy is your student. What comments will you give her—either in conference or in writing—about her research paper? What do you think is strong about her paper? What advice will you give her about its content, organization, and tone?

   b. Rosen encourages students to become independent self-editors. However, sometimes students can't "see" their errors. Teachers can raise students' awareness of errors with minimal marking. Reread Amy's essay, this time paying attention to proofreading errors. Using a minimal marking system you devise for yourself, mark Amy's paper so that she can notice and correct these errors on her own.

Part III

Connecting Grammar and Rhetoric

As you discovered in Parts 1 and 2, the rationale for teaching grammar (especially Hartwell's Grammar 3, 4, but also Grammar 5 [p. 5]), is often framed in terms of writing; that is, most people believe students should study grammar in order to improve their writing. For most people, there's a simple, clearly defined relationship between grammar and writing: good writing is grammatically correct.

In fact, however, the relationship is much more complex. Good writing is more than simply correct grammar. Good writing is persuasively argued, appropriately organized, sufficiently developed, logically coherent, stylistically pleasing, and above all, intellectually engaging. Good writing should be easy for us to read and yet challenge us to think. Good writers know a variety of linguistic features they can use to create these rhetorical effects.

The three chapters in this section explore the intersection between a writer's rhetorical judgment and a text's linguistic features. They address the following questions:

- How do the linguistic and rhetorical demands on the writer change to fit various contexts?
- How do students develop their sense of what is and isn't a sentence?
- How can students learn to build more complex sentences and paragraphs?

6

Understanding Oral and Written Language

As Wolfram, Adger, and Christian (1999) point out, in order to succeed in school, every child, regardless of social or linguistic background, has to learn academic English: that is, they have to expand their existing linguistic repertoire to include the formal, written standard English that's typical of discourse in school. That generally means clearly enunciated pronunciation, Standard English grammar; complex sentences of multisyllabic, Latinate vocabulary; organized and supported arguments; etc. So the general public is on target when it says that students go to school to learn "proper English"; students do indeed generally go to school to learn the language conventions appropriate in formal contexts. What perhaps the general public doesn't say is that students also learn by implication how different contexts make different linguistic demands on the communicator.

Pragmatics

Linguists call a person's understanding of the various linguistic demands of various social contexts *pragmatics* (Yule, 1996). Every time we communicate, we make decisions about how to address our interlocutors (people we communicate with), how formal our word choice will be, how much background information and supporting detail they'll need, etc. (A bilingual child's sense of pragmatics is even more complex because it also includes what language to speak.) We're usually not aware of these pragmatic decisions and shifts because they're intuitive (Hartwell's Grammar 1 [p. 5]), but sociolinguists have made attempts to systematically describe them.

One such description, discussed in the reading for Chapter 1, was developed by Martin Joos in his 1961 book *The Five Clocks*. Just as we have to readjust our clocks when we're in different time zones, Joos argued, we naturally adjust our language in different contexts. Joos identified five levels of formality, which are summarized in Figure 6.1.

FIGURE 6.1   *Theoretical Foundation: Martin Joos' Five Levels of Formality*

Working in the late 1950s, linguist Martin Joos (1961) observed there are five levels of usage style in English. Here is a brief description of each of these styles.

Intimate

Speaking/Writing to family
- Usually a pair.
- Speaker/Writer: supplies little or no background information to be understood.
- Listener/Reader: understands with little or no effort because so much is shared.
- Highly elliptical statements; private language invented from shared experiences (family-isms).

Casual

Speaking/Writing to friends/acquaintances/insiders of social group
- Speaker/Writer: supplies some background information to be understood.
- Listener/Reader: understands with little effort because much is shared.
- Fragments, elliptical statements, slang, or specific group jargon.

Consultative

Speaking/Writing to strangers
- Cannot be strangers for long; must move to casual style or break off communication.
- Based on cooperation to achieve limited goals.
- Speaker/Writer: supplies background information to be understood.
- Listener/Reader: works actively to understand.
- Full sentences, formulaic expressions, brief.

Formal

Speaking/Writing to large group
- Most written texts fall into this category because they must stand alone, but aren't permanent.
- Speaker/Writer: supplies enough background information so "text" stands alone; "text" detached from immediate reality.
- Listener/Reader: participates passively, must be authorized to respond, may not interrupt.
- Purpose of speaking is usually to inform or entertain; form and format important; language precise, fully developed; organized; planned in advance.

Frozen

Writing texts that become classics
- Great literature; expected to be permanent.
- Writer and Reader separated by time and space, so no physical interaction between two.
- Text is often reread, generating new meaning for the reader.

Distinguishing Between Oral and Written Language

A second attempt to systematically explain the differences between oral and written language is found in the reading for this chapter by Wolfram, Adger, and Christian (1999). Some of the differences they focus on include the mechanics of producing language, the relationship between the communicator and the inter-locutors, and the formal properties of the production that results. These differences are spelled out more carefully in the reading, but they are summed up in Figure 6.2.

Developing Pragmatic and Literate Understanding

As Daniels (1983 [See Chapter 1]) points out, pragmatics is the last of the language systems to be learned. By the time they go to school, children have learned how to form and pronounce words (*morphology* and *phonology*) and how to form sentences (*syntax*). But they're still learning to shift their language to meet the demands of different communication situations. School in general, but especially English language arts classes, affords them the opportunities to do just that.

As a result of their school experiences, students' language tends to grow in two directions: to the more formal and to the more literate. Although very young children may have some experiences with written language, much of their initial understanding of language is an understanding of oral language. More specifically, it tends to be an understanding of oral language among intimates, since young children tend to have a limited sphere of interlocutors. Often their interlocutors are already familiar with the topics a toddler might choose since they've shared those experiences. For instance, a parent comes to pick up a child at day care. If the daycare worker says to the child, "Tell your daddy what you did today in art time," she's encouraging him to tell a story, but she generally already knows what happened and can fill in the gaps of the story if needed. Similarly, if the parent invites the child to explain the picture he drew in art time, the picture is in front of them, and Daddy can point to it and ask questions about it.

When children go to school, their sphere of communication opens up considerably, and so does their need to use more formal language. Now, they're less likely to share experiences with their interlocutors—teachers and classmates tend not to share their home life, and parents and siblings tend not to share their experiences in class—so they have to learn to assess how much background information and explicit detail their audience needs to understand their stories. Moreover, older students are increasingly invited to participate in public forums, such as student governments, community activism, and employment, where they need to use more formal language. So while there's much about language children can transfer from their experiences with informal, intimate language, there are some new things they have to learn.

The same is true of their literacy development. As students progress in grade level, they increasingly depend on written texts to learn and on their written texts to demonstrate their learning. (Have you ever heard the adage, "In grades one through three, students learn to read, but in grades four and beyond, they

FIGURE 6.2 *Foundational Theory: Spoken vs. Written Language*

Here are important differences between spoken and written language (Joos, 1961; Wolfram, Adger, & Christian, 1999).

Spoken	*Written*
Mechanics of Producing Language	
• Speech is a string of unbroken sounds.	• Writing is a string of letters broken up into word boundaries; have to understand how words are formed in language; have to know spelling.
• Rising/falling intonation marks phrase and clause boundaries.	• Punctuation marks phrase and clause boundaries.
• Audibility important, but often context can help listeners compensate for inaudible sounds.	• Readability important, but often context can help readers compensate for unreadable text.
Relationship of Communicator to Interlocutor	
• Listener is present; speaker actively seeks interest by addressing listener directly with body language, pronouns *you* or *we*.	• Written for reader who is not present; writer tries to engage reader but not overtly. • In academic writing, use of *you*, *I* often discouraged; usually written with third person pronouns (*he, she, it, they*, etc.).
• Formal markings of beginnings and endings of conversation may happen, but not necessary.	• Clearly marked beginnings, middles, and ends. • Introduction has to orient reader; conclusion has to bring closure; middle has to develop ideas.
• Associative flow of ideas; looser flow of ideas; speaker subject to interruption.	• (Chrono)logical flow of ideas; sustained, uninterrupted presentation of ideas.
Formality of Language	
• Communication is two-way: speakers and listeners take turns playing each role.	• Communication is one-way: from writer to reader.
• Communicators within shouting distance of each other.	• Communicators usually are separated by time and space.
• Instant feedback, so can repair miscommunication.	• Feedback is delayed; few chances to repair miscommunication; text must stand alone.
• Tends to call for intimate or casual style.	• Tends to call for formal or frozen style.

read to learn"?) Again, there's much about oral language that transfers to the written medium, but there are also important differences every child must learn in order to become literate:

- They must learn to break strings of sounds up into words and spell them correctly.
- They must learn to break turns of talk with rising and falling intonation into phrases, clauses, sentences, and paragraphs and punctuate them correctly.
- They must learn the differences between face-to-face, two-way, shared, oral communication and one-way, written communication with a distant audience.

This last difference is probably the most difficult. Their readers are distant both in terms of not being physically present when they write and of not being likely to share their experiences (though it's often the case with school writing that the audience—the teacher—does indeed share the experiences of writer, having read the source text or knowing the subject as well as or better than the student). Thus, because readers aren't around to signal any miscommunication that might occur, writers need to learn to anticipate reader needs by providing sufficient background information, sufficient details, sufficient clues about how to read their texts (such as thesis statement and topic sentences). In short, students need to learn to create texts that stand alone.

Basic Writers

Every child needs to understand the similarities and differences between oral and written language, between their obligations as speakers and as writers, and obviously, the more experiences—and the broader the experiences—they have with oral and written language, the easier it is to sort out these similarities and differences. Students who don't have many experiences with written text struggle to manage the conventions specific to texts. According to basic writing theorist Mina Shaughnessy (1977), inexperienced writers make "errors" because learning to write Standard English is like learning a new dialect. Students can transfer much of their knowledge of the language from speaking to writing, but some features of writing must be learned specifically for a new medium. These features, such as spelling, punctuation, formal vocabulary, and complex syntax, are what give students the most trouble. (See Chapter 5 for tips on prioritizing errors.) For language minority students, writing *is* in fact learning a new dialect, because the grammar of written, academic English is highly aligned to Standard English. In addition to sorting out the differences between speaking and writing, these students must also sort out the differences between their home discourse and the standard discourse of the school.

Like Rosen's (1998) advice in Chapter 5, Shaughnessy (1977) recommends that teachers analyze errors in students' writing, looking for patterns and trying to deduce students' understandings of academic language. She says teachers should encourage students to keep a list of personal grammar troublespots. Like Wolfram, Adger, and Christian (1999), she has these recommendations:

- Help students understand the differences between written and spoken language.
- Give students lots of practice in writing without penalizing them.
- Give students both informal, writing-to-learn kinds of assignments in addition to formal, revised/edited assignments.
- Incorporate peer review and peer editing sessions into the writing process.

This chapter explores the language demands of various contexts, specifically oral language and the formal, written Standard English typically expected in school. Students come to school with many experiences that they can draw on to learn this discourse, but some features are different and must be learned for this new context.

Exploring Your Own Language Experience

1. Before you begin the reading for this chapter, spend five minutes or so writing in your journal about the following:

   a. Think back to the days when you were first learning to write (sentences, paragraphs, and essays in elementary/middle/high school and/or academic papers/professional reports in college). What did you find hard about communicating in writing? What was easy? Why?
   b. Given your experience, what should writing teachers keep in mind when they are working with beginning writers?

2. Reread Daniels (Chapter 1). What does he say about how students learn to meet the various linguistic demands of different communication situations?

Dialects and Written Language

Walt Wolfram, Carolyn Temple Adger, and Donna Christian

This reading is a chapter from Dialects in Schools and Communities *(1999, Lawrence Erlbaum Associates). The book as a whole argues that teachers, students, and the general public alike should understand dialects: what they are, how and why they occur, etc. Teachers especially should understand how dialects impact on students' reading, writing, speaking, listening, and visual interpretation. This chapter of their book examines the impact of dialects on writing. In order to understand this influence, Wolfram, Adger, and Christian begin by explaining important differences between speaking and writing.*

Transforming the spoken (or signed) language system into written forms of communication is challenging for all children. For speakers of vernacular dialects, there are some additional factors to be considered, largely because the gap between the language of their speaking styles and the language of written styles is wider than it is for speakers of standard varieties. The instructional approaches related to writing that practitioners adopt need to differ from those for spoken language because these two productive language processes differ in some fundamental ways. This chapter considers a range of such issues in the teaching of writing to speakers of vernacular dialects.

Oral and Written Language

The contrasts between the spoken language medium and the written language medium present several kinds of difficulty for writers. One area of difficulty stems from the need to learn features of a written language style that contrast with the spoken style. Another is a more general problem of accommodating the special communicative demands of the writing situation.

Developing written language expertise requires learning to make choices about style. One element of the stylistic contrast between spoken and written language relates to formality. School writing is generally more formal than either the spoken style that students use most often or the writing that students do in other settings. For example, the use of a phrase like "a good deal of difficulty" might be preferred in an essay or report over the more commonly spoken "a lot of trouble" that is appropriate for conversation or for a note or an e-mail message. The use of conversational features like *you know* and *well* is quite restricted in writing. In some school writing, it may not be considered appropriate to use the first person perspective: Rather than using the form *I think soccer is very popular*, a writer might say *Soccer seems to be very popular*, or *It seems that . . .*, and so forth. These are just a few samples of the written language style that a student must eventually learn in order to become a successful writer.

A second dimension of the difference between written language and speech is in the actual circumstances surrounding the acts of writing and speaking. The two media place differing demands on the communicator. The fact that writing is received visually means that any information that can be conveyed orally through different voice qualities (such as stress and intonation) has to be provided in another way. For example, the difference between a compound word, as in *a blackbird*, and a phrase, *a black bird*, which is a matter of stress in speaking, is converted to a spacing difference in writing. Similarly, questions that may be indicated by intonation in speech have to be marked by special punctuation in writing (e.g., *Malcolm took the train?*). Writing involves a set of conventions unique to this medium—the mechanics of writing—that determine when to capitalize, place periods, commas, and so forth. These are quite arbitrary, as indicated by the fact that writing systems vary around the world and different languages use different mechanical conventions, but learning to use them is a necessary aspect of learning to write.

The most significant difference between writing and speaking situations is in the role played by the hearer/reader. In speaking, the hearer is usually present and participating in the social interaction. The hearer is not passive: He or she provides feedback through facial expressions and body orientation, through listening behaviors like "Uh huh" and "Yeah," by commenting and questioning. The speaker and the hearer align toward each other in a kind of conversational ballet, each following the other's lead, getting and giving news about whether or not the interaction is succeeding (Tannen, 1993). If something goes wrong, they can adjust appropriately. In writing, on the other hand, the receiver of the communication is absent and the writer must take care to consider the perspective of this absent, and often unknown, reader. Immediate feedback is unavailable. Unless the reader is well known to the writer, assumptions about shared knowledge that is crucial to interpreting the message may turn out to be ill-founded. References must be made explicit so that the reader will not be confused. Taking into account the absent reader can be one of the most difficult tasks for the child who is beginning to write, as well as for the experienced writer. A young writer might report on vacation activities with *We went to visit grandma, Ginger went too* . . . , without making explicit that Ginger is a dog. One of the central tasks of writing instruction is helping children develop their growing awareness of the reader.

Vernacular Dialect and Writing

Speaking a vernacular dialect probably has less direct influence on development of writing skill than was once thought (Wolfram & Whiteman, 1971). Speakers of all dialects encounter writing difficulties like those mentioned. This does not mean, however, that the dialect of English spoken by the student can be ignored in writing instruction. In fact, vernacular speakers may have trouble in several dimensions due to differences between their language skills and those that writing requires.

Some vernacular-speaking students may seem to take longer to acquire some writing skills than others do because they are making a bigger transition. The contrast between spoken language and written styles may be wider for the vernacular dialect speaker than for the Standard English speaker in several ways. For one thing, the written style of language may not be as familiar to these students if they have had fewer experiences with written text in the community. In addition, differences in spoken dialects manifest themselves in writing. Thus, a student may write *a* as the form of the indefinite article before both a consonant and a vowel (e.g., *a teacher* and *a aunt*) if this is how the article is spoken. When faced with a great deal of correction of items that vary between vernacular and standard, students may become frustrated and hesitant to try again. Also, they may make other, different errors in an attempt to avoid certain usages from their spoken dialect, a phenomenon known as **hyper-correction**. For instance, after numerous instances of correction, a student might avoid using a structure or begin using structures like *an car* or *an city*. Such usages, which may also occur to a lesser extent in speech, represent an effort to catch potential errors.

The following paragraph, composed by a ninth grader from an African American working-class community, shows influence of vernacular dialect. It was written in response to a teacher's question on a reading passage:

> I would prefer living the way the Hunzakuts live, because they live a whole lot longer and they don't have no crime and they don't get sick and if you are the age of 60, or 80 you still can play many game like you the age of 6 or 9 and don't have to worry about Cancer or Heartattacks. Its would be a whole lot better living their way.

Given detailed knowledge about the student's spoken dialect, we can identify some instances of direct influence. For example, *they don't have no crime* is an instance of multiple negation, a common feature in vernacular dialects of English. The absence of the plural ending in *many game* is also a candidate for dialect influence, as is copula absence in *like you the age of 6 or 9*. These dialect influences can be contrasted with mechanical errors. For example, if the writer had written *your* for *you're*, as in *your the age of 6*, this would be a mechanical error. All speakers of English share the problem of writing words that sound alike but are spelled differently in various uses (*your* and *you're* are like *break* and *brake* in this respect).

This sample of student writing also shows indirect influence from spoken dialect. Hypercorrection is suggested in the construction *its would be*. A fairly common feature for speakers with backgrounds like that of the writer is the absence of the *are* and *is* forms of the verb *be* in sentences like *they nice* or *she here*. It may be that this feature had appeared in the student's writing and was corrected rather frequently, resulting in a sensitivity to the problem of leaving those verbs out. The unnecessary addition of *s* on *its* in the case of *its would be* may represent an unconscious effort to avoid the mistake of leaving *is* or *are* out, but without a full understanding of the structure in question. This example of hypercorrection illustrates that a dialect can influence production of written forms indirectly.

Indirect influence from a vernacular dialect is also evident when dialect combines with writing problems shared by all inexperienced writers. Writing samples from vernacular dialect speakers reflect only selected features from the spoken dialect; other, equally frequent characteristics of speech are seldom found in writing. Some of those that occur are apparently related to general writing development patterns. One study, which compared a large amount of spoken and written data from both standard and vernacular dialect speakers at all age levels, found that all writers, regardless of dialect background, omitted certain grammatical suffixes to some extent in early writing (Farr & Daniels, 1986). These included the verbal *-s* ending (giving *he walk*), the plural ending (as in *many game* from the sample composition), and the past ending *-ed* (*last summer she move to Texas*). For all groups in the sample, the suffixes were sometimes absent, but the frequency was much higher for the vernacular dialect speakers, who also use these features in their speech to varying extents. This pattern indicates that the absence of suffixes in writing is not solely a product of dialect influence. The influence from dialect combines with a general tendency in writing development to produce a pattern involving nonstandard structures in early writing.

Teaching Writing

How can teachers support the development of writing skills in their vernacular dialect-speaking students? Farr and Daniels (1986) suggested a set of key factors for writing instruction to be effective for secondary school students from vernacular dialect backgrounds that appear to be readily adaptable for students at any level:

Students should have:

1. Teachers who understand and appreciate the basic linguistic competence that students bring with them to school, and who therefore have positive expectations for students' achievements in writing.
2. Regular and substantial practice in writing, aimed at developing fluency.
3. The opportunity to write for real, personally significant purposes.
4. Experience in writing for a wide range of audiences, both inside and outside of school.
5. Rich and continuous reading experience, including both published literature of acknowledged merit and the work of peers and instructors.
6. Exposure to models of writing in process and writers at work, including both teachers and classmates.
7. Instruction in the process of writing; that is, learning to work at a given writing task in appropriate phases, including prewriting, drafting, and revising.

8. Collaborative activities for students that provide ideas for writing and guidance for revising works in progress.
9. One-to-one writing conferences with the teacher.
10. Direct instruction in specific strategies and techniques for writing.
11. Reduced instruction in grammatical terminology and related drills, with increased use of sentence combining activities.
12. Teaching of writing mechanics and grammar in the context of students' actual compositions, rather than in separate drills or exercises.
13. Moderate marking of surface structure errors, focusing on sets of patterns of related errors.
14. Flexible and cumulative evaluation of student writing that stresses revision and is sensitive to variations in subject, audience, and purpose.
15. Practicing and using writing as a tool of learning in all subjects in the curriculum, not just in English. (Farr & Daniels, 1986, pp. 45–46).

One important conclusion to be drawn from these guidelines for teaching writing is that decontextualized skills-based instruction in written Standard English ought to be avoided, just as with teaching spoken Standard English. It does not lead to able writing, and it alienates students from the pursuit of writing. The process approach to writing, which emphasizes language skills that all students can be presumed to have in rich abundance, deals with grammar and mechanics only after the writing is drafted.

We do not mean to suggest that teachers should not teach Standard English forms to students who use vernacular forms in their writing. There is fairly widespread agreement among educators and researchers that the ability to use Standard English for written work is an important skill (Smitherman, 1995). But writing instruction for speakers of vernacular dialects should not be limited to a focus on contrasting forms, and these contrasts should not be addressed out of the context of writing. Furthermore, dialect differences should not be disproportionately weighted in the evaluation of students' ability to express themselves in written form.

Areas of Vernacular Influence in Writing. Although the research base is limited in terms of the role of a student's dialect background in the writing process, some observations on dimensions of language contrast may be useful for teachers. In using a process approach to writing, teachers may find it helpful to distinguish at least three different types of problems that vernacular dialect speakers encounter in writing:

1. *Organization or progression of an argument or narrative.* Difficulties here are quite common to nearly every developing writer. Organization problems may relate to the writer's assumptions about audience that make the writing task very different from spoken language, as well as to culturally based expectations for how to tell a story or make an argument (Cazden, 1988; Gee, 1990; Michaels, 1981). Specific instruction in the organization conventions associated with literacy can occur as minilessons during the critical review phase of the writing process. They should be shaped by the teacher's clear understanding of influences from students' cultural backgrounds. These influences may reflect patterned differences in ways of achieving textual cohesion.
2. *Mechanical aspects of writing.* The conventions of capitalization, punctuation, and spelling are aspects of the system for writing English that all speakers of English must master, regardless of their dialect. The fact that English spelling does not sig-

nify the sounds of the language consistently in a one-to-one relation makes spelling difficult for everyone. Dialect differences, however, introduce an additional set of possibilities for spelling errors. For example, spelling the first vowel sound of *tinder* and *tender* the same way may be related to the fact that these words are pronounced the same in Southern dialects. This would be quite similar to a Standard American English speaker confusing *t* and *d* spellings in a word like *therapeutic* (*therapeudic*) because the *t* and *d* are pronounced similarly in this position. This confusion would not arise for speakers of British English who pronounce *t* and *d* between vowels (as in *latter* and *ladder*) differently.

3. *Grammar.* Grammatical differences between Standard English and the student's dialect may interfere in writing. The use of nonstandard verb forms, as in *The girl knowed the answer*, may come from a spoken dialect that regularly uses these grammatical rules. Similarly, the use of expletive or existential *it* for *there* in sentences such as *It was a new student in the class yesterday* in writing may come from a vernacular speaker's normal use of this form in spoken language.

In the strictest sense, the examples given are not really errors, but rather the reflection in writing of the differences in verbal expression, pronunciation, and grammar between the students' dialect and the standard dialect against which the writing is being judged.

Teachers may want to use the classification scheme just given in classifying students' writing miscues. It might also be adopted by students as they learn the process of self-editing. Understanding precisely what kind of difficulty a writer is experiencing with respect to stylistic and dialectal contrast, students and teachers can move more surely toward achieving proficiency in appropriate written forms. Teachers and students might, for example, prioritize their difficulties and systematically focus on different kinds of writing miscues at different points in the achievement of proficient Standard English writing skills.

Another technique is to focus on a set of items rather than on every dialect error and technical mistake in each piece of writing. If possessives become a target of attention, then attending to apostrophes with singular and plural forms makes sense because these items are related. But when the class focuses on possessives, matters of verb tense, double negatives, and capitalization must be put aside for the time being, even if "we just worked on that!" The message that form is secondary to content is not convincing otherwise. There will be times to insist on perfection, but these occasions should be clearly justified by the objective for writing.

Spelling and Dialect. The problems associated with sounding out words to arrive at their spellings do not appear to be that much greater for speakers of vernacular dialects than for other speakers, although some particular items may be influenced by dialect. All speakers are faced with learning the conventions of English spelling where the sound and spelling relationship is not regular: For example, *could, tough* and *though* cannot be spelled on the basis of sound. It seems likely, then, that a child who pronounces *toof* can adjust to the standard spelling *tooth* as well as another child who says *tuff* learns to spell it *tough*. Vernacular dialect speakers may make different mistakes in attempting spellings at various stages, which may draw undue attention to a spelling problem. This potential difficulty can be overcome if a teacher is well aware of the pronunciation features of the dialects spoken by the students so that the sound differences can be taken into proper account in teaching spelling. For example, a teacher in a Southern setting might have to teach the spelling of *tin* and *ten* like other homophonous words such as *two, to,* or *too.*

Postponing Editing. The writing process approach restricts error correction to the later phases of writing so as to encourage students to write thoughtfully and at length. Because nonstandard features such as the absence of suffixes do not signal lack of conceptual knowledge, writers can make changes during the revision phase rather easily if instances of dialect interference are pointed out to them. As a practical matter, it may be difficult for teachers who themselves learned to write in a sea of red ink to postpone editing, and students may be concerned with dialect features in their own and others' writing when they are supposed to be focusing on content. However, commitment to producing authentic, high-quality writing, rather than writing for display or remedial skill-learning purposes, suggests that editing be relegated to the back burner during the composing phase. This recommendation should not be interpreted as advice to ignore or downplay editing, but to convey to students that attention to the form of language is distinct from and secondary to conceptualizing and drafting.

Teachers are being urged to give their students frequent and varied writing activities for different purposes across the content areas. However, not all writing needs to be refined through the writing process. Jotting down ideas for a structured discussion, annotating written text, taking class notes—all of these are writing. When students are comfortable with writing, they are more likely to feel capable of producing finished written text with Standard English.

Peer Editing. Peer interaction can contribute to developing writing skills when students have been trained to critique each other's writing and to help edit out errors, when the purpose and the nature of the evaluation task is very clear, and when it is directly tied to a whole class project. From peer editing can come topics for general instruction on mechanics and standard dialect features. For example, if it becomes clear from editing sessions that many students have trouble with possessives as in writing *John hat* for *John's hat* (a problem shared to some extent by both standard and vernacular speakers at certain stages of learning to write), then this feature can become the focus of direct instruction and student attention for a time. This approach has at least two advantages: Contrasting dialect and mechanics conventions are explained in context, and students share in identifying writing problems for explicit instruction.

Dialogue Journals. One strategy to encourage writing without dwelling on form that has been found to work with both mainstream and nonmainstream children is the dialogue journal (Peyton & Reed, 1990; Staton, Shuy, Peyton, & Reed, 1988). A dialogue journal is a bound notebook in which a student and teacher communicate regularly in writing over a continuous period of time. Students can write as much as they want about topics of their choice. The teacher writes back each time the student writes—often responding to the student's topics, but also introducing new topics, making comments and offering observations and opinions, requesting and giving clarification, asking questions, and answering student questions. The teacher adopts a role as a participant *with* the student in an ongoing, written conversation, rather than an evaluator who corrects or comments on the writing. There is no overt correction of the student's writing by the teacher, although the teacher may model particular linguistic features or probe for missing information.

The advantage of this method is that students experience writing as an interactive communicative experience in a nonthreatening atmosphere. They also write about topics that are important to them and explore topics in a genre that is appropriate to their current level of proficiency in writing. Many teachers have found that this opportunity encourages students from quite different backgrounds and with quite different experiences in terms of traditional academic success to feel confident in expressing themselves in writing (Peyton, 1990). Students who feel that they have something to say in writing tend to be much more motivated to develop writing skills commensurate with academic success than those who have not overcome the initial hurdle of finding something to write about.

Assessment of Writing Ability

A further difficulty that comes from dialect influence relates to formal assessment. Although errors in writing stemming from dialect features are actually relatively minor in terms of the communicative goal of writing, they often are accorded major importance in formal evaluation. Points of mechanics and Standard English usage are often treated as measures of writing ability, putting the speakers of vernacular dialects at a disadvantage. For example, students' writing ability may be assessed formally by their ability to distinguish between the use of *good* and *well*, or the past usage of *come* (*Yesterday he come to school*) and *came*, rather than the content of their writing.

Such items privilege Standard English speakers and discriminate against speakers of vernacular dialects. In recent years the multiple choice, grammar-based tests that examine students' ability to recognize errors in Standard English usage and grammar have been balanced with writing samples. However, the grammar-based tests continue to focus precisely on those areas where there is likely to be dialect influence from a vernacular dialect. Preparation materials for the writing test in the SAT II include the following sentences as typical items. Students are to determine whether the italicized portion is correct usage:

- By the time Nick arrived at the campsite, the tents had been set up, the fire was lit, and there *wasn't hardly* anything to do except relax and enjoy the mountain air.
- Both novels deal with immigrants from Africa, who, overcoming obstacles, advance *themself* in America in spite of society's unjust treatment towards black people. (Ehrenhaft, 1994, p. 29)

Note the focus on double negatives in the first sentence and plural deletion in the second sentence, both regular vernacular features.

Bias in standardized tests of writing may come from other sources. Items written in a highly literate style, such as the following from the same SAT review manual, may be systematically more difficult to evaluate for students from some social groups:

Although I wish it were otherwise, by this time next week I will have had surgery on my knee, which was injured during a hockey game last winter. (Ehrenhaft, 1994, p. 32)

Those who have less experience with text may have trouble detecting that the verbs in this sentence are correct. Differing conceptions of what constitutes good style according to different cultural groups also may have an effect. For example, an item in which the correct answer requires the choice of "reach my destination" over "get there" appeals to a value on the use of a kind of superstandard English in writing. Thus, objective tests of usage and mechanics may be harder for students from vernacular dialect backgrounds because these tests tend to focus on points of dialect differences in usage. Alternatively, they may require choices based on language experiences that are not shared by all groups.

One might conclude that tests involving samples of student writing are more fair for vernacular speakers than those focusing on particular forms, but there are problems with this approach too. It may be inappropriate to judge an individual's writing ability on the basis of a limited sample of one or two short essays produced in a very short time frame. Although this limitation applies to all students, there may be an even greater effect on students who must attend to dialect choices in their writing. Writing samples present other implications for speakers from vernacular dialect backgrounds. Depending on who is scoring the writing, the writer's use of certain structures that the scorer regards as errors may lead to a lower overall score being assigned, in spite of scorer training. For example, a rater who considers a feature like suffix absence to be a very severe problem may be unable to see positive qualities in a passage when it contains such dialect influence.

There is also some possibility of cultural bias in the topics assigned by the test. For example, a writing prompt for 13-year-olds on the NAEP asked students to describe for a friend a reproduction of a Dali painting. If students could not imagine themselves ever doing such a task, they might not be able to display their writing skills to full advantage. More holistic approaches avoid the unreasonable attention to dialect contrast, but they do not solve the dilemma of assessing writing development in a dialectally diverse population. They also do not necessarily counter the tendency of evaluators to assign lower scores in their overall assessment simply based on the occurrence of some nonstandard dialect forms in writing. Thus, the common but unjustified association of the appearance of dialect features with the inability to express oneself must be recognized and countered by those who engage in holistic assessments. The classroom teacher is probably in a much better position to assess student writing development than the scorer of a large-scale test, both because of being able to track individual progress across time and because of knowing precisely which dialect differences the student is managing. Informal classroom diagnostic assessments serve to help teachers particularize writing goals for students and plan subsequent instructional activities. Portfolio assessment, a more structured approach, has gained a wide following. Students select some of their writings for teacher evaluation and defend them in a conference with the teacher, stating why they value these writings. When this approach is used as intended, students play an active role in assessing their own work and in articulating their personal view of excellent writing.

Further Study

Farr, M., & Daniels, H. (1986). *Language diversity and writing instruction*. Urbana, IL: National Council of Teachers of English.

This resource offers both a theoretical framework and practical suggestions to educators who wish to improve the teaching of writing to secondary-school students who speak vernacular dialects.

Hampton, S. (1995). Strategies for increasing achievement in writing. In R. W. Cole (Ed.), *Educating everybody's children: Diverse teaching strategies for diverse learners: What research and practice say about improving achievement* (pp. 99–120). Alexandria, VA: Association for Supervision and Curriculum Development.

This summary of current thinking on writing instruction does not focus on students' dialect, but it does concern teaching writing to students from outside the mainstream. It is clear and practical.

Shaughnessy, M. P. (1977). *Errors and expectations: A guide for the teacher of basic writing.* New York: Oxford University Press.

Although somewhat dated, this book provides a helpful approach to the systematic study of writing errors. It is not specifically targeted for writers from vernacular dialect backgrounds, but there are many aspects of the approach that will prove useful to teachers of these students.

References

Cazden, C. (1988). *Classroom discourse: The language of teaching and learning.* Portsmouth, NH: Heinemann.

Ehrenhaft, G. (1994). *How to prepare for SAT II: Writing.* New York: Barrons.

Farr, M., & Daniels, H. (1986). *Language diversity and writing instruction.* New York: ERIC Clearinghouse on Urban Education, and Urbana, IL: ERIC Clearinghouse on Reading and Communication Skills.

Gee, J. P. (1990). *Social linguistics and literacies.* New York: Falmer Press.

Michaels, S. (1981). "Sharing time": Children's narrative styles and differential access to literacy. *Language in Society, 10,* 423–442.

Peyton, J. K. (Ed.). (1990). *Students and teachers writing together: Perspectives on journal writing.* Alexandria, VA: Teachers of English to Speakers of Other Languages.

Peyton, J. K., & Reed, L. (1990). *Dialogue journal writing with nonnative English speakers: A handbook for teachers.* Alexandria, VA: Teachers of English to Speakers of Other Languages.

Smitherman, G. (1995). Students' rights to their own language: A retrospective. *English Journal, 84*(1) 21–27.

Staton, J., Shuy, R. W., Peyton, J. K., & Reed, L. (1988). *Dialogue journal communication: Classroom, linguistic, social and cognitive views.* Norwood, NJ: Ablex.

Tannen, D. (Ed.). 1993. *Framing in discourse.* New York: Oxford University Press.

Wolfram, W., & Whiteman, M. (1971). The role of dialect interference in composition. *The Florida FL Reporter, 9,* 34–38.

Questions for Discussion

1. According to Wolfram, Adger, and Christian, why do the differences between spoken and written language give beginning writers trouble?

2. On July 31, 2001, the *Washington Post* published a report on its newsbytes.com Website about a recent study done by Ned Kock of the E-Collaboration Research Center at Temple's Fox School of Business and Management which compared face-to-face and e-mail communication (Bartlett, 2001). Ten groups worked to solve a problem via face-to-face interaction while another 10 groups used e-mail. One conclusion from the study is that communicating by e-mail takes much longer than communicating face-to-face does. According to Kock, "The cognitive effort was about 10 times higher. It might take someone face-to-face or on the telephone about 10 minutes to contribute a 600-word idea to a discussion. It will take over an

hour to communicate the same idea electronically." The article noted that Kock was "surprised" by how much longer it took to write messages than to say them.

Are you surprised by the results of the study? Why/why not? Using what you know about the differences between oral and written language, explain the results of Kock's study.

3. Read the in-class essay by Matt (p. 219).
   a. Imagine that Matt is your student. What comments will you give Matt—either in conference or in writing—to encourage him to revise his in-class essay? What do you think is strong about his essay? What advice will you give him about the content, organization, and tone of his essay?
   b. Perhaps you mentioned the informal, or "oral" tone of Matt's essay in your comments to him. Which features of his text are more characteristic of writing? Which features are more characteristic of speaking? Does the conversational tone of the essay "work"? Why/why not?

4. Read the essays by Jasmine (p. 217) and Drew (pp. 224).
   a. Imagine that Jasmine is your student. What comments will you give her—either in conference or in writing—about her family story? What do you think is strong about her story? What advice will you give her about its content, organization, and tone?
   b. Imagine that Drew is your student. What comments will you give him—either in conference or in writing—about his analysis? What do you think is strong about his paper? What advice will you give him about its content, organization, and tone?
   c. Perhaps you mentioned Jasmine's and Drew's direct address to the audience in your comments to each of them. What relationship does each writer establish with the audience? Does that relationship "work" in each essay? Why/why not?

7

Developing a Sense of Sentences and Their Punctuation

Recently, according to British grammarian Richard Hudson (2000), grammar instruction has been making a kind of comeback. He says "there is now much more enthusiasm in some educational circles for the idea that conscious grammar (resulting from formal teaching) could have the useful benefit of improving writing" (p. 2). However, Hudson adds, certain kinds of structured grammar exercises seem to be more effective than others: namely, those that ask students to produce writing rather than analyze given sentences, and those that focus on grammatical features unique to writing, such as punctuation. In Chapter 8, I describe exercises that focus on producing new kinds of sentence structures. However, before students can produce more sophisticated sentences, they must have a concept of what is and isn't a sentence as well as how to punctuate it. So in this chapter, I look at teaching punctuation—primarily instruction in end punctuation.

Why Punctuation Is Hard

In comparison to spelling, for example, little is written about punctuation, even though it's one of the features of writing students seem to have the most trouble with. Punctuation is an issue that begins in elementary school and continues to cause problems even for adult writers. In my experience, skilled writers, if they make any grammatical mistakes at all, are likely to make punctuation errors, often comma splices. Half of the twenty most common errors in Connors and Lunsford's (1988) study are punctuation errors. Of these, most have to do with identifying sentence boundaries (thereby avoiding fragments, run-ons, and comma splices). In their study, comma splices ranked as the eighth most common error, but as the sixth error most likely to be marked by a teacher. In Beason's study (2001), sentence fragments were the most bothersome error, while fused sentences ranked fourth of five. Likewise, in Hairston's (1981) error attitude study, sentence fragments and run-ons were considered "very serious" while comma splices were only "moderately serious."

There are several reasons punctuation seems so difficult:

- *The rules of punctuation seem to allow for a great deal of personal preference, more so than other features of grammar.* Although some punctuation existed in early texts, most of the marks we know today were introduced into English after the printing press came to England in 1476 (Graddol, Leith, & Swann, 1996). As I noted in Chapter 2, the needs of printers—consistency and efficiency, among others—helped to standardize the language, including the rules of punctuation. However, as David Crystal (1995) points out, punctuation never became as consistent as spelling or grammar, and so rules for punctuation aren't as hard and fast. Moreover, their use is often influenced by the genre of the text: academic writing uses punctuation differently than creative writing does. This means that punctuation is more than a mechanistic, easily learned skill (Cordeiro, 1998).
- *Punctuation is unique to writing, and developing writers cannot always rely on their sense of oral language to help them punctuate.* Transfer from oral language works some of the time, but it also gets them in trouble. As Danielewicz and Chafe (1985) note:

> In writing, punctuation is a device for dividing text into units, or to signal semantic and syntactic relationships. In speaking, such functions are performed by prosody, above all by intonation and pausing. Written punctuation reflects to some degree the intonational and pause boundaries of speech. One might, therefore, expect that writers could learn to punctuate well by relying on their intuitive knowledge of spoken prosody. Unfortunately, the relation between spoken prosody and written punctuation is not a simple one, and this fact creates problems for inexperienced writers who have not yet become familiar with the complexity of the relation. (p. 214)

- *In modern English, we're not entirely sure of the purpose of punctuation,* which contributes in part to the complexity of the relationship between speaking and writing that Danielewicz and Chafe (1985) mention. From the beginning, punctuation has been used to give readers clues about how to interpret a text. But it has differed through history whether that interpretation should be primarily oral or structural (Graddol et al., 1996). Until the eighteenth century, when texts were typically read aloud, punctuation marked suitable places for readers to pause for a breath and guided their inflection and intonation. Gradually, as reading came more and more to be a silent activity, punctuation came to signal grammatical structures. By the end of the century, punctuation in English began to take on a modern look. There remains, however, "an ambiguity in modern English as to whether punctuation should reflect grammatical boundaries or potential reading behavior" (Graddol et al., 1996, p. 63).

For these reasons, new writers—whether children or adolescent/adult basic writers—still struggle to develop a spontaneous, or intuitive, sense of the sentence and how to punctuate it (Hartwell's Grammar 1 [p.5]). That is, they struggle to control punctuation well enough to include it in their text as they're drafting, even though their mind is focused more on content (Cordeiro, 1998). Writers seem to follow a similar sequence: from unmarked texts to texts marked on the basis of sound and meaning to texts marked on the basis of structure (Cordeiro, 1998; Hall, 1996; Ivanic, 1996). This conceptual development takes a long time; however, writers are often expected to punctuate sentences correctly long before they fully understand what a sentence is (Kress, 1982, as reported in Hall, 1996).

Developing a Sense of Punctuation

According to Nigel Hall (1996), a British literacy educator and co-director of The Punctuation Project in the United Kingdom, there are few studies that examine young children's growing understanding of what is and isn't a sentence and how they use punctuation as either writers or readers. Therefore, the conclusions that follow about how children develop an understanding of sentences and of punctuation and of how the two interact are preliminary at best.

It seems that for several years, the concepts of sentence and of punctuation are separate entities in children's minds. Young writers begin by distinguishing writing from drawing or scribbling, but don't distinguish between letters and punctuation marks (Cordeiro, 1998). They may not even see the marks because they're so focused on figuring out sound-symbol relationships, forming letters, and segmenting the letters into words correctly. Gradually, as they gain more experience with writing, they begin to differentiate letters and punctuation. The first to be distinguished are dot-like marks, such as periods and commas. Later, they begin to also see punctuation that looks like letters (i.e., the semicolon, which looks like a lower-case *i*) (Ferreiro & Teberosky, 1984, as reported in Hall, 1996). However, these marks are mainly graphic marks; children don't yet understand completely that they signal syntactic elements (Cordeiro, 1998).

Cordeiro (1998) compared period placement in the writing of first graders, third graders, and sixth graders. There was little difference in accuracy between the first and third graders, meaning that first graders were just as likely to put periods at the ends of sentences as third graders were. This may seem surprising, but consider that first-grade texts are often only one sentence long, so it's fairly easy for first graders to mark the end of a sentence. They generally have more chances to place periods correctly. Third graders, on the other hand, have more chances to place periods incorrectly because their texts are longer, containing more than one syntactic sentence. However, although there was little difference in accuracy, there was significant difference in the kinds of errors each grade made. Even though third graders placed some periods incorrectly, they nevertheless tended to put them at phrase boundaries. First graders, in contrast, put periods at the ends of words, lines, or pages. This difference suggests that third graders see punctuation more syntactically than first graders do.

But Cordeiro (1998) found that for her sixth graders, notions of paragraph development competed with their sense of punctuation. They were confused by the traditional grammar directions to put periods at the ends of sentences, which by definition are "complete thoughts." For them, a "complete thought" became the length of a paragraph, as their ability to generate more details on the same topic increased. They struggled with how to punctuate what they saw as aspects of the same topic. She noted that their texts were full of run-on or comma splice sentences. They seemed to be using the criterion of topic relatedness more than the criterion of syntax. As Cordeiro notes, students' sense of punctuation is always in flux, because once they come to an understanding of it, they push themselves to write more complex sentences and ideas, forcing them to once again experiment with punctuation.

The sequence Cordeiro (1998) describes is applicable to all kinds of texts, but Kress (1982, as reported in Hall, 1996) argues that it may be easier for children to learn to punctuate non-narrative texts than narratives because it may be easier for them to differentiate topics in a report than in a story. Similarly, children can increase their sense of punctuation with a lot of practice in writing. Calkins (1980, as reported in Hall, 1996) compared children in two third-grade classes; one class focused on the writing process, while the other studied traditional grammar. At the end of the school year, students in the writing class understood more about punctuation, could identify more kinds of punctuation, and liked punctuation more than students in the grammar class did. In addition, the writing students talked easily about the various marks, mentioning their effect on the text, while the grammar students struggled to repeat memorized definitions.

It's also possible that students will improve their sense of punctuation with extensive practice in proofreading for punctuation errors. *The Daily Oral Language* proofreading curriculum spotlighted in Chapter 5 includes punctuation as early as the first grade. According to the promotional sampler, lessons from week 12 of the Grade 1 set of exercises cover the following punctuation rules: apostrophes in contractions and possessives, questions marks, commas to set off direct quotes, quotation marks to signal direct quotes, and commas in a series. These skills seem advanced for students, who, research suggests, are still figuring out what is and isn't a sentence. But it may be that because these students are more attuned to punctuation as a result of these exercises, they'll develop their sense of punctuation more quickly. This kind of classroom research is urgently needed.

All of the language arts textbooks that I examined—*Writer's Choice* (Glencoe McGraw-Hill), *Elements of Language* (Odell et al., 2001), and *English* (Rueda et al., 2001)—included in their table of contents a separate section dealing with punctuation. However, they also addressed punctuation elsewhere, if it seemed

appropriate to the discussion. For example, all of the texts included end punctuation in their discussion of declarative, interrogative, imperative, and ex-
clamatory sentences.

The Punctuation of Adult Basic Writers

The developmental process I described above for children learning to write is similar to the process adults use to learn to write. They too begin with a limited
repertoire of punctuation rules. They also use sound and meaning to decide
where to put punctuation marks before they see punctuation as syntactic.

In her landmark study of adult basic writers, Mina Shaughnessy (1977)
makes two observations about the punctuation habits of inexperienced writers:

- Their punctuation repertoire is limited almost exclusively to periods and
  capitalization, and to some extent, paragraph indentation and commas.
- They struggle with punctuation, not because they don't understand sentences, but because they don't always know how to write sentences down.

Danielewicz and Chafe (1985) note that since we generally develop a proficiency in oral language before we do so in written language, our experience
in writing inevitably develops out of our experience in speaking. As competent
speakers, we know the difference between what they call *period intonation* (a
falling pitch to indicate the end of a sentence) and *comma intonation* (a rising
pitch to indicate the end of a phrase). Generally, we can transfer this knowledge to writing, using commas to indicate comma intonation and periods for
period intonation. In fact, inexperienced writers can do this so well it sometimes gets them into trouble. They're not always aware of when the transfer
doesn't work.

Danielewicz and Chafe (1985) argue that "normal" speaking patterns lead
basic writers to "erroneous" punctuation. Comparing the speech of educated
adults with the writing of developmental students, they identify several cases in
which writers' analogies lead them astray. For example, a speaker may hold a long
string of descriptive sentences together with comma intonation, using period intonation only to signal the end of the description. Rather than using period punctuation at the end of each syntactic sentence, speakers use it to signal the end of the
turn-of-talk or the paragraph. Inexperienced writers who follow this same pattern
end up with comma splices. Another example is the speaker who ends a sentence
with period intonation, but then adds an afterthought. The period intonation can't
be undone—unless the speaker repeats the entire sentence—so the speaker
presses on anyway. Students who use this analogy in punctuating their writing
end up with sentence fragments.

Danielewicz and Chafe (1985, p. 225) urge teachers to see nonstandard
punctuation as "inappropriate extensions" of oral language into writing and to
point out to students specific ways in which writing differs from speaking.

While Danielewicz and Chafe (1985) infer students' understanding of punctuation from their writing, Ivanic (1996) asks students to explain their reasoning directly. In "Linguistics and the Logic of Non-Standard Punctuation," British instructor Roz Ivanic reports on the explanations basic writers give for using/not using periods and commas and evaluates whether these reasons lead to correct judgments. Ivanic was especially interested in punctuation, she says, because it makes many borderline candidates fail standardized English exams in Britain—as it no doubt does in the U.S. as well. Ivanic asked 10 students in an adult education writing skills refresher course to write an essay on a topic of their choice. As soon as possible after they had completed their drafts, she interviewed them to learn why they had chosen to punctuate their essays as they had. Their responses fell into four broad categories: *reasons of quantity* (the need for punctuation after a certain number of words); *sound* (the need for pauses or breaks); *meaning* (a switch in topic); and *structure* (an understanding of how sentences are constructed). Later she identified whether each instance of punctuation was accurate (based on the expectations of standardized English test writers and graders) and correlated the results to the reasons writers gave. Altogether, she looked at 150 instances of commas and periods.

Ivanic (1996) came to several conclusions about the reasons her 10 basic writers used to guide their judgments about periods and commas:

- *Writers formed many more correct sentences than not.* Almost three-fourths (74 percent) of the periods were correctly placed. Likewise, 80 percent of the commas were correctly used. As Noguchi reminds us in the reading for this chapter, teachers have to remember that there is more to praise in students' writing than to fault.
- *Sound (the need for pauses) was the criterion most often used to place commas, while meaning (a switch in topics) was most often used for placing periods.* For commas, sound and meaning were equally good in helping students judge correct placement. For periods, on the other hand, meaning and structure were more successful criteria. This suggests that only the first half of the common rule of thumb "use commas for short pauses and periods for long ones" is useful; the second half leads writers astray. It also suggests that teachers recommend to students that they use different strategies in editing for commas than they would for editing for periods.
- *There may be a developmental sequence to reasons writers give for judging whether to use punctuation at any given junction.* The least proficient of Ivanic's writers used quantity most frequently as the criterion, but more often than not the punctuation was placed incorrectly. This writer seemed to feel a pressure to write long sentences, but couldn't control them. The most proficient writer, on the other hand, relied solely on meaning and structure to make punctuation decisions. This sequence seems compatible with the sequence described above for young writers: writers who use quantity to decide where to place punctuation see marks more graphically than semantically or syntactically.

- *Comma splices represent writers' judgments about the degree of relatedness between sentences.* Ivanic's writers were completely accurate in putting periods at the ends of sentences when the next sentence indicated an obvious switch in topics. They were far less accurate when the switch in topics was less obvious, such as when subsequent sentences developed ideas begun in the first. When the cohesive ties between sentences were very strong—for example, when the second sentence restated the topic of the first with the pronouns *it, this,* or *they*—then writers were more likely to use commas than periods. Again, Ivanic's findings about adult students parallel those about children. These kinds of comma splices represent semantic distinctions rather than syntactic ones.

This chapter explores how students use punctuation, especially why they make comma splices.

Exploring Your Own Language Experience

1. Before you begin the reading, spend five minutes or so writing in your journal about the following:
   How comfortable you do feel about your ability to punctuate sentences correctly? What do you think contributed most to your understanding of punctuation?
2. Review Rosen (see Chapter 5) and your notes about the reading. What does she recommend for helping students become more aware of their punctuation?

Run-ons, Comma Splices, and Native-Speaker Abilities

Rei R. Noguchi

> *In this reading, Noguchi tries to figure out why and how native speakers of English—who, by transformational-generative grammar definitions, understand completely how to form sentences correctly—will nevertheless misform them by punctuating them incorrectly. He also tries to figure out ways to tap into their intuitions about language to help them edit their own writing. This reading is excerpted from a longer chapter on the same topic in his book,* Grammar and the Teaching of Writing: Limits and Possibilities *(1991, National Council of Teachers of English). Noguchi's chapter is also interesting because it's clearly written from the point of view of a transformational-generative grammarian. His writing gives you a sense of the concerns of that particular school of grammar.*

For teachers of writing, probably no stylistic error creates as much frustration as run-ons and comma splices. By a "run-on" or a "run-on sentence" (or alternatively, a "fused sentence"), I mean a sequence of two or more sentences written as one, with no punctuation between the independent clauses (e.g., *Jack and his relatives plan to visit Disneyland they leave next Wednesday*). By a "comma splice," I mean two or more sentences written as one, with a comma joining the independent clauses (e.g., *Jack and his relatives plan to visit Disneyland, they leave next Wednesday*). Run-ons and comma splices occur at all grade levels, from elementary school to college and even beyond. Parris (n.d., 1), in *Sisyphus and the Comma Splice*, states, "The comma splice, for years, was the most frequent violation of traditional punctuation rules I encountered, a violation committed by my students at all levels, whether in freshman composition, advanced expository, or upper-level business and technical writing classes." Connors and Lunsford (1988), in their study of the twenty most frequently occurring formal errors in college writing, place comma splices eighth and run-ons eighteenth. At the elementary and secondary school level, run-ons and comma splices, in all likelihood, occur with even greater frequency. If for no other reason than their relatively high degree of occurrence and their problematic character, run-ons and comma splices deserve scrutiny, particularly with respect to their status as errors, their causes and, most important, their remedies.

The Problems in Treating Run-ons and Comma Splices

Finding a way to eliminate run-ons and comma splices presents a formidable challenge. The pedagogical problems are both obvious and daunting. If run-ons and comma splices, by definition, consist of two or more independent clauses misjoined by incorrect or no punctuation, the problem is made at least doubly difficult by the fact that treatment requires the isolation of not just one independent clause but two or more of them in sequence—and without the help of punctuation and capitalization (since they are incorrect to begin with). To make matters worse, an effective remedy must not only provide a means of identifying independent clauses but also an easy way of locating the point of illicit merger so that the appropriate punctuation can be added. Finally and worst of all, run-ons and comma splices require recognition of the grammatical category "sentence" or "independent clause," by far the most complex of all syntactic categories. As many teachers can attest, a sentence or an independent clause is not a structure which can be easily and transparently defined for students.

Traditional definitions of a clause or a sentence prove opaque or, at best, unwieldy because of their vagueness or their interlinkage with definitions of other grammatical categories. For example, defining a sentence as a sequence of words having "a complete thought" only shifts the problem to the equally perplexing task of defining "a complete thought." Defining a sentence as a unit with a complete subject and complete predicate (or, alternatively, with a noun-phrase subject and a verb phrase), necessitates defining "subject" and "predicate" (not to mention the notion of "complete") and eventually "noun," "verb," and probably "verb complement" (e.g., direct object, indirect object). What starts off as a seemingly simple task of defining a sentence results in rapidly proliferating definitions of the parts of the sentence, with the misunderstanding of any one of the parts likely to lead to the misunderstanding of the whole.

Five Kinds of Native-Speaker Abilities

If the pedagogical task of defining a sentence were not vexing enough, the problem of run-ons and comma splices becomes all the more frustrating if we consider that run-ons and comma splices seem to be errors that ought not to occur in the first place, at least not among native speakers of English. Native speakers of English, by virtue of being native speakers, have the following linguistic abilities:

1. The ability to distinguish a grammatical sentence from an ungrammatical one: e.g., *The cook put the soup on the stove* versus **The cook put the soup* or **Cook the put soup the on stove the*

2. The ability to produce and understand an infinite number of new sentences of potentially infinite length: e.g., *Jack went home, and he fixed himself a sandwich, and he cleaned his room, and he turned on his stereo, and . . . .*

3. The ability to recognize ambiguous sentences: e.g., *My mother hates boring guests* (i.e., 'My mother hates to bore guests' or 'My mother hates guests who are boring').

4. The ability to recognize synonymous sentences: e.g., *Alice and Tom washed the car* versus *The car was washed by Alice and Tom.*

5. The ability to recognize the internal structure of sentences: e.g., *Julia is eager to help* versus *Julia is easy to help.* (In the first sentence, Julia does the helping; in the second sentence, someone helps Julia.)

If native (but not non–native) speakers of English already possess the prodigious syntactic and semantic abilities illustrated in (1–5), then what becomes especially puzzling—and frustrating—is that these very abilities all hinge on a knowledge of what constitutes a sentence, precisely the knowledge which seems lacking in students who write with run-ons and comma splices (and fragments). That is, whatever run-ons and comma splices are, they, as written units, constitute nonsentences of the language.

A Curious Paradox and Its Repercussions

If native writers, by virtue of being native speakers of English, possess the ability to produce and recognize what constitutes a legitimate sentence of their language, then we confront a curious paradox with run-ons and comma splices. The paradox can be stated somewhat expansively as follows: native writers frequently write with run-ons and comma splices, which, by definition, are not genuine sentences; yet, given that these writers already know and can recognize sentences of English by being native speakers of English, such errors should not occur, or, at least, not with the frequency that they do. The source of the errors cannot lie in speakers' not knowing the correct end product. While writers may commit usage errors—such as ending a sentence with a preposition, splitting an infinitive, using *hopefully* as a sentence modifier, or using *ain't*—they usually do so because they do not realize that such features may violate some prescriptive rules of writing. That is, given the choice of writing *Hopefully, it will not rain during our baseball game* or *We hope it will not rain during our baseball game* or *It is hoped that it will not rain during our baseball game*, these students most likely would not know, without formal instruction, which sentence violates the prescriptive rule. These same students, by virtue of being native speakers of English, however, would readily recognize without formal instruction that *The cook put the soup on the stove* is a legitimate sentence of English while **The cook put the soup* is not.

That native-writer run-ons and comma splices seem to run counter to the very notion of native speakerhood helps explain, to some extent, not only the high degree of frustration they create but also their high degree of stigma. Hairston, in her survey of reactions to nonstandard writing features among nonacademic professionals, places comma splices in a group of errors she labels "moderately serious," but run-ons and fragments fall in a group of errors she labels "very serious." Such features in formal written discourse often evoke harsh criticism among professionals, nonacademic and academic, because in their eyes, sentences constitute the building blocks of formal writing; that is, formal written discourse is composed of or at least constructed from well–formed (i.e., genuine) sentences. Formal writing containing such nonsentence sequences as unintentional run-ons comma splices, and fragments, however, strikes at the very heart of this strongly held belief. Hence, native writers who write with run-ons, comma splices, and fragments encounter far harsher condemnation than non-native writers. (Indeed, the only native writers exempt from harsh criticism here are very young writers—preschool or elementary school level—who are in the beginning stages of acquiring the conventions of writing.)

Resolving the Paradox

Why is it that native speakers of English, despite their native-language abilities, frequently write with run-ons and comma splices, or, put somewhat cryptically, why is it that native speakers, who ought to know better, don't? I believe that a large part of the answer, perhaps the largest, lies in some crucial physical differences between speech and writing. While both modes of communication use a system of verbal symbols to convey virtually any kind of message (from philosophical treatises to sweet nothings), writing is distinguished from speech by, among other things, different conventions to mark sentence boundaries. Where speech utilizes phonological signals (intonation and pauses) to mark sentence boundaries, writing usually marks these boundaries graphologically with an initial capital letter and appropriate end punctuation (e.g., a period or a question mark). When writers produce run-ons and comma splices, however, they, knowingly or unknowingly, violate this writing convention, or put in another way, the phonological sentence does not coincide with the graphological sentence. (See Bamberg 1977 for one possible way to increase writer awareness of the phonological sentence.)

While the boundary markings of the phonological sentence have probably remained constant throughout the history of English, the same cannot be said of the graphological sentence. Indeed, from what language historians can gather from the punctuation of early written texts, today's run-ons and comma splices (and fragments) may not have been infelicities at all in centuries past. W. F. Bolton (1982) points out that Old English not only had different writing conventions but that these conventions varied so much among individual writers that extracting a set of commonly shared conventions proves, if not impossible, at least difficult. He writes, "The only mark of punctuation in the *Beowulf* manuscript was the period, and that appeared rarely; when it did, it was almost always at the end of the verse line; the same was true of many early Chaucer manuscripts: they were punctuated only with the period, and it appeared only at the end of the verse lines, whether or not a sentence ended there . . . . The manuscripts of Wyclif [i.e., John Wycliffe, c. 1330–84] were more heavily punctuated, but the system of punctuation was not ours" (177–78). Punctuation of formal written discourse two hundred years after Wycliffe still shows significant differences from today's conventions. Walter J. Ong (1944) argues that late sixteenth- and early seventeenth-century punctuation was a mixture of two systems, neither of them identical to the modern system, one being a system based on elocution and the other based on an earlier tradition in which the punctuation indicated "neither the syntax nor the niceties of delivery, but is rather a device serving primarily the exigencies of breathing in discourse, considered basically as oral, with due respect only secondarily for the demands of sense" (354–55). All this is not to claim that students who write without sentence-final punctuation write like Chaucer, Wycliffe, or the *Beowulf* poet, but these students do share one fact with writers of earlier periods, namely, that their conventions for marking sentence boundaries differ from today's written standard.

Interestingly, remnants of the earlier traditions of marking sentence boundaries still persist among beginning writers. Since the earlier systems of punctuation have their roots in speech, and given that beginning writers often view writing as just a transcription of speech, it is highly likely, indeed probable, that their unconventional system of punctuation reproduces, to some extent, part of the earlier systems. If we look at Irene Brosnahan's (1976) "A Few Good Words for the Comma Splice," particularly her criteria for permissible comma splices—criteria based, she claims, on actual usage of writers—the connection to earlier traditions, particularly to one based on meaning, becomes more apparent:

> *Rule*: The comma alone is used to separate independent clauses, without any accompanying conjunction, under the following conditions:
>
> 1. Syntax—the clauses are short and usually parallel in structure though they can be in any combination of affirmative and negative clauses.
> 2. Semantics—the sentence cannot be potentially ambiguous, and the semantic relationship between the clauses is paraphrase, repetition, amplification, opposition, addition, or summary.
> 3. Style—the usage level is General English or Informal English.
> 4. Rhetorical—the effect is rapidity of movement and/or emphasis. (185)

Where Brosnahan's main rule and first condition reflect a syntactic basis for determining acceptable comma splices, the other conditions reflect more a meaning basis (cognitive, social, and rhetorical) and hence connect more closely to an earlier system of punctuation. Students produce and punctuate run-ons and comma splices on the basis of these conditions; they continue a historically earlier tradition that was institutionally supplanted but never completely died. Significantly, the historic development of a semantically based punctuation system into a syntactically based one is also found in the way young children acquire the present system. As Patricia Cordeiro states, "Meaning structures are not bounded by orthographic structures or syntactic sentences. Children, in attempting to learn how to punctuate the ongoing stream of writing are in actual fact learning a new form of language organization: the sentence" (1988, 72).

We should not, however, believe that students who have already learned how to read but who write with run-ons and comma splices are completely unaware of the syntactically based system of marking sentence boundaries. To dispel this erroneous view, we need only to cite the greater number of correctly demarcated graphological sentences that usually do appear in their writing. I suspect, however, that, during the multifaceted task of putting words on paper, students who know the syntactically based system yet write with run-ons and comma errors allow the syntactically based system to recede from immediate consciousness, thus making it easier for the competing, and in many ways more natural and more expressive, semantically based system to exert itself. Note how readily and frequently even skilled writers, during the onrush of ideas, merge into one sentence what should be two separate sentences or how these same writers punctuate what are clearly (i.e., syntactically) questions with periods. Stated in another way, the surge or grip of ideas sometimes proves strong enough to override the constraints of form.

A Proper Perspective on Run-ons and Comma Splices

From a strictly practical perspective, how should teachers view run-ons and comma splices? For one thing, teachers need to keep in mind that good writing can and should accommodate intentional nonsentence sequences. A skilled writer might deliberately use a comma splice to convey a closely connected series of events (e.g., *We came, we saw, we conquered*) or a run-on to create a sense of prolixity and mechanical prattle (as in e.e. cummings's poem "next to of course god america i") or a sentence fragment to create emphasis and a sense of informality (as in many contemporary magazine advertisements). Brosnahan (1976) argues for other writing situations where comma splices might be contextually appropriate, as do Kline and Memering (1977) for the sentence fragment.

Second, teachers need to keep in mind that unintentional run-ons and comma splices, even if they occur in large numbers, are not indicators of a defective concept of the sentence, at least, not among native writers. Writers, particularly developing ones, will write with run-ons and comma splices as they experiment with more complex structures in the written medium, but these errors may indicate a transitional stage of development.

Treating Run-ons and Comma Splices

Given that run-ons and comma splices today stand a greater chance of evoking not only more negative reaction than in earlier centuries but negative reaction of a much higher degree, and given that unintentional run-ons and comma splices will garner far more negative reaction than intentional ones, what can we do to help students eliminate the unintentional ones? Do we, as in the past, simply administer heavier doses of grammar? No, I do not believe this is the easiest or even the most practical solution. Rather, the solution lies in extracting from students the unconscious knowledge of sentences that they already possess. By so doing, teachers can not only turn what, at first, seems a mysterious "gap" in native-speaker abilities into a pedagogical asset but also demonstrate to themselves and to their students that native speakers do, in fact, have an underlying knowledge of what constitutes a sentence of their language.

If given a set of genuine (declarative) sentences, native speakers of English can easily transform them into the corresponding tag and yes-no questions. For example, if given the (a) sentences below, native speakers can turn them into the corresponding (b) and (c) sentences.

1. a. Your next-door neighbor is going to sell his car for $400.
   b. Your next-door neighbor is going to sell his car for $400, isn't he?
   c. Is your next-door neighbor going to sell his car for $400?
2. a. Nancy, who couldn't wait, ripped open the cellophane wrapper on the box.
   b. Nancy, who couldn't wait, ripped open the cellophane wrapper on the box, didn't she?
   c. Did Nancy, who couldn't wait, rip open the cellophane wrapper on the box?
3. a. For the past six months, Linda and Sue have run five miles every day.
   b. For the past six months, Linda and Sue have run five miles every day, haven't they?
   c. For the past six months, have Linda and Sue run five miles every day?
4. a. Ed and his cousin will buy two tickets each.
   b. Ed and his cousin will buy two tickets each, won't they?
   c. Will Ed and his cousin buy two tickets each?
5. a. You weren't in class for a whole month.
   b. You weren't in class for a whole month, were you?
   c. Weren't you in class for a whole month?

As quick and automatic as this exercise may seem, forming proper tag and yes-no questions requires knowledge of some complex descriptive rules. For example, yes-no question formation involves a rule which moves the first auxiliary (i.e., "helping") verb (if there is one) and the contracted negative *–n't* (if there is one) to the immediate left of the subject; if there is no first auxiliary verb, the appropriate form of *do* (*do, does,* or *did*) is instead added to the immediate left of the subject; if the main verb of the original declarative sentence is *be* (in some dialects, also *have*) and there is no first auxiliary verb, then the main verb *be* (or the main verb *have*) is moved to the immediate left of the subject. Tag-question formation involves knowledge of an even more complex descriptive rule. Roughly stated, if the original declarative sentence is positive, the first auxiliary verb in contracted negative form and the subject in pronominal form are copied in that order to the immediate right of the original declarative sentence; if the original declarative sentence is negative, only the first auxiliary verb and the subject in pronominal form in that order are copied to the immediate right of the original declarative sentence; if there is no first auxiliary verb to copy, then the appropriate form of *do* is added in lieu of the first auxiliary verb to the immediate right of the original sentence; if the main verb of the original declarative sentence is *be* (in some dialects, also *have*) and there is no first auxiliary verb, then the main verb *be* (or the main verb *have*) is copied in lieu of the first auxiliary verb to the immediate right of the original declarative sentence.

Complicated as the yes-no and tag-question rules are, there is no need to teach these two rules formally. Students already have them in their heads. If they did not, they would be unable to produce grammatical tag and yes-no questions in examples 1–5 above or, more tellingly, in everyday conversation. Indeed, because students already possess an unconscious knowledge of these two descriptive rules, they have the capacity to produce an infinite number of grammatical tag and yes-no questions. Even with this prodigious ability, however, they will find it next to impossible to transform the following sequences into their proper and corresponding tag and yes–no questions:

6. Your next-door neighbor is going to sell his car for $400 he should sell it for $800.
7. Nancy, impatient as always, ripped off the cellophane wrapper of the package the icing of the cake came off with it.
8. For the past six months, Linda and Sue have run five miles every day, they really want to win the city championship badly.
9. Ed and his cousin will buy two tickets each, Hank will buy six.
10. You weren't in class for a whole month, it isn't fair.

The reason students cannot transform sequences 6–10 into proper and corresponding tag and yes–no questions lies in the simple fact that the tag and yes–no question rules work only on genuine declarative sentences. Sequences 6 and 7, being run-ons, and sequences 8–10, being comma splices, are nonsentences and, hence, disallow the correct operation of the tag and yes–no question rules. Put more succinctly, tag question and yes–no question formation operate successfully only on real sentences, not nonsentences. Although students are not consciously aware of this fact, they know it intuitively. If this is so, then students can use their unconscious knowledge of tag and yes-no question formation to help detect and correct run-ons and comma splices. Although either tag-question formation or yes–no question formation will help isolate run-ons and comma splices from genuine sentences, using both in combination brings better results.

Two Scenarios. In working with sample sequences like (6–10), teachers can expect two different but related scenarios. In one, students will be unable to transform the run-ons and comma splices into both proper and corresponding tag questions and proper and corresponding yes–no questions. This, of course, is the clearest indication that such sequences are nonsentences of the language. When teachers—and students—reach this assessment, then the stage is set for actually correcting the nonsentence sequences. However, a second and, perhaps, even more revealing scenario may occur. Some students may find that for some nonsentence sequences they cannot form yes–no questions but they can form tag questions. Take, for example, the run-on in (7) above. For this nonsentence sequence, some students may claim, indeed, insist, that the proper and corresponding tag question is (11):

11. *Nancy, impatient as always, ripped off the cellophane wrapper of the package the icing of the cake came off with it, didn't it?

Responses such as (11) shed further light on the basic conflict between the conventions of writing and speech, the validity of native-speaker abilities, and, in the end, the value of using both yes–no questions and tag questions as a means of eliminating run-ons and comma splices. The conflict between the conventions of writing and speech, already apparent in the sequence in (7), becomes even more conspicuous in the response in (11), where the graphological sentence comes in conflict with the phonological sentence. Teachers can show this conflict very easily by writing the sequence in (11) on the chalkboard and then having one or two students read it orally at normal (or slightly slower than normal) speed. After having heard the sequence students will notice that one part of the sequence (call it the first part) sounds like a statement, but the remaining, or second part, sounds like a question. While some students may encounter difficulty in detecting run-ons and comma splices in writing, they all, as native speakers of English, should experience no difficulty in distinguishing a question from a non-question in speech. More than that, if asked to locate the point where the statement ends and the question begins, they can do so without effort.

The teacher should mark on the chalkboard the separation point between the statement and the question contained in (11) as follows:

12. Nancy, impatient as always, ripped off the cellophane wrapper of the package // the icing of the cake came off with it, didn't it?

Teachers might here point out that, though the tag question in (12) seems a proper (i.e., grammatical) one, it corresponds to only the part to the right of the double slash (//). Teachers should ask students to transform the statement part of the sequence (i.e., the first part) into a tag question and a yes-no question, a task which should yield, *Nancy, impatient as always, ripped off the cellophane wrapper of the package, didn't she?* and *Did Nancy, impatient as always, rip off the cellophane wrapper of the package?* To verify that the second part of (12) is also a sentence, teachers can ask students to provide the yes–no question counterpart (*Did the icing of the cake come off with it?*). After having accomplished these tasks—tasks which come easily because they rely on linguistic knowledge that native speakers already possess—students come to see more clearly not only why sequences like (11) actually consist of misjoined sentences but also precisely where the misjoining occurs.

Some Practical Benefits

Although the approach described above may not work for all students (e.g., students in the lower primary grades or non-native students who lack fluency in English), it can potentially work for all others. If native writers know how to form tag and yes–no questions—which they should as native speakers of the language—they possess an easily accessible and always available means of checking for run-ons and comma splices without first having to undergo formal instruction in grammar. They simply use what they already know. For teachers, this means less time and effort spent on formal grammar instruction and more time and energy to devote to other and more important aspects of writing. Although unconventional features such as run-ons and comma splices require attention at some stage in the writing process (preferably during the rewriting or proofreading stages), teachers should bear in mind that treatment of such errors should comprise neither the principal activities of a writing program nor its principal goal.

For students, the benefits can be no less significant. First, the proposed approach relieves students from many hours of difficult and often tedious lessons in grammar where rote memorization seems more important than principles. The approach proposed here not only greatly shortens the time allotted to formal grammar study but offers a more interactive and, I believe, a more interesting way to learn about grammar. Because traditional approaches to grammar have generally failed to build on underlying linguistic abilities, teachers have not only made their task more difficult and time-consuming but also alienated a large number of students who might otherwise pursue grammar study with greater enthusiasm. Second, the proposed approach enables students to learn more about their remarkable abilities as native speakers of the language. By generating their own language data, forming hypotheses, and testing them with their native-speaker intuitions of the language, students come to learn more not only about language and inductive reasoning but also about themselves—of what it means to possess knowledge *of* a language rather than possessing knowledge *about* a language. Finally, the proposed approach promotes greater self-confidence and self-reliance. Instead of ignoring underlying linguistic abilities or viewing such abilities negatively (i.e., as a lack or defect in such abilities), the proposed approach enables students to demonstrate and verify for themselves the prodigious and often untapped linguistic abilities they bring to the classroom every day.

References

Bamberg, B. (1977). Periods are basic: A strategy for eliminating comma faults and run-on sentences. In O. Clapp and the Committee on Classroom Practices (Eds.), *Classroom practices in teaching English 1977–1978: Teaching the basics—really!* Urbana, IL: National Council of Teachers of English.

Bolton, W. F. (1982). *A living language.* New York: Random House.

Brosnahan, I. T. (1976). A few good words for the comma splice. *College English, 38,* 184–188.

Connors, R. J., & Lunsford, A. A. (1988). Frequency of formal errors in current college writing, or Ma and Pa Kettle do research. *College Composition and Communication, 39,* 395–409.

Cordeiro, P. (1988). Children's punctuation: An analysis of errors in period placement. *Research in the Teaching of English, 22,* 62–74.

Hairston, M. (1981). Not all errors are created equal: Nonacademic readers in the professions respond to lapses in usage. *College English, 43,* 794–806.

Kline, C. R., Jr., & Memering, W. D. (1977). Formal fragments: The English minor sentence. *Research in the Teaching of English, 11,* 97–110.

Ong, W. J. (1944). Historical backgrounds of Elizabethan and Jacobean punctuation theory. *PLMA, 59,* 349–360.

Questions for Discussion

1. What paradox does Noguchi find in comma splices and run-on sentences? What does he recommend as a solution? How does his approach differ from that of traditional grammarians? How compatible is it with the suggestions that Rosen makes?

2. Hall (1996) explains that The Punctuation Project was founded in part as a response to national curriculum reform in Britain. Early elementary teachers didn't worry too much about the punctuation skills of their students, recognizing that their skills in correctly marking sentence boundaries would improve with time and practice. The new curriculum, however, stated explicitly that 7-year-olds were expected to punctuate most of their sentences correctly. Teachers asked for help in teaching this skill. The Punctuation Project supplies not only pedagogical support but also does research into children's developing sense of punctuation.

   Consult your state's curriculum guidelines. What kind of punctuation does your state want teachers to teach? At which levels? If your state has mandated assessments to measure educational progress, is knowledge of punctuation assessed? If so, how?

3. Read the essays by Nick (p. 219) and Adam (pp. 224).
   a. Imagine that Nick is your student. What comments will you give him—either in conference or in writing—about his journal entry? What do you think is strong about his journal? What advice will you give him about its content, organization, and tone?
   b. Imagine that Adam is your student. What comments will you give him—either in conference or in writing—about his analysis? What do you think is strong about his paper? What advice will you give him about its content, organization, and tone?
   c. Perhaps you mentioned Nick's and Adam's comma splices/run-on sentences in your comments to them. To what extent do their hypotheses about sentence boundary punctuation complement those of the basic writers described by Noguchi, Shaughnessy, and Danielewicz and Chafe? What advice can you give Nick and Adam that would help them better see their comma splice errors?

8

Building More Complex Sentences and Paragraphs

One theme that's evident in Chapter 7 is that writers grow in their understanding of what is and isn't a sentence and in their abilities to write more complex sentences and more developed paragraphs. Theoretical linguists, rhetoricians, and English language arts teachers have sought to learn more about these abilities and their implications for writing and grammar curricula. One particularly fertile time for this research was the 1960s. During that time, transformational-generative linguists sought to explain what enabled native speakers to *generate* and *transform* grammatical sentences (see Chapter 2). Also, during the same decade, rhetorician Francis Christensen (1967) studied the sentences and paragraphs of contemporary writers to define a modern prose style for the late twentieth century. Meanwhile, syntactician Kellogg Hunt (1965) was interested in describing the changes in students' writing over time. He sought to identify which syntactic structures appeared in the writing of older students that did not appear in the writing of younger ones. These grammatical elements made up what he defined as a "mature style."

Transformational-Generative Grammar's Model of Sentence Transformations

In the late 1950s/early 1960s, transformational-generative grammarians came up with a model of language and of language use that distinguished between the *deep* and *surface structures* of a sentence. According to this model, ideas start out deep in our brains as simple, positive, declarative propositions (the *deep structure*); they typically undergo a number of transformations before they eventually get articulated (the *surface structure*). For example, the deep structure proposition "Shakespeare wrote *Hamlet*" may be expressed as "Shakespeare wrote *Hamlet*.," but it may also be transformed into the passive sentence *"Hamlet* was written by Shakespeare." Or further condensed into "Shakespeare's *Hamlet*." A writer's context and purpose determine which stylistic variation—which surface structure, which transformations—is most effective.

In addition to transforming single propositions, we may condense and embed propositions within our sentences. For example, we may embed the two propositions *"Hamlet* is a popular play." and "Shakespeare wrote *Hamlet*." into any number of surface structures, such as:

- *Hamlet*, which was written by Shakespeare, is a popular play.
- *Hamlet*, a popular play, was written by Shakespeare.
- Shakespeare wrote *Hamlet*, a popular play.
- Shakespeare's *Hamlet* is a popular play.

Again, context, purpose, and stylistic effect determine which surface structure a writer chooses. The embedded structures are dependent clauses and phrases—to use traditional grammar terminology—and the resulting sentences are complex sentences.

Hunt's Research on Syntactic Complexity

While the transformational-generative grammarians were developing a model of generating, transforming, and embedding sentences, Kellogg Hunt (1965, 1977; Hunt & O'Donnell, 1970) was researching how students grow in their abilities to perform these functions. Hunt's name is synonymous with research into the syntactic development of student writers. He examined the writing of students from around the country at various grade levels. One element he measured was the length of sentences, defined as the number of words per *t*-unit. A *t*-unit is a single independent clause plus all the dependent clauses associated with it—in essence, a correctly punctuated sentence. Hunt created this unit of measure because he realized early on that he couldn't trust the way students punctuated their own sentences. That is, he couldn't simply count the number of words between periods in students' papers, because younger children tended to create a lot of comma splices or to string sentences together with *ands*; this made for long, but not very complex sentences. So he repunctuated the sentences by determining *t*-units and then counted the number of words per *t*-unit. He found that as they grew older, students were able to write longer and longer sentences. His findings on *t*-units are summarized in Figure 8.1.

Hunt measured the *t*-units in writing students did under two different conditions: what he called *freewriting* and *rewriting*. By *freewriting*, Hunt meant writing that children did on their own. He noted that when they wrote for themselves, they wrote longer individual sentences and longer themes in general. By *rewriting*, Hunt meant writing students did as part of his studies. He gave students various paragraphs, each containing many short sentences, and

FIGURE 8.1   *Theoretical Foundation: Hunt's Research on Syntactic Complexity*

This chart summarizes Hunt's (1965, 1977; Hunt & O'Donnell, 1970) research into students' syntactic development. He uses three measures to determine each student's level of development:

- Length of sentence, or number of words per *t-unit* (defined as an independent clause and all the dependent clauses attached to it);
- Density of sentence, or consolidation (defined as the number of propositions per *t-unit*); and
- Syntactic structures used.

Hunt found that as they get older, students are able to write longer sentences that use a greater variety of structures to pack in more ideas.

	Grade 4	Grade 8	Grade 12	Skilled Adult
	Length of Sentences			
freewriting (words/*t*-unit)	6.7	10.2	12	13
rewriting	5.4	9.8	11.3	14.8
	Density of Sentences			
consolidation (propositions/*t*-unit)	1.1	2.4	3.2	5.1
	Syntactic Structures Writers Able to Use			
Coordinating Sentences (*I went to the store, and I bought milk.*)	primary strategy	✓	✓	seldom used
Compound Predicates (*I went to the store and bought milk.*)	✓	✓	✓	✓
Clauses Reduced to Pre-Noun Adjectives (the car *that's blue* → the *blue* car.)	✓	explosion of growth	explosion of growth	✓
Subordinate Clauses (I was upset, *because I couldn't go.*)		✓	✓	✓
Appositives (Lora, *my sister who's an artist*, lives in New Zealand.)		✓	✓	frequently used
Participial Phrases (My sister *living in Iowa* is interested in sustainable agriculture.)			✓	✓

asked them to "study the passage and then rewrite it in a better way. You may combine sentences, change the order of words, and omit words that are repeated too many times. But try not to leave out any of the information" (1977, p. 103). Here are the first few sentences of his most famous exercise, often referred to simply as the "Aluminum" paragraph:

Aluminum

(1) Aluminum is a metal. (2) It is abundant. (3) It has many uses. (4) It comes from bauxite. (5) Bauxite is an ore. (6) Bauxite looks like clay.

The value of this kind of exercise was that every student wrote essentially the same thing, so the paragraphs could be compared. Hunt found that older students were able to consolidate more of the short sentences into a single sentence, so their sentences were denser. He developed what he called a *consolidation score*: the average number of short exercise sentences combined into a single rewritten sentence. Consider this consolidated version by a fourth grader:

Aluminum is a metal and it is abundant. It has many uses and it comes from bauxite. Bauxite is an ore and looks like clay (Hunt, 1977, p. 95).

Compare it to a version written by a skilled adult:

Aluminum, an abundant metal with many uses comes from bauxite, a clay-like ore (Hunt, 1977, p. 95).

The fourth grader was able to do little more than simply rewrite the sentences and to combine them with *and*, while the skilled adult could combine six short sentences into one. The average consolidation scores for various levels of students are reported in Figure 8.1.

Hunt (1977) found that older students wrote denser, more consolidated sentences because they had many more syntactic structures in their repertoire. Hunt found, for example, that fourth graders rely on coordination—either of full sentences or of predicates—a great deal because it's one of the few syntactic strategies they have at their command. Skilled adults, on the other hand, seldom use that strategy because they have so many more structures to choose from. Figure 8.1 charts the structures that Hunt found in students' writing at various ages.

I should note here that Hunt's findings don't represent hard-and-fast stages of development that every student goes through. Rather, they're general guidelines that may help teachers decide which ways to encourage specific students to write more complex sentences than they might do on their own.

Sentence Combining Exercises

Hunt's research showed that students seem to develop a natural ability to transform, condense, and embed structures in their writing. However, it also showed that these abilities "could be enhanced" by introducing students to syntactic structures and giving them practice in combining and embedding smaller ideas into more complex ones (Hunt, 1977, p. 101).

Interest in students' abilities to transform and combine sentences led to development of sentence combining curricula in the 1970s and early 1980s, especially on the college level. One popular text at the time was William Strong's *Sentence Combining: A Composing Book*. Kerek, Daiker, and Morenberg (1980) compared the writing of first year college students using Strong's book to the writing of a control group of students who studied traditional grammar. The experimental sections showed syntactic growth while traditional sections did not. A follow up study done more than two years later showed the gains lasted.

There are two kinds of sentence combining exercises:

- *Structured exercises,* in which students are given directions in how to combine the sentences, and
- *Free exercises,* in which students are given a passage of short sentences and asked to combine them in a way they find effective.

An example of a structured exercise is this pair of sentences:

1. a. The boy had outgrown his old jacket.
   b. His mother wanted to buy him a new one. [, **and**] (Glencoe McGraw-Hill, 2001, p. 517)

Here students are directed to combine these sentences with the connecting word *and*. Note that in this type of exercise, students are taught not only new grammatical options but also how to punctuate them. An example of a free structure exercise is this paragraph:

The boy wore the jacket for three long years. He was unhappy for most of that time. He wished for a jacket of a different color. His family could not afford a black leather jacket. This was America. Children in America did not wear jackets like this. He wanted another jacket badly. He wore the ugly one.

The directions for this exercise say simply, "Rewrite the following paragraphs, combining sentences as you think necessary" (Glencoe McGraw-Hill, 2001, p. 518). Because there are so many possible combinations in this kind of exercise, it's important to discuss the rhetorical effect of students' choices.

Sentence-combining exercises differ from traditional grammar exercises in two important ways:

- *Sentence-combining exercises ask students to produce sentences—to actively write—* while traditional grammar exercises ask students to analyze and label existing sentences—usually by underlining or circling specific parts of speech or by filling in a blank.
- *Writers are encouraged to combine sentences in several different ways.* Because sentence-combining exercises can result in several different answers, these exercises must include discussions of the rhetorical effects of one choice over another. The goal is to develop not only fluency and flexibility, but also the

writer's sense of rhetorical judgment. Traditional grammar exercises, on the other hand, usually seek one right answer, or a limited number of answers. Although traditional grammar units might include writing practice, the emphasis is typically not on writing and on developing rhetorical judgment, but on analyzing existing sentences.

In essence, sentence combining is a grammar curriculum based on a writer's point of view. That's one reason these kinds of exercises lead to more improvement in student writing than traditional grammar exercises.

Although it's no longer popular as a curriculum on the college level, sentence-combining exercises continue to be mixed with more traditional grammar exercises in all three English language arts texts I surveyed. For example, Glencoe McGraw-Hill's *Writer's Choice: Grammar and Composition (Grade 6)* has a separate chapter devoted to sentence combining that appears at the end of the section on grammar, usage, and mechanics. The practice includes both structured and free exercises. However, in spite of this chapter on sentence combining, *Writer's Choice* remains a fairly traditional text, centered more on analyzing sentences than producing them. The bulk of the exercises tend to use the traditional format in which students are asked to underline the part of speech or the point of grammar under study.

In contrast, Houghton Mifflin's *English* (Rueda et al., 2001) includes sentence combining as one kind of exercise throughout the book. A chapter on sentences, for example, begins with a fairly traditional exercise on identifying kinds of sentences, but then asks students to proofread a text formatted as a skit and to write a skit of their own. The next section, labeled "Revising Strategies," suggests that writers make their sentences sound less repetitive by combining sentences with similar subjects or predicates.

Similarly, *Elements of Language: Introductory Course* (Odell et al., 2001) discusses sentence combining as a revision strategy. In a chapter on writing effective sentences, the authors introduce sentence combining as a way to achieve sentence variety and avoid an "entire paragraph of short sentences [, which] make writing choppy" (p. 269).

One commercially available curriculum that focuses exclusively on sentence combining is *Daily Sentence Composing*. A counterpart to *Daily Oral Language*, this program is a series of five-minute, daily mini-lessons based on model sentences written by published authors. There are five kinds of exercises: chunking, unscrambling, imitating, combining, and expanding. Figure 8.2 describes the program in more detail.

Christensen's Analysis of Modern Style

A third exploration of English sentences and paragraphs was done in the 1960s by Francis Christensen (1967). Christensen defined style in terms of the writing of modern, published authors. Christensen believed that the hallmark of twentieth century skilled writing was linguistic compactness. And the kind of

FIGURE 8.2   *Spotlight on Curriculum: Daily Sentence Composing*

Author(s):	Don Killgallon and Jenny Killgallon
Author's(s') Credentials:	Teachers; Don Killgallon is the author of the *Sentence Composing* Series published by Heinemann; Jenny Killgallon is co-author of the elementary school portion of the series
Published By:	Great Source Education Group
Available:	181 Ballardvale Street
	Wilmington, MA 01887
	1-800-289-4490
	www.greatsource.com

Daily Sentence Composing is just one of the *Dailies* programs published by the Great Source Education Group. Other *Dailies* include *Daily Oral Language, Daily Oral Language Plus, Daily Phonics, Daily Vocabulary, Daily Spelling, Daily Analogies, Daily Geography, Daily Mathematics,* and *Daily Science Workout*. All follow the same five- to ten-minute lesson format.

Daily Sentence Composing includes drills on sentence variety and syntactic maturity, using five sentence-composing techniques:

- *Chunking*: Students distinguish meaningful from meaningless sentence parts.
- *Unscrambling*: Students learn the inter-connectedness of related sentence parts.
- *Imitating*: Students identify sentences with similar structures.
- *Combining*: Students assemble a list of sentences to match the structure of a professionally written model.
- *Expanding*: Students add a sentence part to a professionally written sentence from which that same sentence part has been deleted.

These drills are based exclusively on professionally written sentences as models for students to imitate through repeated practice. As students manipulate sentences, they become more aware of and familiar with various sentence structures. They learn to add these sentence structures to their own writing, thus improving it dramatically. These lessons were written for grades six through eight. This example of a *chunking* exercise comes from Week 2 of the Grade 6 set:

Directions:	Unscramble and write out the sentence chunks below to name a sentence with the same chunks as the model. Then write a sentence of your own that imitates the model.
Model:	Then a stone gave way, / leaving a hole / in the wall.
	Gaston Leroux, *The Phantom of the Opera*
	Chunks: on the table / spilling some milk / once a pitcher fell over
Result:	Once a pitcher fell over, spilling some milk on the table.
	After students share their sentences, have them describe the process they used to write their sentences.

This example of an *unscrambling* exercise comes from Week 3 of the Grade 7 set:

FIGURE 8.2 *Continued*

Directions:	Unscramble the sentence parts, or chunks, to make a sentence that makes sense. Write out the sentence. Punctuate correctly.
Model:	a. and sat in her chair by the window b. unsteadily c. across the room d. she limped
Result:	Unsteadily she limped across the room and sat in her chair by the window. Eleanor Coerr, *Sadako and the Thousand Paper Cranes* *Accept other arrangements that make sense.*

This example of an *imitating* exercise comes from Week 7 of the Grade 8 set:

Directions:	Unscramble and write out the sentence parts to imitate the model.
Model:	Finally, she made her decision, drew a long, rattling breath, picked up the phone again, and dialed. Ronald Rogers, *The Good Run* a. he opened the book b. slowly c. got out his crayons again, and drew d. chose an entertaining, colorful illustration
Result:	Slowly, he opened the book, chose an entertaining, colorful illustration, got out his crayons again, and drew. *Reassure students that it may take several tries before they successfully unscramble the sentence.*

In addition to sentence exercises like these, the promotional materials promise exercises in punctuation, especially in identifying comma splices and in using commas with non-essential sentence parts. However, no examples of these exercises were provided.

Description based on promotional materials from Great Source Education Group. Used with permission. (See Chapter 3 for a description of *Daily Oral Language*.)

sentence that best typified effective writing style was the cumulative sentence: a sentence with a bare bones independent clause with several modifying phrases hooked on, usually at the end or the beginning. He noticed that sentences carried their narrative or descriptive material not in the subject and predicate, but in the modifying phrases attached to it. These phrases were often appositives, participial phrases, and absolutes.

Christensen cited a William Faulkner sentence as an example of a cumulative sentence:

> Calico-coated, small bodied, with delicate legs and pink faces in which their mismatched eyes rolled wild and subdued, they huddled, gaudy, motionless and alert, wild as deer, deadly as rattlesnakes, quiet as doves (as cited in Weaver, 1996, p. 132).

In this sentence, *they huddled* represents the independent clause; the phrases before and after it are modifiers. The clause itself has been stripped down to only the essential elements of subject and verb, but the modifiers add layers of additional details. Faulkner uses a variety of structures to supply this detail: participial phrases (*calico-coated*), prepositional phrases (*with delicate legs and pink faces*), relative clauses (*in which . . . subdued*), adjectives (*gaudy, motionless, alert*), etc.

Christensen also noticed that modern paragraphs have a similar texture—a bare bones general statement developed with additional layers of details. In a typical paragraph, an idea is stated—often in (a) topic sentence(s)—and then is developed through a series of coordinating and subordinating ideas. According to Christensen, coordinating sentences paraphrase, contrast, or connect to previous sentences with the same level of generality, while subordinating sentences expand, explain, or define the previous sentence at a more specific level. Christensen recommends at least three levels of specificity in a paragraph.

For example, the previous paragraph can be analyzed into three levels of specificity. The analysis appears in Figure 8.3.

FIGURE 8.3   *Theoretical Foundation: Using Christensen's Paragraph Texture to Analyze a Paragraph*

Francis Christensen (1965) analyzed the writing of twentieth century authors to identify a modern style. Among his conclusions was that modern paragraphs typically have several layers of texture. That is, paragraphs may begin with a general statement that introduces the topic—what we often call a *topic sentence*. Other sentences develop the topic at a more specific level. Here's an example of how a paragraph might be analyzed according to Christensen's ideas of paragraph texture.

---

1. A second strategy for achieving flow is to work for what Francis Christensen (1967) calls *paragraph texture*.
   2. Texture refers to paragraphs having sentences of various levels of generality.
   2. In a typical paragraph, an idea is stated—often in (a) topic sentence(s)—
   2. and then it's developed through a series of coordinating and subordinating ideas.
      3. According to Christensen, coordinating sentences paraphrase, contrast, or connect to previous sentences with the same level of generality,
      3. while subordinating sentences expand, explain, or define the previous sentence at a more specific level.
      3. Christensen recommends at least three levels of specificity in a paragraph.

Christensen (1967) argued for a grammar curriculum that taught students how to expand bare bones sentences and how to use structures for rhetorical effect. He inspired a number of present-day teachers including Constance Weaver and her colleagues (2001 [See Chapter 3]) and the authors of Daily Sentence Composing, Don Killgallon (1998) and Jenny Killgallon (See Figure 8.2).

Another teacher who was inspired by Christensen is Harry R. Noden (1999), author of *Image Grammar: Using Grammatical Structures to Teach Writing*. Noden (1999, 2001) likens grammatical structures to an artist's paintbrush—they're the tools writers use to create images in the minds of readers. Following Christensen, he looks specifically at the structures of the participle, the absolute, the appositive, and adjectives shifted out of order. Noden uses copies of paintings, photographs, and live models to teach students to "paint with grammatical structures" (2001, p. 10). He also uses passages from published writing as models for the kind of sentences and paragraphs he wants his middle school students to produce.

Rhetorical Grammar

One theme that's common to the examination of sentences by transformational-generative grammarians, Hunt (1965, 1970, 1977), and Christensen (1967) is the importance of discussing with students not only how to write more complex structures, but also what rhetorical effects various structures have on the rest of the text and on readers. This is what Martha Kolln (1996; 1999; Kolln & Funk, 2002) calls *rhetorical grammar*. Kolln (1996) argues that introducing grammar in a rhetorical or functional way—sentence combining is one such approach; another is Katie Wood Ray's reading-like-a-writer approach (See Figure 4.1)—has a greater influence on our teaching of the writing process than traditional grammar does. Not only do students develop a broader repertoire of structures to use in their writing and, in the process, develop a vocabulary for talking about writing (Hartwell's Grammar 5 [p. 5]), but they also deepen their sense of rhetorical judgment.

One aspect of rhetorical grammar that Kolln is especially interested in is readability—that is, in how writers can structure sentences to complement—or take advantage of—the processes readers use to comprehend their texts. For example, in the reading for this chapter, Kolln and Funk discuss what they call *end focus*, the tendency for readers to look to the ends (i.e., the predicates) of sentences for important ideas. Writers who are aware of this reading convention can structure their sentences to put their main ideas in the predicates. That way they can feel more confident readers will get their point.

End focus is a natural extension of the *known-new* (or *given-new*) *contract*, an obligation writers have to connect each sentence to what has gone before it. According to Colleen Donnelly in *Linguistics for Writers* (1994), the known-new contract is based on the assumption that every sentence contains some material that's familiar to readers—the *known* or the *given*—and some material that's unfamiliar—the *new*. Material is familiar to readers, either because they've read previous portions of the text or because they can easily infer an idea from what they already know about the topic. Material is new because the writer adds (an) additional element(s) to the ongoing story, description, or argument. The new information in a sentence often becomes the given in subsequent sentences. To keep readers on an even keel, the known portion is generally the subject of the sentence while the new is generally the predicate. That's why readers focus on the ends of sentences. That's also why savvy writers do too. In addition to readability and emphasis, the known-new contract has another important role: it helps writing "flow," that is, it helps link ideas together into unified paragraphs.

Another important element of rhetorical grammar is how to use stylistic devices effectively. In the reading for this chapter, Kolln and Funk discuss such stylistic features as word order variation, appositives, and deliberate sentence fragments.

This chapter explores techniques for helping students compose more sophisticated sentences and paragraphs as well as understand the rhetorical effects of their choices.

Exploring Your Own Language Experience

1. Before you begin the reading, spend five minutes or so writing in your journal about the following:

   To what extent did you study "style"—that is, how words were put together for emphatic or aesthetic effect—in your writing or literature classes?

2. Review Weaver, McNally, and Moerman (see Chapter 3) and your notes about the reading. How do these instructors teach students to write more effective sentences? What value do they believe these exercises have?

Rhetorical Grammar

Martha Kolln and Robert Funk

> *This reading is an excerpt of a chapter entitled "Rhetorical Grammar" from Kolln and Funk's* Understanding English Grammar *(2002, Longman, 6th ed.). An earlier version of this chapter was developed in Kolln's* Rhetorical Grammar: Grammatical Choices, Rhetorical Effects *(1999, Allyn and Bacon, 3rd ed.). Kolln's name is synonymous with the phrase* rhetorical grammar *and with a conviction that teachers could talk to students in more sophisticated ways about writing if the latter were more familiar with grammar and grammar terminology. In essence, she's an advocate for Hartwell's* Grammar 5; *that is, for a vocabulary of stylistic and rhetorical options. This condensation focuses on how students can use sentence structure and rhythm to make their writing more readable.*

Chapter Preview
Rhetoric refers to the linguistic choices we make in a given speaking or writing situation. Here is a description of rhetoric:

In the written language, what is appropriate or effective in one situation may be inappropriate or ineffective in another. The language you use in letters to your family and friends is noticeably different from the language you use when applying for a job. Even the writing you do in school varies, depending on the situation. The language of the personal essay you write for your composition class has an informality that would be inappropriate for a business report or a history research paper. As with speech, the purpose and the audience make all the difference.

If this description of rhetoric sounds to you like plain old common sense, you're absolutely right. You've always understood that the person you're talking to or writing to—in other words, your audience—will have an effect on what you say and the way you say it.

In terms of writing, then, rhetoric means that the situation—the topic, the purpose, and the audience—will make a difference in the way you write. And to a great extent that rhetorical situation will determine the grammatical choices you make, choices about sentence structure and vocabulary, even about punctuation. Rhetorical grammar is about those choices.

In this chapter we will discuss the ways in which a knowledge of grammar can make a difference to you as a writer. We will begin by considering sentence patterns; we will see how the features of those patterns, including their transformations, can heighten your awareness of the effect your writing has on your audience. We will then take up the grammatical choices and rhetorical effects of other sentence features.

Sentence Patterns

Cohesion. Sentences consist of a series of slots, some required and some optional, filled by structures of various forms. Your understanding of the slots can be helpful in thinking about sentence **cohesion**, the ties that connect each sentence to what has gone before—the glue that gives a paragraph and an essay unity. Part of that glue is provided by information in the sentence that the reader knows or expects, information that has already been mentioned.

Let's look at the paragraph you just read as an example of that cohesive glue and reader expectation. The first sentence introduces the topic of sentence slots, with a brief description. You can be fairly certain that the next sentence will say something further about sentence slots. And, yes, it does: The subject of the next sentence is *Your understanding of the slots*. In other words, the sentence opens with old, or known, information. You don't expect to get to the new information, the purpose of the sentence, until you get to the predicate slot. And there it is in the predicate—new information, even a new term, *cohesion*, and the descriptive *glue*. And the third sentence? Again, you're not surprised to see known information—this time, *glue*—in the subject slot.

This known-to-new sequence is fairly typical for cohesive paragraphs, where the new information of one sentence becomes the known information of the next. In fact, the known-new sequence is so pervasive a feature of our prose that it is sometimes referred to as the ***known-new contract***. The writer has an obligation, a contract of sorts, to fulfill expectations in the reader—to keep the reader on familiar ground. The reader has every right to expect each sentence to be connected in some way to what has gone before, to include a known element.

One of our most common known elements, certainly as strong as the repeated noun or noun phrase, is the pronoun. Consider how often the subject slot of the second sentence in a passage is filled by a pronoun, such as *she* or *he* or *it* or *they*. That pronoun is automatically tied to its antecedent, a previously mentioned nominal that it stands for. If there is no obvious antecedent, then the pronoun is not doing its cohesive job.

In the following passage, part of the opening paragraph of an essay by Annie Dillard, the first sentence introduces the topic, *a weasel*, in the subject slot. And, as you can see, the subject slots of the next three sentences are filled by the pronoun *he*:

> A weasel is wild. Who knows what **he** thinks? **He** sleeps in his underground den, his tail draped over his nose. Sometimes **he** lives in his den for two days without leaving. Outside, **he** stalks rabbits, mice, muskrats, and birds, killing more bodies than **he** can eat warm, and often dragging the carcasses home.

The pattern of known and new information in this passage, which is fairly common in descriptive writing, has a different schema from the earlier paragraph discussed. The earlier one, where the new information in one sentence becomes the known information of the next, might be diagrammed in this way:

A—B, B—C, C—D

In the weasel paragraph, where succeeding sentences repeated the subject, the schema would look like this:

A—B, A—C, A—D

Cohesion can also be enhanced by the information in an opening adverbial slot. For example, the opening of the fifth sentence in the weasel passage, *Outside*, provides a cohesive tie by contrasting with the "inside" designation *in his den* of sentence four. In narrative writing, adverbials of place or time often serve as the glue that connects sentences and paragraphs.

How can the known-new principle of cohesion help you as a writer? Are you supposed to stop after every sentence and estimate the cohesive power of your next subject? No, of course not. That's not the way writers work. But when you are revising—and by the way, revision goes on all the time, even during the first draft—you will want to keep in mind the issues of the known-new contract and reader expectation. You can learn to put yourself in your reader's shoes to see if you've kept your part of the bargain.

Sentence Rhythm

One of the most distinctive features of any language—and one of the most automatic for the native speaker—is its sense of rhythm. Our language has a rhythm just as surely as music does—a regular beat. That sense of rhythm is tied up with the sentence patterns and with the known-new contract. If you read the opening sentence in this paragraph out loud, you'll hear yourself saying "one of the most" in almost a monotone; you probably don't hear a stressed syllable, a beat, until you get to *distinctive*:

one of the most disTINCtive

And you probably rush through those first four words so fast that you pronounce "of" without the *f* making "one of" sound like the first two words in "won a prize."

The rhythm of sentences, what we call the **intonation** pattern, can be described as valleys and peaks, where the loudest syllables, those with stress, are represented by peaks:

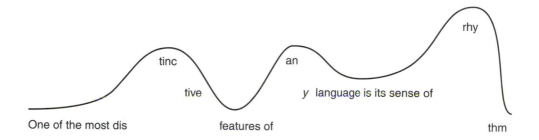

Not all the peaks are of the same height—we have different degrees of stress—but they do tend to come at fairly regular intervals. As listeners we pay attention to the peaks—that's where we'll hear the information that the speaker is focusing on. As speakers, we manipulate the peaks and valleys to coincide with our message, reserving the loudest stress, the highest peak, for the new information, which will be our main point of focus.

End Focus. The rhythm of a sentence is closely tied both to its two-part subject-predicate structure and to the known-new contract. The topic, or theme, stated in the subject will usually be a valley or low peak in the intonation contour, especially if it is known information; the prominent peak of stress, the focus on the new information, will come in the predicate; it will be close to the end of the sentence. Linguists describe this common rhythm pattern as **end focus**. It is a rhythm that experienced writers are sensitive to. Good writers, you can be sure, are tuned in to the rhythm of their own inner voice as they write; they understand how to manipulate sentences in order to control the way the reader reads them and to prevent misreading.

Read the following passage aloud and listen to the intonation pattern you give to the underlined sentence:

> Did you hear what happened? <u>Barbara wrecked her motorcycle yesterday.</u> She was on her way to work when the car in front of her stopped suddenly—and she didn't.

You probably read that second sentence with the stress on *motor*. In a different context, however, the rhythm could change if the purpose of the sentence has changed. In the following passage, the known information has changed. Again, read it aloud and listen to the intonation:

> Sue told me that Barbara had an accident this morning on her way to work. But I think she got her facts wrong. <u>Barbara wrecked her motorcycle yesterday.</u>

This time you probably put the main stress on *yesterday*; in this context it would make no sense to stress *motorcycle*. Try reading the passage that way, and you'll easily recognize the problem: All the information in the last sentence up to the word *yesterday* is already known. In this context it is old information: "Barbara wrecked her motorcycle" is a repetition, albeit more specific, of "Barbara had an accident." As a reader, you know intuitively that it's not time to apply stress until you get beyond that old information, until you get to *yesterday*, the new focus.

You'll note, however, that the principle of end focus is still operating, with the main stress on the last sentence element. But imagine how awkward the sentence would be if the adverb *yesterday* were shifted to the beginning of the sentence. It would certainly be grammatical from a structural point of view; as you know, adverbials are movable, especially adverbials of time. Even in opening position the reader might recognize *yesterday* as the new information and give it main stress. But the sentence would certainly have lost its natural rhythm. Read the passage aloud, and you'll hear the problem:

> Sue told me that Barbara had an accident this morning on her way to work. But I think she got her facts wrong. Yesterday Barbara wrecked her motorcycle.

While sentence variety is certainly commendable, you won't want to shift an adverbial to the opening slot just for the sake of variety—certainly not if that adverbial is the new information.

Sentence Transformations

Because end focus is such a common rhythm pattern, we can think of it as a part of the contract between writer and reader. The reader expects the main sentence focus to be in the predicate unless given a signal to the contrary. And we do have several such signals at our disposal.

Several sentence transformations allow the writer to shift the focus of the sentence, pointing the reader to a particular slot. The *it*-cleft transformation is one of the most versatile. Here are three variations of the sentence about Barbara, each of which guarantees that the reader will put the emphasis exactly where the writer intends for it to be:

1. It was Barbara who wrecked her motorcycle yesterday.
2. It was her motorcycle that Barbara wrecked yesterday.
3. It was yesterday that Barbara wrecked her motorcycle.

If sentence 3 had been included in that earlier passage about the accident, it would have been impossible for the reader to miss the new information; in the cleft transformation the emphasis is clearly on *yesterday*.

The *it*-cleft is not a structure you will want to overuse, but it certainly is useful—and almost foolproof—when it comes to controlling the rhythm of a sentence and directing the reader's focus.

Another cleft transformation uses a *what* clause to direct the reader's attention. In the following sentence you will probably put the emphasis on *bothers*:

> Mike's cynical attitude toward the customers really bothers me.

Here are two variations using the *what*-cleft:

> What bothers me is Mike's cynical attitude toward the customers.
> What bothers me about Mike is his cynical attitude toward the customers.

While all three versions mean essentially the same thing, the choice in a particular context will be determined in part by what the reader already knows—and consequently expects.

Another common sentence variation is the *there* transformation, which allows the writer to focus on the subject by shifting it to the slot following *be*—either the predicating *be* or the auxiliary *be*.

> Several hundred people were crowding the courtroom.
> There were *several hundred people* crowding the courtroom.
>
> Another big crowd was in the hallway.
> There was *another big crowd* in the hallway.

Do writers consciously call up such rhythm controlling devices from their grammar tool kits as they write? Do they tell themselves, "Time to use my trusty *it*-cleft, or should I delay this subject with the *there* transformation?" No, they probably don't. They may not even know labels like "transformation" and "cleft." But as experienced writers and readers, they're tuned in to sentence rhythm as they compose—especially as they revise. And you can be sure that in reading their own prose, whether silently or aloud, they are paying attention to sentence rhythm.

Unfortunately, the *there* and the cleft transformations are often misunderstood in handbooks and style manuals: They are seen as wordy, indirect ways of conveying ideas rather than as alternatives that give the writer a choice, that enable the writer to control the sentence focus. It's true, of course, that you won't want to overuse these transformations. You will want to consider the larger context, to pay attention to how many other *it* or *what* or *there* sentences occur in proximity. But certainly these kinds of sentence manipulations are valuable tools for the right occasion.

The Passive Voice. Another transformation to achieve end focus is the passive voice made by adding *be + -en* to the verb and shifting the object to subject position. Here's an example:

> Active: *The committee discussed the report.*
>
> Passive: *The report was discussed by the committee.*

It's certainly possible that everything you've read in other books or heard from teachers about the passive voice has been negative—admonitions to avoid it because of wordiness or vagueness. In fact, however, the passive voice has a legitimate role to play in every kind of writing.

As with cleft sentences and the *there* transformation, the passive voice enables the writer to shift emphasis in the sentence, so that the reader will put the focus where it should be—on the new information. That passive shift can also provide transition between sentences. When the object of the action is the known information, the passive transformation can shift that information to the subject slot, where we generally find it.

In the earlier discussion of cohesion we looked at the pattern of known and new information in the paragraph about sentence slots. The subject of the third (and last) sentence includes the word *glue*, the known information from the previous sentence:

> Part of that glue is provided by information in the sentence that the reader knows or expects, information that has already been mentioned.

Part of that glue functions as the subject—but it's not the agent. We put the agent, the "doer" of the verb provided, in end-focus position because it is the new information. We used the passive transformation to do so.

The passive voice certainly has a place in every kind of prose. To avoid it simply for the sake of avoiding it often results in a stilted, unnatural voice. The choices we make when we write should always be made on the basis of rhetorical effectiveness, not on the misguided notion that certain structures are inherently weak or wordy or vague. When we read in our handbooks,

> The passive voice should be avoided,

we should celebrate the fact that the authors have found a way to put their most important word, *avoided*, in the position of end-focus and have used an efficient tool for doing so: the passive voice.

Style
Everything we write, we write "with style," in one sense of the word—when the word refers simply to an individual's way of writing. You have your own style of writing, just as you have your own style of walking and whistling and wearing your hair. We also use the word *style* to characterize the overall impression of a piece of writing, such as the plain style, the pompous style, the official style.

The word *style* is also used in connection with variations in sentence structure, with the structural and punctuation choices that you as a writer can use to your advantage. For example, in the second sentence of the previous paragraph, three verb phrases in a series are connected with two *ands* and no commas:

> walking and whistling and wearing your hair
>
> It could have been written with two commas and only one *and*:
>
> walking, whistling, and wearing your hair
>
> Or only commas
>
> walking, whistling, wearing your hair

Such stylistic variations have traditionally occupied an important place in the study of rhetoric. In fact, the Greeks had names for every deviation from ordinary word order and usage, and Greek orators practiced using them. Some of the more common ones you're familiar with, such "figures of speech" as simile, metaphor, and personification. But many of them, you probably don't even notice—such as the shift, in both this sentence and the previous one, of the direct object to opening position. In this section we will examine the rhetorical effects that these and other variations in sentence structure and punctuation can have.

Word Order Variation. Variation from the standard subject-verb-object word order is fairly common in poetry; it can be effective in prose as well, partly because it is uncommon. In the following sentence, Charles Dickens made sure that the reader would hear the contrast between *has* and *has not*:

> Talent, Mr. Micawber has; money, Mr. Micawber has not.

Robert Frost used this variation, too, in the first line of his famous poem "Stopping by Woods on a Snowy Evening":

> Whose woods these are, I think I know.

Notice that all these variations put special emphasis on the verb, the slot that would normally be in a valley when the sentence has a direct object.

With certain adverbs in opening position, the subject and the auxiliary can be reversed:

> Never before had I seen such an eerie glow in the night sky.
> Rarely do I hear such words of praise.

The Introductory Appositive Series. In the following passages, the sentence opens with a series of noun phrases that act as appositives to the subject. In the first example, Churchill describes Queen Victoria:

> High devotion to her royal task, domestic virtues, evident sincerity of nature, a piercing and sometime disconcerting truthfulness—all these qualities of the Queen's had long impressed themselves upon the mind of her subjects.
>
> Ravagers, despoilers, pagans, heathens—such epithets pretty well summed up the Vikings for those who lived in the British Isles during medieval times.

Notice, too, in these examples that the series does not include a conjunction before the last member.

The Deliberate Sentence Fragment. The sentence fragments that composition teachers flag with a marginal "frag" are the unintentional kind, usually the result of punctuation errors, the most common being the subordinate clause punctuated as a full sentence. But not all fragments are errors. Experienced writers know how to use them effectively—noun phrases or verb phrases that invariably call attention to themselves. The first two examples are from novels of John le Carré:

> They remembered the tinkling of falling glass all right, and the timid brushing noise of the young foliage hitting the road. *And the mewing of people too frightened to scream.*
>
> *The Little Drummer Girl*

> Our Candidate begins speaking. *A deliberate, unimpressive opening.*
>
> *A Perfect Spy*

Repetition. Repetition has both a positive and a negative sense. On the positive side, repetition gives our sentences cohesion: The known-new contract calls for the repetition, if not of words, then of ideas. It is part of the glue that holds sentences together. But we also have a negative label for repetition when it has no purpose, when it gets in the reader's way: Then we call it redundancy. If you've heard warnings about redundancy, if you've seen "red" in the margins of your essays, you might hesitate to use repetition deliberately. But don't hesitate. It's easy to distinguish redundancy from good repetition, from repetition as a stylistic tool.

The Greek rhetoricians had labels for every conceivable kind of good repetition—from the repetition of sounds and syllables to that of words and phrases in various locations in the sentence. We'll confine our discussion to repetition in coordinate structures that will make the reader sit up and take notice.

Consider the Gettysburg Address. Which of Lincoln's words, other than "Fourscore and seven years ago," do you remember? Probably "government of the people, by the people, and for the people." It's hard to imagine those words without the repetition: "Of, by, and for the people" just wouldn't have the same effect. And think about President Kennedy's stirring words, with his repetition of *any*:

> [W]e shall pay any price, bear any burden, meet any hardship, support any friend, oppose any foe to assure the survival and the success of liberty.

Notice, too, that the conjunction has been omitted before the last member of the series. He seems to be saying, "I could go on and on with my list."

You don't have to be a president to use that kind of repetition, nor do you have to reserve it for formal occasions. Whenever you use a coordinate structure, there's an opportunity for you to add to its impact with repetition, simply by including words that wouldn't have to be included. The following sentence, from an essay in *Time* by Charles Krauthammer, could have been more concise, but it would have lost its drama:

> There is not a single Western standard, there are two: what we demand of Western countries at peace and what we demand of Western countries at war.

These uses of repetition, as well as the other stylistic devices we have taken up in this chapter, will invariably call attention to themselves. For that reason, you will reserve these structures for important ideas, for those times when you want your reader to sit up and take notice. But, like the gourmet cook who knows that too many spices can overwhelm a dish, you won't want to overwhelm your reader. But you will want to recognize that, like the spice that turns a bland sauce into fine cuisine, these stylistic tools can make the difference between ordinary and powerful prose.

Questions for Discussion

1. According to Kolln and Funk, why should students study rhetorical grammar? In what ways are their ideas compatible with those of Weaver, McNally, and Moerman? What can teachers do to help student writers develop their sense of rhetorical judgment?

2. To test the claims of Kellogg Hunt, read the pieces written by fourth graders (Jasmine [p. 217], Alexsandra and Edgar [p. 218]) and the pieces written by tenth graders (The In-Class Essays [pp. 219–222]). What structures appear in the writing of the older students that don't appear in the younger students' essays? How does your analysis compare to Hunt's?

3. To test the claim of Francis Christensen that the cumulative sentence is the typical sentence of the late twentieth/early twenty-first century, examine some of your favorite passages by your favorite authors writing today. How often do these writers use cumulative sentences? What (other) kinds of sentences are (also) typical? Based on the passages you've chosen, what kind of sentences reflect current tastes?

4. Return to the textbooks and state curriculum guidelines you examined in Chapter 2. To what extent do they deal with style? How do they treat it? If your state has mandated assessments to measure educational progress, is knowledge of style assessed? If so, how?

5. Writers can take advantage of the known-new contract by transforming sentences to create end focus and by working for a pleasing balance of given and new information.
   a. Reread the essay by Adam (p. 224), paying particular attention to the way he tells the story of Trent's tattooing a dragon on the inside of his lip in paragraph 3. Does he make the most effective use of end focus in sentence 2? Why/why not? Is the cleft construction in sentence 3 effective? Why/why not? What advice would you give Adam about editing his sentences to make them easier to read?
   b. Reread Amy's paper (p. 226), paying particular attention to her description of the date rape drug rohypnol in the second half of paragraph 2. Does she have a pleasing balance between given and new information? Why/why not? What advice would you give Amy about editing her sentences?
   c. Read Mario's introduction to his literary analysis (p. 228). Does he effectively use passive voice and cleft sentence transformation in his opening sentence? Why/why not? What advice would you give to Mario about his introduction?

6. Read the kitchen descriptions by Alexsandra and Edgar (pp. 217–218).
   a. Imagine that Alexsandra is your student. What comments will you give her—either in conference or in writing—about her description? What do you think is strong about her paper? What advice would you give her about its content, organization, and tone?

   b. Imagine that Edgar is your student. What comments will you give him—either in conference or in writing—about his description? What do you think is strong about his paper? What advice would you give him about its content, organization, and tone?

   c. According to Kolln and Funk, there are several strategies writers can use to make their sentences cohesive. One strategy is to repeat a phrase. These parallel phrases create a pattern in the reader's mind. What do you notice about the way the writers tie the paragraphs of their description together? Does this strategy "work"? Why/why not?

7. Read the essay by N. Finklberry (p. 220–221).

   a. Imagine that N. Finklberry is your student. What comments will you give her—either in conference or in writing—to encourage her to revise her in-class essay? What do you think is strong about her essay? What advice will you give her about its content, organization, and tone?

   b. There are a number of fragments in the essay. Kolln and Funk discuss the deliberative sentence fragment, suggesting that fragments can be effective. Are these fragments effective? Do they "work"? Why/why not? In conferencing with the author, would you call attention to them? Why/why not? If so, what would you say about them?

Part IV

Working with Language Minority Writers

In the first three sections of the book, I described the students who make up the heart of English language arts classrooms only in general terms because the issues of grammar teaching I discussed were important for all students. In this section, however, I describe in detail the language backgrounds of linguistic minority students, those students whose home languages aren't Standard English *and who struggle in school as a result.* These students are native speakers of vernacular varieties of English or of other languages. But they're expected to use academic English in school with the same degree of facility as any native speaker of Standard English. Most vernacular-English speaking and bilingual students are equally comfortable in their home and school languages. But many others aren't. They struggle in school in part because the gap between the expectations and conventions of their home languages and those of school language are too wide to bridge without specific instruction.

The two chapters in this section focus on techniques mainstream English language arts teachers can use to help linguistic minority students bridge that gap. They address the following questions:

- Who are vernacular English speakers? English Language Learners (ELLs)?
- What is the process of learning a second dialect? a second language?
- What approaches can teachers use to specifically instruct linguistic minority students about the conventions of academic English?

9

Working with Language Minority Students— Vernacular English Speakers

Chapter 6 argues that in order to succeed in school, every child, regardless of social or linguistic background, has to learn academic English: that is, they have to develop an equal comfort with casual language *and* formal language, with the oral medium *and* the written medium, with the conventions of their home discourse *and* the conventions of school discourse.

Language Minority Students

Some students, however, have an easier time developing this comfort than others do. Students, regardless of background, who read a lot develop this comfort most easily, because they unconsciously absorb the vocabulary, rhythms, and conventions of written language as they read. For the most part, texts are written in Standard English, so readers absorb the grammatical features of Standard English as well as features unique to writing, such as spelling and punctuation. Moreover, texts read in school contexts, such as social studies and science textbooks, help students learn the style and conventions of academic English. This is why Constance Weaver (1996) recommends students do a lot of reading.

Even among those who don't read much, some students will feel more comfortable with written academic English than others. Students whose home language is Standard English are likely to have a relatively easy transition because their home language forms the basis of academic discourse. So it's students whose home languages aren't Standard English—that is, students who speak another dialect of English or who speak another language—who are most likely to struggle in school. These students are often called language minority students (Baugh, 1998; Hagemann, 2001).

Hagemann (2001) points out that language minority students may be monolingual speakers of vernacular dialects of English, such as African American Vernacular English (AAVE) or Chicano Vernacular English (CVE). Or they may be bilingual students who speak these dialects in addition to another language. However, you should note that not all students who belong to an ethnic or racial minority fall under the umbrella of *linguistic minority student. Only* those students who struggle in school as a result of their home language fall into this category.

Linguistic Sensitivity in the Classroom

In the past, teachers made little effort to understand linguistic minority students and to develop ways to help them learn academic English more successfully.

Unfortunately, for many students, some teachers still do. As Sharroky Hollie (2001) points out:

> Still, many [linguistic] minority students will walk into classrooms and be discreetly taught in most cases, and explicitly told in others, that the language of their forefathers, their families, and their communities is bad language, street language, the speech of the ignorant and/or uneducated. (p. 54)

In actuality, these dialects aren't ignorant or uneducated—they're perfectly logical and expressive in their own ways. However, it's common for people to automatically assume that when the grammar of a dialect is DIFFERENT from the standard, it's DEFICIENT. This is the same prejudice revealed in Maxine Hairston's (1981) attitudinal survey of errors (See Chapter 5). Hairston asked professionals to rate various sentences to determine how much the "errors" in the sentences would cause the study participants to lower their perception of the writers. All of the errors she deemed most serious—that is, the errors that were most likely to exact a social tax—are features of vernacular dialects of English. These features include non-standard verb forms (*I seen*), subject-verb disagreement (*Jones don't think it's acceptable*), using object pronouns as subjects (*Me and him were the last to leave*) and double negatives. Many of these features have a historical precedence in earlier forms of English. Thus, the "error" isn't in the forms themselves but in violating reader expectations, in using vernacular forms when standard forms are expected. Knowing pragmatics and knowing the history of English then leads to a greater understanding—and it's hoped, a greater tolerance—of the various dialects of English, which is one of the goals of Andrews' (1998) Language Exploration and Awareness curriculum (See Chapter 3).

Fortunately, more and more teachers—if not necessarily the general public—are becoming sensitive to their students' home languages and are searching for ways to help linguistic minority students. They've been inspired by the

Students' Right to Their Own Language (SRTOL) resolution adopted in April 1974 by members of the Conference on College Composition and Communication (CCCC) and later by the entire NCTE. The resolution states the following:

> We affirm the students' right to their own patterns and varieties of language—the dialects of their nurture or whatever dialects in which they find their own identity and style. Language scholars long ago denied that the myth of a standard American dialect has any validity. The claim that any one dialect is unacceptable amounts to an attempt of one social group to exert its dominance over another. Such a claim leads to false advice for speakers and writers, and immoral advice for humans. A nation proud of its diverse heritage and its cultural and racial variety will preserve its heritage of dialects. We affirm strongly that teachers must have the experiences and training that will enable them to respect diversity and uphold the right of students to their own language.

The resolution holds two essential principles: (1) that teachers should learn as much as they can about the home languages of their students, and (2) that teachers should respect and value the home languages of their students.

This emphasis on teacher training and linguistic tolerance is also part of the CCCC Statement on Ebonics, adopted by the CCCC Executive Committee in 1998 in response to the Oakland, California, Ebonics Debate, which erupted in December 1996. At that time, the Oakland School Board issued what came to be called "The Oakland Ebonics Resolution." The essential purpose of the resolution was to encourage schools in the district to recognize the legitimacy of African American Vernacular English (AAVE, as linguists prefer to call it) or Ebonics (as the general public typically refers to it) as the home language of many of their students; to adopt second language pedagogical strategies and programs in working with AAVE-speaking students; and to commit school district funds to improving the school success of its African American students (Oakland, CA, Board of Education, 1996/1998; Olszewski, 1996). The goal was to help raise the reading scores of African American children, which lagged behind the scores of other children. The general public misunderstood the resolution, thinking that it called for teachers to teach Ebonics, and it reacted loudly and negatively, arguing that teachers in Oakland, California, shouldn't teach African American children Ebonics because it was "slang" or "street talk."

In response, professional organizations, such as the Linguistics Society of America (1997) issued official statements affirming the legitimacy of AAVE as a systematic and rule-governed dialect of English and denouncing the negative— sometimes vitriolic—public characterizations of AAVE as "incorrect and demeaning." The CCCC (1998) went on to advocate that teachers and other school and curriculum officials:

> undergo training to provide them with adequate knowledge about Ebonics and help them overcome the prevailing stereotypes about the language and learning potential of African American students and others who speak Ebonics. Teachers

in particular must be equipped with the fundamental training and knowledge that will enable them to be effective in teaching language and literacy skills to Ebonics speakers.

This means that teachers need to become more familiar with the features of vernacular dialects of English. A brief list of the most common features can be found in Figure 9.1.

FIGURE 9.1   *Theoretical Foundation: A Brief Inventory of Grammatical Features of Vernacular Dialects of English*

This list of some of the most common grammatical features of vernacular dialects of English was adapted from Wolfram and Schilling-Estes (1998) and Rickford (1999).

Irregular Verbs
1. past (*-ed*) as participle (*-en*) form
2. participle (*-en*) as past (*-ed*) form
3. base form as past (*-ed*) form
4. different irregular form
5. regularized past of irregular verb

I *had went* there as a kid.
I *seen* her yesterday.
She *come* over to visit.
He *drug* in mud all over the house.
Everybody *knowed* he did it.

Notes: 1, 2, 3, and 4 are common in many varieties of English. 5 is more common in second-language-influenced varieties (e.g., Vietnamese English).

Special Auxiliary Verb Forms
1. habitual *be*
2. remote time *béen* (stressed, pronounced BIN)
3. absence of *is/are* (where SE can contract *is/are*)

My nose *be itching* all day.
I *been known* her all my life.
You ugly.

Notes: Found in African American English (AAVE) varieties.

Past Tense Absence
1. as a result of consonant cluster reduction
2. when context clearly indicates past tense
3. when describing habitual action in the past

Yesterday he *mess* up.
He *play* a new song *last night* that I like.
In those days, we *play* a different kind of game.

Notes: Found in African American, Vietnamese, and Native American varieties of English.

Subject-Verb Agreement
1. *-s* absence on third person singular present tense main verbs
2. *-s* absence on third person singular present auxiliary verbs

She like to sit on the porch and drink iced tea.
She don't like to stay indoors.

FIGURE 9.1   *Continued*

3. present tense forms of *be* become *is*   *We is* keeping cool in spite of the heat.
4. past tense forms of *be* become *was*   The *dogs* was behind the house.
5. past tense negative forms of *be* become *were*   *She weren't* at the dance last night.
6. *is/was* with *there*   There *was* only five people there.
     There's two men here to see you.

Notes: 1 is most common in AAVE. 2 and 4 are found in all varieties of English. 6 is found in all varieties, and some linguists say it's becoming standard.

Negation

1. multiple negation—subject and auxiliary verb   *Nobody don't* know what's going on.
2. multiple negation—auxiliary verb and object pronouns   The police *wasn't* saying *nothing*.
3. multiple negation—across clause boundaries   There *wasn't* much that I *couldn't* do. (meaning "There wasn't much I could do.")
4. use of *ain't* for *be* + *not*, *have* + *not* or *did* + *not*   She *ain't* here now.
     I *ain't* seen her in a long time.
     I *ain't* go to school yesterday.

Notes: 1 is common to all varieties of English. 2 is mainly AAVE. 3 is common across all varieties of English, though substituting ain't *for* do + not *is found only in AAVE.*

Plurals

1. absence of plural suffix (*-s*), esp. when plural is obvious from context   All the *girl* went shopping.
2. regularized forms of irregular plurals   The *childrens* ate the ice cream.

Notes: 1 is more common in second-language-influenced varieties (e.g., Vietnamese English), and to a lesser extent, AAVE. 2 is common in many varieties of English.

Possessives

1. absence of the possessive suffix, esp. when ownership is clear from context   *John coat.*

Notes: Common in AAVE.

Pronouns

1. use of plural form of *you*   *y'all* (southern), *youse* (northern), *you'uns* (Appalachian)
2. use of object forms in coordinating subjects   *Me and him* love to play football.
3. use of object forms as demonstratives   *Them* tools you're looking for are in the garage.

(continued)

FIGURE 9.1   *Continued*

4. use of *that* in relative clauses modifying a person	The *person that* I was telling you about is here.
5. use of *it is* for *there is/are*	*It's* a dog in the yard.
6. use of *which* as a coordinating conjunction	They gave me this cigar, *which* they know I don't smoke cigars.

Notes: 1, 2, 3, 4, and 5 are common in all varieties of English. 6 is common in the south, AAVE and spreading to other varieties.

Adjectives/Adverbs

1. use of *-er* or *-est* suffix on multisyllable adjectives	*beautifulest, awfulest*
2. regularized forms of irregular adverb	*badder, mostest*
3. absence of *-ly* suffix on adverbs	She's *real* nice. She's *awful* mean.

Notes: 1 and 2 are common to all varieties. In the case of many adverbs, 3 is becoming standard.

The principles emphasized in the SRTOL (NCTE, 1974) and Ebonics (CCCC, 1998) Resolutions—namely, "build[ing] teachers' knowledge, understanding, and positive attitude toward nonstandard languages and the students who use them"—also forms the first goal of the Linguistic Awareness Program (LAP) in Los Angeles (Hollie, 2001, p. 54). LAP is a "comprehensive nonstandard language awareness program designed to serve the language needs of African American, Mexican American, Hawaiian American, and Native American students who are not proficient in Standard American English" (Hollie, 2001, p. 54). The LAP has five other key instructional approaches:

1. Integrate linguistic knowledge about nonstandard language into instruction.
2. Utilize second language acquisition methodologies to support the acquisition of school language and literacy.
3. Employ a balanced approach to literacy acquisition that incorporates phonics and language experience.
4. Design instruction around the learning styles and strengths of Standard English Language Learners [students learning Standard English as another dialect].
5. Infuse the history and culture of Standard English language learners into the instructional curriculum. (54–55)

LAP's Approaches 1 and 5 here seem to be compatible with Andrews' (1998) Language Exploration and Awareness curriculum. Both advocate teaching students about the history of English and about how and why dialects come into being as a way to increase linguistic tolerance and to motivate students to learn Standard English as the Language of Wider Communication. LAP's Approach 5 is also compatible with NCTE's 1986 Task Force on Racism and Bias in the Teaching of English. In its official statement, entitled *Expanding Opportunities: Academic Success for Culturally and Linguistically Diverse Students*, the task force called for teachers of writing to, among other strategies, "incorporate the rich backgrounds of linguistically and culturally diverse students" and to "provide a nurturing environment for writing."

Contrastive Analysis

Hollie (2001) doesn't say specifically which second language acquisition methodologies LAP uses in response to Approach 2, but one such methodology is Contrastive Analysis, or the systematic study of the differences of two languages. Contrastive analysis came from the marriage of linguistics and behaviorism in the 1950s (Danesi & Di Pietro, 1991). Key to this theory is the hypothesis that adolescents and adults use their native language as a kind of filter through which they learn the linguistic rules of their second language, especially in the early stages of the process. They transfer patterns from their native language to the new language, sometimes consciously, but more often unconsciously. When aspects of the two languages are similar, this interlinguistic connection has a positive effect on learning (which contrastive analysts call *transfer*); when aspects are different, this connection tends to have a negative effect (called *interference*). Contrastive analysis proponents originally thought that they could systematically contrast any two languages, determine ahead of time where native speakers of a given language would have trouble learning a given second language, and then design curricula to especially address these troublespots. These initial hopes for an *a priori predictive* tool did not pan out because students didn't always make the errors that were predicted. However, as Danesi and Di Pietro note, contrastive analysis nevertheless remains a valuable *a posteriori explanatory* tool. That is, teachers cannot always predict with 100 percent accuracy where students will make errors, but once students have made one, teachers can determine if it was possibly caused by interference from their first language. (See Chapter 10 for a discussion of the kinds of errors English Language Learners make.)

Contrastive analysis can also serve as an organizing framework for developing curriculum. It's a useful approach for introducing or reviewing concepts in the new language—i.e., academic English—by explicitly contrasting them to what students already know—i.e. their home language(s). This technique is based on the premise that students' use of a second language is governed by rules that they're working to sort out—whether they can articulate these rules or not. If we help students become aware of their rules, we can help them identify the ones that transfer successfully to Standard Academic English and revise the ones that don't. To me, the advantages of this kind of approach are intuitively obvious: it simply makes a lot of pedagogical sense to begin with what students know and to help them move toward what they don't know or haven't had the opportunity to practice much.

There are, however, empirical studies that prove this as well (Siegel, 1999). Siegel (1999) reported on his review of almost two dozen studies from around the world which compared students in a traditional grammar program with students in a program whose teachers respected the home languages of their students, allowed students to use their home languages, and overtly compared elements of their home dialects with the standard. In each study, the experimental students did as well as or better than the control students did on standardized reading and writing tests.

One program similar to the studies Siegel (1999) describes is the Standard English Proficiency (SEP) program (Miner, 1998). Endorsed by the State of California, this program acknowledges the systematic and rule-governed nature of AAVE while helping students learn Standard English. The basic premise of the SEP program is that teachers are teaching Standard English as an additional dialect, not "fixing" the home language students brought with them to school.

According to Carrie Secret, a fifth-grade teacher who teaches in an SEP program in Oakland, California, the ultimate goal is to help students learn standard English, but to use students' home language(s) to do that (as reported in Miner, 1998). Secret uses the metaphor of translation to help her students realize that they have transferred first language structures—in the case of Secret's students, AAVE structures—into their second, Standard Written English. Secret says:

> When writing, the students are aware that finished pieces are written in [Standard] English. The use of Ebonic structures appears in many of their first drafts. When this happens I simple say, 'You used Ebonics here. I need you to translate this thought into [Standard] English.' This kind of statement does not negate the child's thought or language.
>
> Before I [started teaching using the SEP program approach], my approach was different. I used the 'fix-something-that-was-wrong' approach. I was always calling for the children to say something correct or to fix something to make it right. I now approach the same task from a different perspective that has a more positive effect on my children. (As reported in Miner, 1998, p. 81.)

Another program based on contrastive analysis is the "School Talk/Friend Talk" curriculum developed by Mary I. Berger of The Speak Standard, Too Institute in Chicago. Berger designed a series of 95 scripted lessons that contrast features of Standard English with various vernacular dialects of English and with other languages. Berger urges her students to not give up their native dialect(s), but to take on Standard English as an additional form of communication. She urges them to use appropriate talk among friends, but also to switch to use appropriate talk in school or the workplace too (Nicklin, 1994). A brief description of the School Talk/Friend Talk curriculum can be found in Figure 9.2.

The comparative approach that Berger and Secret use also works well with literature. For example, Terry Meier (1998) explains how the children's story

FIGURE 9.2 *Spotlight on Curriculum: School Talk/Friend Talk*

Author(s):	Mary I. Berger
Author's(s') Credentials:	Speech Pathologist, College Instructor, Teacher-Trainer
Published By:	Orchard Books, Inc.
Available:	2222 North Orchard Street
	Chicago, IL 60614-5244
	1-800-528-5244

The *Teach Standard, Too* teacher's manual includes the *School Talk/Friend Talk* course and the student writing journal, *Write Standard, Too.*

School Talk/Friend Talk

The *"School Talk/Friend Talk"* course is comprised of 95 scripted lessons that emphasize how and when the pronunciation and/or grammar of Standard English (School Talk) differs from various vernacular dialects of English (Friend Talk). The goal of the course is to consciously contrast equivalent features in standard and nonstandard styles so that students can begin to hear the differences, to practice School Talk, and to learn to switch from one to the other when the occasion demands. Working to combat the discrimination some students face because of their home dialect, the course teaches students that their dialects are merely DIFFERENT from Standard English, and NOT DEFICIENT versions of it.

Each lesson begins with a linguistic explanation of the difference under study intended for the teacher. It also includes an opening story the teacher can read to elicit contrasting sentences from students. After discussing the difference(s) they hear and see in their sentences, students practice the equivalent School Talk and Friend Talk features and learn to identify each.

This example comes from a unit on *be* verbs:

Friend Talk	School Talk
She pretty.	She is/'s pretty.
She nice.	She is/'s nice.
He funny.	He is/'s funny.

After an opening story in which two students describe their teacher, students discuss the difference in these sentences (i.e., the presence or absence of the *be*-verb), which sentences represent School Talk and which represent Friend Talk, and when it's advantageous to use either. Then, students are asked to generate sentences describing their friends. These sentences are analyzed the same way. Students practice "translating" sentences from one "talk" to the other. Finally, they end up with a drill in which they listen to the teacher pronounce some sentences and identify whether they used Friend Talk or School Talk. Question-answer and other oral drills follow.

Although the exercises were originally written for younger children, appendices in the teacher's manual show how the lessons can be adapted for adolescent and adult students.

Description based on promotional materials from Orchard Books, Inc. Used with permission.

Flossie and the Fox by Patricia McKissack can be used effectively to develop elementary students' metalinguistic awareness. The book, set in the rural south probably in the early 1900s, tells the story of a young girl named Flossie who uses language to outwit a fox blocking her path. The fox speaks Standard English, but Flossie, her grandmother and the narrator of the story use a rural southern dialect. Meier offers a number of language and writing activities that encourage students to become more aware of the different conventions of these two dialects:

- *Rewrite the story from the fox's point of view.* This exercise not only requires students to re-see events in the story from another point of view, it also requires them to "translate" narration and dialogue from one dialect to another. In order to translate accurately, students have to know the conventions of Standard English.
- *Comment on Flossie's use of language.* How did she outwit the fox? What grammatical, rhetorical, and stylistic features did she use to achieve her purpose? This exercise draws students' attention not only to the strategies one might use to defend one's self, refute arguments, persuade, etc., but also to how those strategies are encoded in language.
- *Focus on word endings.* This exercise asks students to compare word endings (i.e., Flossie's *chile* to Fox's *child*, Flossie's *heap o' words* to Fox's *top of the morning*) in order to better understand the differences in pronunciation between the two dialects. Students also take turns playing various roles in the story so they practice the pronunciation of both dialects.

These activities help students understand the content of the story more thoroughly while they attend to the language of the characters, and by extension, their own language.

Because Meier (1998) works with inner city African American students, her goal is to help them feel comfort speaking not only AAVE but also what she calls Standard Black English, a variety of English that follows standard grammar but also allows speakers to reflect their ethnic identity. According to Meier, Standard Black English has such ethnic markers as:

characteristic intonational patterns; metaphorical language; concrete examples and analogies to make a point; rhyme, rhythm, alliteration, and other forms of repetition, including word play; use of proverbs, aphorisms, biblical quotations, and learned allusions; colorful and unusual vocabulary; arguing to a main point (rather than from a main point); [and] making a point through indirection. (p. 99)

Martin Luther King was such a speaker.

Other such standard varieties exist as well, though they're not as well defined.

This chapter explores contrastive analysis and other teaching strategies that support language minority students in achieving proficiency in academic English.

Exploring Your Own Language Experience

1. Before you begin the reading, spend five minutes or so writing in your journal about the following:

   In her discussion of language attitudes entitled *Verbal Hygiene*, Deborah Cameron (1995) says that language attitudes are inevitable because they're derived from our natural ability to judge language. As a native speaker, we have (and need) the ability to judge whether language is grammatical, elegant, appropriate to its context, etc. However, this ability to make judgments has important implications when we use it to make judgments about the language of others—when, for example, we make assumptions about a student's intelligence or competence based on how they talk. What kind of language attitudes do you have? How do you react when you hear someone speaking "with an accent" that's different from yours? Does it depend on which dialect they're speaking? On the context? Would you say you're a linguistically tolerant person? Why/why not?

2. Reread Wolfram, Adger, and Christian (See Chapter 6). What teaching strategies do they offer to teachers to support language minority students?

A Bridge from Home to School: Helping Working Class Students Acquire School Literacy

Julie Hagemann

> *This article was published in a March 2001 "And Language for All" theme issue of* English Journal. *In this article, Hagemann first identifies who language minority students are and then describes the process of learning a second dialect. She goes on to describe some ways she uses this process to help language minority students feel more comfortable with academic language.*

It's the middle of the semester in my basic writing class, and I'm getting to know my students and their writing abilities. I'm discovering anew that this class is like many others I've had at my urban Midwestern university: most of the students are working class, many of them language minority students. These are students whose home language is not Standard English and who struggle in school as a result (Baugh). Most of them speak a vernacular variety of English, but some are bilinguals who've had little practice with writing English. They're in my class because they need additional help in preparing to do university work and in mastering Standard English. Not all working class students struggle with Standard English, nor do all language minority students struggle to feel comfortable in school. But my students do. Primary and secondary school wasn't easy for them, but they're willing to try again in college. A new school, a new start. This time they're hoping they'll succeed.

Adam, Tameka, and Bobby are representative of the vernacular speakers of English who are enrolled in college basic writing courses. Adam is a burly student from the rural southern part of Indiana, and he speaks in a way that many people associate with southern accents. He was a football star at his high school, and the ease he felt on the field gave him some respite from the discomfort of the classroom. He had hoped to play football on the main campus, but those dreams were shattered when his SAT scores came back. He didn't score high enough for a scholarship. Now he's at our branch campus, hoping in a few years to transfer. Adam appears uncomfortable in the city and in a college classroom—unless he's talking about his family's love of football. "Me and my brothers all played," he said proudly, "and my dad seen every game. He never missed a one." Adam is especially uncomfortable with the literacy demands of the university. "I don't 'do' textbooks," he says with such finality that our class discussion of critical reading is momentarily brought to a halt. Writing comes hard to him, too.

Across the room from Adam is Tameka, who's from an urban, industrial part of the state. She can write a fine essay in Standard English, if given enough time. She needs to write her ideas first in familiar language and then translate them into Standard English. Her speech has the rhythm, intonation, and features of African American Vernacular English (AAVE), the language, she says, "we speak at home, you know, in our community." She's probably the most sociolinguistically savvy student I've ever taught. She knows that AAVE is a dialect with as much legitimacy as Standard English. She also knows that in school a different kind of English is expected.

Behind her sits Bobby, who speaks Chicano English, a version he learned growing up in a predominantly Hispanic neighborhood. Both of Bobby's parents emigrated from Mexico as teens. The whole family speaks mainly English now, but they maintain their Spanish by communicating with relatives in Mexico. Like Adam and Tameka, Bobby's speech carries the rhythms and intonation of his cultural heritage. Though his accent may share some of the same features as the accent of a Spanish speaker learning English, Bobby is a native speaker of English and has a native speaker's intuitive sense of what's grammatical in his home language. Even so, like Adam, he's not much of a reader and writer—either in English or Spanish. As a result, when he writes formal English, his essays sound very oral, and he pays little attention to punctuation. Bobby is struggling not only in my class, but in others, as well, because he hates to read his textbooks. He does fine in classes in which the tests cover the lecture material, but in classes where the reading material is different from the lecture material, he fails. He forms a study group for each of his classes so he can listen to his group mates talk about the material and learn it orally, but his strategy doesn't work well enough to get him through the academic babel. He's on probation and may have to leave the university at the end of the semester.

Adam, Tameka, and Bobby want to succeed in school, and in order to do so, they must learn Standard English as well as the specific conventions that characterize formal academic writing. *All* students have to work to master the conventions of written academic English, but some have an easier time of it than others. Pérez says that school is an institution "primarily designed for children from middle class English literate homes" (21). For these children, the transition to academic English is relatively easy. Their home language is closer to Standard English and overlaps to a larger extent with academic English. However, for working class, language minority students who typically speak various Englishes that are considered nonstandard, the transition is much more difficult.

The rules of their home discourses don't overlap as much with those of the academic world. As a result, many language minority students struggle with the rules and conventions of speaking and writing "school talk."

What Adam, Tameka, and Bobby need is what all basic writers need: a curriculum that prepares them for the literacy practices of the academy. They need to learn, for example, to be critical readers and writers, to state claims they can support persuasively, to deal with conflicting points of view in texts, and to re-present those ideas in texts to achieve their own purposes. But they also need what middle class students already have: access to formal, written, standard American English, to supplement their home discourses. They need a detailed awareness of how their home discourse is similar to and different from Standard American English and an ability to shift smoothly from their home discourse to academic English whenever they want or need to.

We can help working class, language minority students learn this new discourse by drawing on what we know about sociolinguistics and about adolescents learning an additional language. Research in second language learning suggests that we can facilitate learning if we explicitly present the conventions of academic writing and Standard English in ways that help students sort out the similarities and differences between "school talk" and "home talk." Overtly comparing home discourse and school discourse helps students focus attention on what they already know and what they still need to learn. It values their home languages and uses them as a bridge from home to school.

The Linguistic Background of Working Class Students

Most working class, language minority students are native, monolingual speakers of a vernacular, or nonstandard, dialect of English. These dialects may be regional (such as Appalachian English), ethnic (such as AAVE), or the result of languages that have come into contact with each other (such as Chicano English, Puerto Rican English, Vietnamese English, or Navajo English). The dialects of English are mutually intelligible, but they differ in phonological, lexical, and grammatical features. By far the greatest number of differences are differences in sound—what we commonly think of as accent—and vocabulary. In comparison, there are relatively few differences in grammar, but it's these differences that typically impact student writing the most.

Generally speaking, the vernacular dialects of English such as those spoken by Adam, Tameka, and Bobby are characterized by grammar rules that differ from those standardized in dictionaries, handbooks, and other sources of authority and that, as a result, attract a social "stigma" (Wolfram & Schilling-Estes). Some vernacular features represent variations that are "socially conspicuous" and seldom used by middle class speakers such as multiple negation (*I didn't do nothing*), different subject-verb agreement rules (*Janie talk with her hands alot*), and regularization of irregular verbs (*I knowed he could do it*). Other features such as dropping the final *g* in *ing* verbs (*I went swimmin' today*), represent items that both middle class and working class speakers use, but because the latter use them to a much larger degree, they're stigmatized. Many of these features represent historical divergences—that is, the working class preserved some features, while the middle class adopted new ones, or vice versa.

Another significant difference between vernacular dialects and Standard English is that the former are informal, spoken dialects, while the latter tend to be drawn from formal writing. That's in part why the writing of vernacular dialect speakers tends to sound oral and informal and is often considered inappropriate in the academy.

The best known of the vernacular dialects is AAVE or Ebonics. A thorough discussion of the features of AAVE can be found in John Rickford's *African American*

Vernacular English, while a thorough discussion of dialects in general can be found in Wolfram and Schilling-Estes's *American English*.

The Process of Learning a Second Dialect

We know much more about the processes that students use to learn a second language (i.e., English) than we do about the processes that native vernacular speakers like Adam, Tameka, and Bobby use to learn a second dialect (i.e., Standard English). But as Siegel points out, recent research in psycholinguistics suggests that the processes overlap in fundamental ways. Whether students acquire two languages or two dialects, their success depends on their ability to develop a different mental representation for each system. Most psycholinguists who research second language acquisition agree that fluent bilinguals sort out their two languages into separate linguistic subsystems and store them at least partially in different places in their brain. With separate subsystems, bilinguals can draw on either language whenever they want to.

Imagine that fluent bilingual speakers had in their brains a train station with trains waiting on parallel tracks to take off. An idea is conceived, and one train (say, an English train) leaves the station, rushing past stations for planning and formulating the idea to its destination to articulate it. It could just as easily have been the other train (say, a Spanish one) that left the station, since the tracks are parallel. The context in which the idea is conceived determines which train leaves the station—and in which language the idea will finally be articulated.

Not yet fluent bilinguals, on the other hand, have in their brains a train station with one fully laid set of tracks (their first language [say Spanish], which they already know) and one partially laid set of tracks (their second language [say English], which they're learning). They may conceive an idea and send the Spanish train rushing out of the station, but it'll have to stop at the planning or formulating stations so that passengers can switch to the English train and head for their final stop. This switch takes time, and it's possible that some of the passengers will get lost in the transition. It's also possible that the English tracks have gaps, which derail the train before it gets to its destination. According to Siegel, this language model works as well with speakers of two different varieties of English. This is why, for example, Tameka needs the extra time to write her essays.

Ironically, it may be easier for nonnatives to learn Standard English than it is for natives. For Adam, Tameka, and Bobby, the task of learning Standard English is made harder by the fact that they're already native speakers. For them, the task of sorting and separating the two dialects is much harder because the dialects share so much grammatically. Students may have a general sense that there's a difference between the dialect they speak at home and the one they're expected to use at school, but they may not notice which specific features are different. Moreover, they're less likely to be motivated to make the effort to learn and use Standard English because they can already be understood by English speakers. (Helping working class students acquire Standard English is not a matter of intelligibility but of image-management; we're helping students create a certain status with their academic audience.) Thus, they may not be able to monitor their own language very well for instances of dialect interference.

A Pedagogy of Overt Comparison

Because developing separate subsystems is such an integral part of language learning, a successful language pedagogy helps students separate their target language (i.e., Standard English) from their home language. As Siegel says, in order to learn a particular feature, students first need to *notice*, or *pay attention to*, it. Sometimes this means pointing out features students may not know because they haven't encountered them before. This may be the case with less commonly known rules, such as the distinction between *few* and *less* or *like* and *as*, or with sophisticated punctuation marks, such as semicolons and colons. Sometimes this means raising students' level of awareness of features they already know. They may know that in Standard English their subjects and verbs must agree, but they just can't "see" their mistakes when they proofread their papers.

Second, students need to *compare* this feature with their existing knowledge of English. They're more likely to accept new information and adjust their current thinking when they see how it differs from their prior knowledge. This step requires an increased understanding of the feature in question, an understanding that can be facilitated by overtly comparing how it works in their home language to how it works in Standard English. Adam, for example, found it helpful when we compared irregular Standard English verb patterns (i.e., *go, went, has/have/had gone*) with his own more regularized ones (i.e., *go, went, has/have/had went*). He even found it interesting that English has two ways to form tense in verbs (by changing the stem vowel sound and by adding *ed*). At one time in its history, changing the stem vowel was a common process, but now we generally add *ed* (i.e., *microwaved, faxed, e-mailed*, etc.)

Finally, students need to *integrate* this feature into their growing Standard English subsystem through practice and use. It would seem then that a pedagogical approach that encouraged students to notice, compare, and integrate new features into their linguistic systems would facilitate their language learning.

Perhaps it seems counterintuitive to develop a language curriculum that makes use of what many see as "substandard" dialects to learn Standard English. It certainly did to the general public in the 1996–97 uproar over the Oakland Ebonics decision. The public argued, among other things, that time spent studying students' nonstandard home language(s) was time away from study and drill in Standard English. Moreover, many believed that the study of such language(s) would actually interfere with students' learning of the standard. However, these fears are unfounded, according to Siegel, who reviewed almost two dozen psycholinguistic and educational studies from the US and around the world. Each study compared a control group of students whose teachers taught only the standard dialect with an experimental group whose teachers made use of their home dialects as a medium of instruction or as an object of study or who allowed them to express themselves in either language. In all the studies Siegel reviewed, the experimental group mastered the standard equally well or better than the control group. He concludes:

> All the available studies and reports [I've] described demonstrate various positive results of making use of the students' own varieties of language in education: greater participation rates, higher scores on tests measuring reading and writing skills in standard English, and increases in overall academic achievement. (710)

What makes a pedagogy of overt comparison so effective, Siegel argues, is that students become more aware of the differences between their home dialect and the standard and begin to separate them into two distinct linguistic systems in their brain. It has affective advantages as well. Using home languages in the classroom legitimizes them, and this in turn increases the self-esteem of the students who speak them.

We use this pedagogy of overt comparison often throughout the course of the semester in basic writing to help students learn both the more global features of academic writing and the more sentence-level features of Standard English. Some of these lessons are described below.

Motivating Students to Learn Standard English

Within a few weeks, I could see that all of Adam's papers looked pretty much the same—five paragraphs, usually narrative. He also avoided incorporating sources, even though the assignment called for it. His introductions even looked the same—two sentences in which he introduced the topic and then a sentence in which he announced "In this paper, I will . . . ". His conclusions always began with "In conclusion . . . ". When I suggested he try a new format, one that would enable him to be more analytical and make use of the readings we had discussed in class, he complained. "I can be myself when I'm telling stories," he said, "but not when I do academic writing. I can't quote those authors," he went on to say. "They use such big words. That just ain't me."

I can appreciate Adam's resistance. His identity and social and cultural affiliations are intimately tied to his language (Wolfram, Adger, and Christian). If he continues to tell stories and use "everyday" vocabulary—that is, to rehearse what he already knows well—then he maintains the identity he came to school with. But being analytical and using sources aligns him more fully with the academy. To Adam, that meant giving up or changing a significant portion of his identity. I tried to reassure him that I wanted him to expand his repertoire and sense of self—not erase it.

I thought it might help reassure Adam if I could help him become aware that he naturally shifted identities when he spoke, so one day in class we compared the way we spoke in various situations. As part of the lesson, I asked my students to role play describing a car accident they were in to three different audiences: an insurance agent, their grandparents, and a friend. It was a task they could do fairly easily. Depending on the audience, they chose different words, added/deleted particular details, used a different tone, etc. The students readily agreed they had to craft different versions of the same event for the three different audiences.

Then I did some role playing of my own—as devil's advocate. I asked which version was the "right" one, knowing it was a setup because there is no "right" one. Adam spoke right up: "The insurance agent's." "Why?" I asked. "Because the words you use to speak to an insurance agent are in the dictionary." "Well," I asked, "you told me you used different language with your friend. Does that mean that the way you talk to your friend is 'wrong'?" At first, Adam said yes; he wanted to hold onto the dictionary as the arbitrator of right and wrong language. But Tameka disagreed. "If you talk to your friend the same way you talked to your insurance agent, the friend would be insulted," she said. "And the insurance agent wouldn't take you seriously if you talked to him the way you talked to your friend."

Then I asked, "Which version of the story allows the 'real you' to come out? Which kind of language expresses your true self, and which are added on?" Again, Tameka spoke up. "All three are 'me,' " she said. "Yeah, I feel more relaxed when I talk to my friend, but I'm just as much 'Tameka' when I talk to the insurance agent. I don't become a different person."

Finally, we came to two conclusions about the nature of language and identity. First, we discovered that "good" or "right" English is not necessarily standard language but language appropriate to the audience and the context. Sometimes it's appropriate to be formal, sometimes not. Because we find ourselves in many different situations, we need to have many languages at our command. We shift so naturally in speaking that we're usually not aware of it. I pointed out that we need to be just as flexible in our writing. One "formula" for writing isn't enough. Second, we play many roles and project different selves at different times. Some are more comfortable than others, but all of them are our "true" selves. Learning academic English isn't giving up one's self-identity, it's adding on another role, another identity.

What I hoped Adam would notice about his own language use in comparing speaking to writing was that he was already quite flexible, able to adjust his language as the context demanded. I hoped that with this awareness he would give himself permission to experiment with more academic language. Indeed, there were sources in his next paper. It was a start.

Sorting Out the Conventions of Academic Writing

For the last writing project of the semester, my students researched the problem of parking on campus. They first wrote a description of the problem in order to clarify for themselves what the issues were. Then their assignment was to write a letter to the director of facilities asking him to take action to solve the problem. (We had invited him to class to present our ideas in person, but he was unable to attend.) But the letter proved to be a challenge to Adam, Tameka, and Bobby. They not only had to figure out what they thought was the best solution, but also how to persuade the director to take action. They were both eager and anxious because the audience was real, as was the potential for meaningful results.

Again, I wanted them to become aware of what they already knew about persuasion, so we compared persuasion strategies they use in the real world with what academics said about how to persuade. We began by telling stories—about persuading their little brother to take out the trash or clean the fish tank, their parents to lend them some money or the car for the evening, a police officer to give them a warning and not a traffic ticket, their girlfriend to marry them—and tried to articulate why they were successful. We discovered that they use the same kinds of arguments that academics use—at least according to the ancient Greeks and their theories about persuasive appeals. They already knew about ethos (*Do it because I'm the mom, and I say so!*), pathos (*Pleeeease! All my friends are going!*), and logos (*You shouldn't drink so much diet cola; I saw on the Internet that it could cause seizures*). In other words, we discovered that they already knew a great deal about how to persuade. What they didn't know or hadn't practiced much was persuading in the medium of a formal, written letter. I promised to teach them the vocabulary and syntax of formal, written persuasion ("*We propose . . .*" and "*This is the most feasible solution because . . .*") and to help them understand their audience, but I assured them that in many ways they could trust their instincts about what worked. Moreover, they even discovered that they already knew how to concede and refute. It's the "yes, but what about" response so common in discussions. We talk about how to "translate" that phrase into academic English with words like *"Granted . . . but nevertheless."*

This kind of overt comparison helps students know which elements of their current linguistic fund of knowledge can be transferred to the new context of academic writing and which elements might interfere with their success at persuading an academic audience. It taps into—and values—what they already know. It also helps them to see that taking on the role of academic writer is not as foreign as they once thought. They're more willing to take on that language when they realize it's analogous—at least in some ways—to what they already know.

Teaching Students to See Their Errors

Bobby's essays were like those of his classmates—informal and undeveloped. But he seemed to have more trouble than the others with grammar and mechanics. He had a lot of spelling mistakes—both the kind of mistakes typical of all vernacular speakers, such as improper homonyms for the context—and the kind of mistakes typical of Chicano Vernacular English speakers, such as writing *choose* for *shoes* (Wolfram and Schilling-Estes). He also had many comma splices and sentence fragments. He would plan a sentence in his head before he wrote it down. He wrote what he heard, and he put periods and commas where he heard himself pause, not necessarily where the syntax indicated. Bobby preferred to learn by ear. He also preferred to write by ear. His papers had a pleasing rhythm and voice, but he couldn't see the lack of, or erroneous, formal features unique to writing. When he proofread his papers, they sounded fine to him, but they looked unconventional to an academic audience. What Bobby needed to notice and pay particular attention to were his words as marks on a page and not as ideas to communicate. (This was one time when Bobby couldn't avoid reading.) We used overt comparison in a number of ways to help Bobby develop his proofreading skills.

First, Bobby and I compared proofreading to critical reading. Bobby didn't know that proofreading requires a different *kind* of reading from the critical reading he's typically urged to do—even though, as Madraso points out, both words share the root word *reading*. In critical reading, we don't really look at each word. Instead, we use our knowledge of the topic and of English grammar to predict what's likely to come. Then we glance at the text only long enough to confirm it is, in fact, what we predicted. In proofreading, on the other hand, we have to look at each word and judge whether we've chosen the best word, expressed an idea clearly, spelled and punctuated correctly, used correct grammar, etc. Successful critical readers read fairly quickly, but in proofreading, they slow down to focus on each word. I suggested that Bobby read his paper aloud, following along with a pencil. This would force him to focus more on what he saw and less on what he heard.

Second, we compared the way that writing sounds to the way that writing looks. When we read critically, we project sounds onto the words. This sound helps us connect written words to concepts we already know. When we proofread, on the other hand, we have to distinguish spoken words from written ones. We have to distinguish, for example, between what's acceptable in informal speaking and what's acceptable in formal writing. A sentence may sound fine to us because we hear people say it all the time, but it's too informal for academic writing. We also have to distinguish between the way words sound and the way they're spelled, such as homonyms and phrases like *used to*, in which the *d* is seldom pronounced. Finally, we have to distinguish between places where we pause when we speak and places where we punctuate. Many of Bobby's sentence fragments were the result of subordinating connectors (e.g., *because, when, after*). He heard himself pause at the ends of these clauses, so he used a period. But a subordinator makes the clause dependent, and so he has to attach it to another sentence with a comma. Bobby's comma splices typically marked an instance when he had a follow-up comment to make about a topic he had just raised. He would restate the topic, usually as a pronoun, and then make his second comment (*We visit my grandparents every Christmas, they live in Mexico.*). Because he rushed to attach another idea to his first, he used a comma. But Bobby had two different sentences, because he had two different comments, and he needed to use a period between them.

Third, we contrasted Bobby's vernacular grammar with formal, Standard English grammar, as Berger suggests. His home dialect, for example, allows for double negatives and object pronouns as subjects (*Us little people don't get nothing.*). It also allows for question word order in indirect questions (*I asked her could I go with her?*). Standard English grammar requires single negatives, subject pronouns before the verb, and standard word order (and periods) with indirect questions.

Bobby made remarkable improvement in his ability to proofread over the semester. Through editing conferences and proofreading and grammar minilessons Bobby learned to pay attention to his writing in ways he'd never been able to before. Comparing critical reading to proofreading, speaking to writing, and vernacular English to Standard English helped Bobby become aware of, sort out, and integrate a number of linguistic strategies into his already complex linguistic system. It raised Bobby's metalinguistic awareness and accelerated his learning.

A colleague of mine noticed this same heightened sense of metalinguistic awareness in her at-risk ninth graders when she started using a formal grammar program based on a pedagogy of overt comparison. Jocelyn Riley uses the "School Talk/Friend Talk" curriculum developed by speech pathologist Mary I. Berger of The Speak Standard, Too Institute in Chicago with her freshmen, who are all linguistic minority students. She says this method works better than her traditional grammar books did. They regularly do minilesson drills based on one of Berger's ninety-five lessons that contrast features of Standard English with various vernacular dialects of English and with other languages.

Riley says she's noticed that students monitor their own language and the language of their friends better than they did with traditional grammar drills. She hears them say to one another, "Hey, you're using Friend Talk and we're in school now. You have to use School Talk." She says students appreciate frank discussion about dialects, how dialects come about, and how they achieve status—or the lack of it—that accompany these drills. They also appreciate the status that Riley accords to the way they talk at home. It's not denigrated; it's simply the way they talk. As a result, they're ready to listen to discussions about "School Talk." They also seem to respond to the explicit contrast between academic English and the way they talk at home. Riley is quite pleased with the program and its results.

Psycholinguists say that fluent bilinguals keep their languages in two separate, but fully developed, subsystems in their brains so that they can easily tap into whichever system is appropriate for the context—or switch between the two systems if they want to. A pedagogy of overt comparison makes this development possible for our working class, linguistic minority students. It helps them become aware of and sort out the differences between their home language—vernacular dialects of English—and school language—Standard English. It also helps them understand and integrate into their linguistic repertoires the conventions of academic literacy. It's a productive bridge from home to school for students like Adam, Tameka, and Bobby.

Works Cited

Baugh, John. "Linguistics, Education, and the Law: Educational Reform for African-American Language Minority Students." *African-American English: Structure, History and Use*. Eds. Salikoko S. Mufwene, John R. Rickford, Guy Bailey, and John Baugh. New York: Routledge, 1998. 282–301.

Berger, Mary I. *Teach Standard Too: Teach Oral and Written Standard English as a Second Dialect to English-Speaking Students*. Chicago: Orchard, publication date unknown. Available by writing to The Speak Standard, Too Institute, 2222 North Orchard Street, Chicago, IL 60614-5244. 1-800-528-5244.

Madraso, Jan. "Proofreading: The Skill We've Neglected to Teach." *English Journal* 82.2 (1993): 32–41.

Pérez, Bertha. "Language, Literacy, and Biliteracy." *Sociocultural Contexts of Language and Literacy*.

Ed. Bertha Pérez. Mahwah, NJ: Lawrence Erlbaum, 1998. 21–48.

Rickford, John R. *African American Vernacular English: Features, Evolution, Educational Implications.* Malden, MA: Blackwell, 1999.

Riley, Jocelyn. Personal Interview. 10 March 1997.

Siegel, Jeff. "Stigmatized and Standardized Varieties in the Classroom: Interference or Separation?" *TESOL Quarterly* 33.4 (Winter 1999): 701–28.

Wolfram, Walt, and Natalie Schilling-Estes. *American English: Dialects and Variation.* Malden, MA: Blackwell, 1998.

Wolfram, Walt, Carolyn Temple Adger, and Donna Christian. *Dialects in Schools and Communities.* Mahwah, NJ: Lawrence Erlbaum, 1999.

Questions for Discussion

1. According to Hagemann, why might it be harder for speakers of vernacular English to learn Standard English than it'd be for non-native speakers? What advice does she offer teachers about how to help such students learn academic English? How does her advice compare to the advice given by Wolfram, Adger, and Christian?

2. Research the Oakland, California, Ebonics Debate that erupted in December 1996. (One source is the *San Francisco Chronicle*, which can be accessed via its Internet address: www.sfgate.com.) According to The Linguistic Society of America Resolution on the Oakland "Ebonics" Issue, the "Oakland School Board's decision to recognize the vernacular of African American students in teaching them Standard English is linguistically and pedagogically sound." Explain why it's a sound policy, in spite of the controversy it generated.

3. Research the School Talk/Friend Talk curriculum. What are the advantages and disadvantages of the method? What kind of credentials does the author have? What kind of evidence does she offer to support the soundness of her methods? How credible is the evidence? Why?

4. On February 13, 1999, the *Chicago Tribune* published an Ann Landers column, in which E. E., a retired secretary of 50 years with a high school education and "impeccable" English, wrote to complain about ungrammatical verb phrases. E. E. was especially dismayed to hear a TV reporter, a lawyer, and the narrator of a political commercial use these phrases. E. E. asked Ann to remind her readers that these phrases are ungrammatical. Among the phrases E. E. complained about were these:

   - woulda came
   - coulda went
   - shoulda did
   - woulda took
   - had went
   - hadn't came
   - had threw
   - I seen

For humor, Ann replied with another commonly heard verb string: "Thanks for writing. I shoulda thunk to tell them off myself" (p. 28).

What do you notice about the verb phrases E. E. complains about? Is it surprising that a TV reporter and an attorney would use these phrases? Why/why not? If you were on Ann Landers' staff, how would you urge her to respond to the letter?

5. Reread the creativity paper by Drew (p. 224), keeping in mind that Drew is a native speaker of African American Vernacular English. What do you notice about the way Drew marks plural nouns and past tense verbs? To what extent do they seem to be a transfer from his home language (African American Vernacular English)? What advice would you give Drew that would help him better "translate" his essay into Standard English?

10

Working with Language Minority Students—English Language Learners

Although Chapter 9 points out that the largest share of language minority students are native born, monolingual speakers of vernacular English, a significant portion are non-native multilinguals. According to the 1990 Census (the latest available at the time of this writing), there are about six million school-aged children in the United States who speak another language at home, though it's not reported in these statistics how many were born outside the United States. Of those, more than five million report they speak English well or very well. But that still leaves one million children who are struggling to become bilingual.

English Language Learners (ELLs)

Valdés (1992) identifies two kinds of non-native born, bilingual students: incipient bilinguals and fluent bilinguals. Incipient bilinguals are in the process of becoming bilingual. That is, they're learning English. Their writing is marked by simple syntax, many grammatical and mechanical "errors," and much transfer from their first language. They may be able to write only on limited topics and may have little awareness of audience (Valdés, 1999). They can benefit from—in fact, they need—formal instruction in English as a Second Language, either in an ESL program or a bilingual program.

A second category of bilingual speakers is the fluent bilingual. These students have learned English, but there are still "non-native-like" features in their speaking and writing (Valdés, 1992). This is especially true if they learned English as adolescents or as adults. They may spell words as they pronounce them—with an accent—such as spelling *one's* as *once*. Furthermore, they may not organize their writing the way American readers expect (Connor, 1996), or they may confuse

192

idiomatic expressions, so readers have a sense that something doesn't "sound quite right" (Yorio, 1989). These features may result because fluent bilinguals often learn much of their English orally—they're what Joy Reid (1998a) calls "ear learners"—so they may not have had much practice in English spelling and punctuation. Perhaps the most difficult features of English to learn—and the ones most marked as "non-native writing"—are articles and prepositions. The misuse of these features doesn't indicate that students don't know English—only that they're non-native speakers. Although fluent bilinguals have outgrown ESL programs and should be mainstreamed into regular classes, they still need help in general editing skills and in identifying and mastering the specific non-native features they retain (Valdés, 1992, 1999).

Learning a Second Language

As you yourself may have experienced, the process of learning another language is long and complex, especially if the goal is learning the language well enough to use it as the medium of learning, as bilingual students in the United States have to do. Research in the United States and Canada has shown that it generally takes non-native speaking children three to five years to develop oral proficiency in English and four to seven years to develop academic English proficiency (Hakuta, Butler, & Witt, 2000; Teachers of English to Speakers of Other Languages [TESOL], 1997).

There are many factors that determine whether learners will succeed at learning another language (Walqui, 2000):

- their attitudes toward the target language;
- their goals for learning it;
- the level of support they receive from their family and peers;
- the presence of positive role models;
- their level of schooling and literacy in their first language; and
- their age, gender, and class.

These factors combine with language learning strategies to influence a student's success. Second language learners use a number of strategies to develop a second, separate linguistic system in their brains—just as second dialect learners do. At first, they use their native language as a guide to learning the linguistic rules of their second language (Lightbown & Spada, 1999). In essence, because they have so little of the second language, they have to rely on their first to carry most of their ideas. Beginning language learners "borrow" rules and vocabulary from their native language, sometimes consciously, but more often unconsciously. They, for example, pronounce English words using Spanish pronunciation rules. When aspects of the two languages are identical, this interlinguistic connection usually has a positive effect on learning. However, when aspects are different, or are similar but not identical, this connection may have a negative effect. Spanish speakers, for example, have an easier time learning English third person gender pronouns (i.e., *he/him/his* and *she/her/her*) than do Mandarin Chinese speakers, because Spanish uses these pronouns much like English does, while Chinese dialects don't make a gender or case distinction in pronouns. Spanish speakers can successfully transfer their understanding of third-person pronouns to English, but Chinese speakers can't because they have little experience with them. Other times, the languages may be "close enough"—but not identical—so learners don't notice that they've substituted their first language for English, as in the case of the Spanish speaker who writes *the tiempo of the music* for *the tempo of the music*.

As a result of these difficulties, some students may be afraid to try some structures because the structures look so different from their native language. Or some students may stay in some developmental stages longer than others, because that developmental stage is most like their native language. For example, one of the developmental stages of forming negatives in English is to simply put *no* in front of the verb, as in *I no speak English*. Students whose first languages use this strategy tend to stay in this developmental stage longer than students whose first languages use a different negation strategy (Lightbown & Spada, 1999). Or they may learn the rules but not use them in the same contexts a native speaker would. Chinese speakers may use *he* regardless of the gender of the person they're referring to, or Spanish speakers may ascribe gender to inanimate objects in English because all nouns in Spanish have gender.

As students gain proficiency in a second language, they no longer need to borrow as much from their first language. They rely instead on their knowledge of the second language. More advanced learners make active efforts to create and test out hypotheses about their new language, reasoning that some features are analogous (Lightbown & Spada, 1999). When they accurately apply a principle to the appropriate features, their reasoning has a positive effect on learning. However, if they don't realize certain exceptions exist, they may extend the analogy to inappropriate contexts and thus make errors. When students learn, for example, that past tense in English is typically marked by adding -*ed* to the verb, they begin to apply that rule to new verbs they learn. With regular verbs, such as *cook* and *bake*, this application succeeds. However, with irregular verbs, such as *eat* and *drink*, this rule doesn't apply in the standard variety and so they err.

The Development of Writing

Thus far, the focus of this discussion has been on learning grammar, but the same discussion applies to language learning on the rhetorical level as well. Researchers have contrasted the rhetorical conventions of writing from various languages and have noted significant differences in organizational patterns, in writerly obligations to make arguments explicit, and in the value of using proverbial wisdom, among others (Connor, 1996). For example, English speakers in India tend to be more formal and to use more Latinate vocabulary than English speakers in the United States. This may be because English was used mainly in formal realms such as schools and government offices when it was first widely used in India. Differences in vocabulary choice, style, and structure can impact the transfer of writing skills in the same way differences impact transfer of grammatical knowledge.

However, most of the research done on contrastive rhetoric has been done with international students on the college (often postgraduate) level. These students have long school histories in their native countries, so presumably, they've been steeped in the rhetorical and academic tradition of their home languages. It's less clear to what extent these research findings can be applied to bilinguals who are educated in American middle and high schools, and who may not be literate in their heritage language.

In fact, it's been only fairly recently that researchers have turned their attention to how immigrant ELLs, especially those in middle and high schools, become bilingual and biliterate. Much of the previous research on second language learning examines the processes used by adults or elementary school children. But more and more studies are examining secondary ELLs (Faltis & Wolfe, 1999; Harklau, 1999a, 1999b; Peregoy & Boyle, 1997; Valdés, 1992, 1999, 2001). Perhaps the best-known researcher in this area is Guadalupe Valdés (1992, 1999, 2001), who has followed the English development of several Latino students in American schools. Figure 10.1 summarizes her observations on how writing ability—both rhetorical and grammatical—develops.

Valdés (1999) doesn't indicate in this chart how she'd distinguish incipient and fluent bilinguals, but the descriptors at the various levels suggest that Level 7

FIGURE 10.1 *Theoretical Foundation: Developing Writing Abilities in Secondary English Language Learners*

Valdés (1999) describes how the Spanish-speaking students in her studies develop their abilities to write in English. This development is initially characterized by translation from students' first language and an inability to focus much on formal or rhetorical elements. Gradually students gain more and more control of vocabulary and sentence structure so they can focus more cognitive attention on meeting audience needs. It's important to acknowledge these are Spanish speakers, because a student's first language has some impact on their learning process. We must be cautious in extrapolating this process to secondary ELLs from all language backgrounds.

Levels	Communicative Tasks Performed	Organization	Mechanics
Level 1	Displays familiarity with English words.	Writes lists of familiar English words.	Spells some words correctly.
Level 2	Attempts to display information.	• Writes simple unconnected sentences that they can produce orally.	• Sentences reflect transfer from Spanish. • Spelling errors are frequent.

(continued)

FIGURE 10.1   *Continued*

		• May also attempt to write by translating from Spanish.	• Uses Spanish spelling conventions to spell English words. • Doesn't attend to capitalization and punctuation.
Level 3	Provides personal information.	Can write very short connected discourse (two or three sentences) about which they can produce connected oral discourse (e.g., family, self, school).	• Sentences continue to reflect transfer from Spanish. • Doesn't attend to capitalization and punctuation. • Spelling errors are frequent. • May still use Spanish spelling conventions to spell English words. • Writing may reflect oral language pronunciation resulting in both spelling errors and non-native-like features.
Level 4	• Displays limited amounts of information. • Explains at a very basic level.	Can write very short connected discourse (a paragraph) on a limited number of academic topics about which they can produce connected oral discourse.	• Sentences continue to reflect transfer from Spanish. • Begins to attend to capitalization and/or punctuation. • Spelling errors are frequent. • Writing may still reflect oral language pronunciation resulting in both spelling errors and non-native-like features.
Level 5	Displays larger amounts of information.	• Can write longer segments of connected discourse.	• Sentences continue to reflect transfer from Spanish.

FIGURE 10.1   *Continued*

	• Writes single, very long paragraphs. • Includes many unrelated ideas in the same paragraph.	• Some basic syntactic patterns still aren't mastered. • Begins to write compound sentences. • Capitalization and punctuation still aren't mastered. • Uses an exclusively oral style.
Level 6	• Displays information to show they can read and understand. • Explains. • Expresses personal opinion. • Justifies opinion. • Recounts experiences in writing.	• Demonstrates little or no audience awareness. • Has little notion of text organization, but begins to use several "paragraphs." • Continues to include unrelated ideas in the same paragraph. • Uses idiosyncratic, unconventional criteria for selection of supporting details.	• Sentences continue to reflect transfer from Spanish, but basic syntactic patterns have been mastered. • Punctuation may still not be mastered. • Uses an exclusively oral style.
Level 7	• Displays information to show they can read and understand. • Explains more fully. • Expresses personal opinion. • Justifies opinion. • Recounts experiences in writing. • Expresses feelings in writing. • Narrates.	• Sense of audience begins to develop. • Growing sense of text organization emerges.	• Growing ability to choose language for its precise meanings begins to emerge. • Awareness of variety of styles used in writing for different purposes emerges.

Adapted from Valdés, G. (1999). Incipient bilingualism and the development of English language writing abilities in the secondary school. In C. J. Faltis & P. Wolfe (eds.), *So much to say: Adolescents, bilingualism and ESL in the secondary school* (pp. 138–175). New York: Columbia University Teachers College Press. Used with permission.

writers have significantly mastered the grammar and rhetorical conventions of written English. She recommends that students who are fluent bilinguals be treated as mainstream students, but continue to receive instruction in identifying and correcting "non-native-like" features in their writing. Moreover, if bilinguals are also contact variety speakers of English, they should also receive instruction comparing their dialect of English to Standard English to help them correct non-standard features.

Valdés (1992, 1999, 2001) makes her recommendations as a result of her study of Spanish-speaking adolescents. But even though a student's first language has some impact on their learning process, there nonetheless seem to be some universal principles that mainstream teachers can apply to their instruction of ELL writers. Valdés' recommendations are echoed by Hartman and Tarone (1999), who studied how well Southeast Asian American students were prepared for college writing. All three teacher/scholars recommend that teachers of bilingual writers should:

- *Focus more on content than on form.* Valdés (1992, 1999, 2001) and Hartman and Tarone (1999) encourage teachers to spend more instructional time on organization and development than on grammar. They argue that the primary readers of ELL writers are mainstream teachers and these teachers are most concerned about what students say. Valdés and Hartman and Tarone also urge teachers to provide students with experiences with a variety of genres, especially academic ones, so that they become familiar and comfortable with the most common genres in school. And finally, they recommend that students read many authentic models—both published and student writing—in order to learn more about written English.
- *Make use of the language skills that students bring with them to support their learning of new skills.* If students are literate in their first language, they can to some extent transfer what they already know about writing and about texts to writing in English. Valdés laments that "very little attention" in school has been given to how ELLs "can be taught to use their first language strategically in learning to write English" (1999, p. 173). Moreover, teachers can make use of students' oral skills in English, which are typically stronger than their written skills. As Valdés points out, "when [students] could display information orally, they were then able to begin to display this information in writing as well" (1999, p. 173).
- *Be tolerant of students' grammatical and mechanical errors, because with time most of these errors will disappear.*

Helping Fluent Bilinguals in Mainstream Classrooms

Teachers of mainstreamed fluent bilinguals often feel inadequately prepared to help students address the "non-native-like" rhetorical and grammatical features in their students' writing. But as Valdés' (1992, 1999, 2001) and Hartman and

Tarone's (1999) recommendations above indicate, they can approach their bilingual writers in much the same way as they approach their monolingual writers—at least to some extent. Just as they would with their native-speaking students, teachers should:

- *Help students develop their sense of rhetorical judgment in English.* Use models of English writing to help students learn the genres and rhetorical/pragmatic conventions that English readers expect. Like any other developing writer, ELLs must learn to anticipate the needs of their readers. However, they may have a more difficult time doing so because they're less likely to share the same cultural conventions as their readers. They may need more explicit instruction in rhetorical conventions. Katie Wood Ray's reading-like-a-writer approach is useful here (See Figure 4.1).
- *Focus on higher-order concerns, such as organization and development, before lower-order ones, such as grammar and usage.* Above all, fluent bilinguals are writers, and like any other students, they most need feedback in how effectively they're communicating their message and meeting their readers' needs. In fact, according to Ferris (1999b), ELLs appreciate teacher comments, take them seriously, and say they're helpful in revising. However, ELLs are more likely to make errors in sentence structure and word choice that impact on the meaning of the essay, so it's likely teachers may have to make more editing comments in initial drafts than they might with their native-speaking writers.
- *Accentuate the positive.* As with their basic writers, teachers must remember that fluent bilinguals are likely to have more well formed sentences than flawed ones (Noguchi, 1991). As teachers/readers, we usually don't notice these places because we take smooth communication for granted. But as Straub (See Chapter 4) points out, we should praise what's good in students' papers.
- *Analyze errors so that they can understand how to more productively help students control their errors.* One approach that teachers can borrow from their mainstream repertoire is error analysis. Rosen (see Chapter 5) suggests teachers look for patterns in students' errors, and try to figure out what underlying "rules" they're using. Then they'll know better how to discuss the errors with students. However, error analysis may be more complex for ESL writers because there seem to be more causes for linguistic errors because bilinguals are working with two languages. Reid (1998b) identifies four kinds of linguistic errors that ELLs typically make: a) performance errors; b) competence errors that result because students' hypotheses about (academic) writing in English are inaccurate or incomplete; c) interference errors that result when students inappropriately transfer what they know from one situation to another; and d) errors that result because some features of English are difficult to learn. These are discussed in more detail in Figure 10.2.
- *Help students "see" errors and sort out the differences in their two language systems by explicitly comparing features of their home language to comparable ones in English.* Just as dialect speakers must sort out their two dialects, bilinguals must sort out their two languages. To help students see these differences,

FIGURE 10.2   *Theoretical Foundation: Identifying English Language Learning Errors*

According to Joy Reid (1998b), ESL writers make errors for four basic reasons that evolve from linguistic factors:

1. *Errors that seem to result from first-language interference.* This kind of error is language-centered because students who share native languages are likely to make the same errors. According to contrastive analysis, students are likely to make errors in places where home languages are different from English. Some of these differences are listed in Figure 10.3.

2. *Errors that seem to result from difficult features of English.* This kind of error is also language-centered, but the problematic language is English. There are some features that are difficult for students of all languages to learn; they may never fully master these features. Such features include articles, prepositions, gerunds, and infinitives.

3. *Errors that seem to result from overgeneralization of English language rules.* This kind of error may be more learner-centered because each student's hypothesis may be different. According to error analysis, learners apply the hypotheses about English that they're developing to inappropriate situations. For example, when ELLs learners understand that English forms its past tense by adding -*ed*, they might add -*ed* to all verbs, including irregular ones. They might say *goed* until they learn the exception *went*.

4. *Performance errors.* This kind of error is learner-centered. According to transformational-generative grammar, learners make mistakes because of haste, distraction, selective attention, etc. They generally know the rules, but in specific instances, they make mistakes.

Ferris (1995) indicates that when these errors are addressed individually, rather than in large class settings, students are more likely to master them.

---

teachers can develop (mini)lessons that compare the two languages, using the contrastive analysis approach that Hagemann (see Chapter 9) describes. In order to understand where students are likely to have trouble learning English because of first-language interference, it's useful to know something about other languages. A brief list of how some of the features of some common languages differ from English can be found in Figure 10.3.

- *Set priorities for the kinds of errors they want students to address.* In the reading for this chapter, Ferris urges teachers to identify patterns of error that students can work on. She suggests beginning with errors that are global (interferes with meaning), frequent, and stigmatizing (exacts a social tax from the writer [see Chapter 5]). She has identified a limited number of errors that she wants her students to master by the end of the term. All of the errors are "treatable"—that is, students can consult a handbook to help them edit. Other errors—"untreatable" errors—have a lower priority because they are less rule-governed and require more teacher support. Articles and prepositions fall into this latter category.

Reid (1998a) argues that English Language Learners (ELLs) make four kinds of errors when writing English: 1. First-language interference errors; 2. Errors because some features of English are difficult; 3. Errors because students apply a rule in a context where it doesn't work; and 4. Production or performance errors. This chart helps teachers recognize the first two kinds of errors. It briefly identifies differences between English and several other languages and makes global predictions about which rules of English beginning ELLs are likely—but not guaranteed—to incorrectly transfer from their first language. The last column also shows where the rules of English are difficult: the last column repeats a number of features difficult for speakers of many different languages, which suggests these features are inherently difficult. This chart was adapted from Stephanie Coffin and Barbara Hall's *Writing Workshop: A Manual for College ESL Writers* (© 1998 by McGraw-Hill Primis Custom Publishing, pp. vii–ix) and is reproduced with permission of the McGraw-Hill Companies. It also draws on Raimes and Sofer (1996) and Gordon (1998, personal communication).

Language	Word Order	Verb System	Nouns/Articles	Other	Predicted Errors
English	SVO; rigid word order; ADV moveable; ADJ before N; REL CL after N.	Extensive tense and aspect system with auxiliary V and modals; wide use of passive voice.	Count/ non-count N; pl N marked with -s; some demonstrative ADJ-N agreement; complex indefinite/definite ART system.	Alphabetic; inconsistent spelling due to infusion of other languages.	
Arabic	VSO (formal); SVO and VO (informal); ADV moveable; ADJ after N; object PRO retained in REL CL.	Past, present, future and some perfect tenses; no *be* in present tense; V contains subject; no modals.	Definite, but no indefinite ART; N have gender; pl N marked; agreement rules different.	Uses Arabic alphabet; right to left writing; spelling is phonetic; no fixed punctuation rules.	Spelling; punctuation; V tense; V form; agreement; number; indefinite ART.
Chinese (Mandarin)	SVO; ADJ and REL CL before N; ADV before V and ADJ.	Uses ADV to indicate tense; *be* rare; no auxiliaries; modals different; different concept of time.	No ART; count/ non-count N different; pl N not marked.	Uses non-alphabetic characters; writing may go from left to right or from top to bottom/right to left; 4 tones.	Word order; V tense; V form; agreement; number; ART; parallelism; post-N modifiers.

(continued)

FIGURE 10.3 *Continued*

Japanese	SOV; REL CL before N, with no REL PRO; has postpositions instead of prepositions.	V contains subject and object; no *be*; passive voice different; modal follows V.	No distinction between count/non-count N; pl N not marked; no ART.	Uses Chinese characters and Japanese alphabet; many English words in lexicon.	Word order; V tense; V form; agreement, number; ART; PREP; parallelism.
Russian, Serbian	SVO & OVS; ADJ and REL CL before N; no *there is/are; it is* implied.	*Be* can be omitted; no perfect and progressive tenses; no auxiliaries; passive voice different.	Some count/non-count N differences; no ART.	Uses Cyrillic alphabet.	Word order; V tense; V form; agreement; ART.
Spanish	SVO, VSO and V; ADV moveable; ADJ after N; double negatives.	Range of tenses and composite forms; V have endings; passive voice; V contains subject.	ART, ADJ and N are marked for pl and gender; definite ART has wider use; no gerunds.	Spelling very phonetic; many English cognates.	Spelling; word order; missing subjects; gerunds/infinitives.
Vietnamese	SVO; ADJ and REL CL after N; no *it is, there is/are.*	Uses ADV to indicate tense; *be* rare; passive voice rare.	Pl N indicated by quantity ADJ; ART different.	Alphabetic; 6 tones.	V tense; V form; agreement; number; ART; parallelism.

A Key to Abbreviations:

S = subject	N = noun/nominals	ART = article	CL = clause
V = verb	ADJ = adjective/adjectivals	PRO = pronoun	REL CL = relative clause
O = object	ADV = adverb/adverbials	PREP = preposition	pl = plural

Whether students are monolingual or bilingual writers, mainstream teachers should expect them to be responsible for correcting at least some of their errors and should teach them how to be better editors of their own writing. Ferris argues that it's just as important for ELLs to become independent self-editors as it is for native-speaking students. However, editing may be a more difficult skill to learn for ESL writers—depending on their school histories and on how they primarily learned English. Students who learned English orally through contact with native speakers—Reid's (1998a) "ear learners"—rely on what sounds "right" in the same way native speakers do. If their English is a vernacular variety, then they may struggle with academic writing conventions, especially with punctuation. These students may need teachers to minimally mark errors they can't "see" as they proofread. Students who learned English through classroom instruction-Reid's "eye learners"—rely on their explicit knowledge of grammar. This knowledge works well when they're editing rule-governed, treatable errors, but it's less successful with "untreatable" errors such as sentence structure, when there are few rules to rely on. These students may need more direct correction strategies. Figure 10.4 discusses treatable and untreatable errors in more detail.

FIGURE 10.4   *Teaching Tip: "Treatable" and "Untreatable" Errors in the Writing of English Language Learners*

Ferris (1999a) makes a distinction between what she calls *treatable* and *untreatable* errors. Treatable errors are errors that students can learn to self-edit because the errors are violations of easily articulated rules that can be found in handbooks (e.g., subject-verb agreement or verb forms). Students can use either their intuitive knowledge of grammar (Hartwell's Grammar 1 [p. 5]) or explicitly learned rules of grammar (Hartwell's Grammars 3 and 4) to find and correct these errors.

Untreatable errors, on the other hand, fall into two categories:

- Writers misuse grammatical elements of English that are difficult; our rules about them are arbitrary so they just have to be memorized. Why, for example, does the verb *enjoy* take a gerund, but the verb *like* take an infinitive (*I enjoy reading.* vs. I *like to read.*)? Other examples are uses of articles, uses of prepositions, and idioms.
- Writers express ideas in ways that native speakers wouldn't. Their ideas may be easily understood, but they sound "foreign" to native ears. For example, this is the opening sentence of John's essay (p. 227) on how to play chess:

There are several indoor games that we cherish to spend our pastimes.

Granted, we understand the gist of his sentence and there's a certain amount of charm to it, but native speakers would probably phrase it in a different way:

There are several indoor games we enjoy playing to pass the time.

The rules for these errors aren't easily articulated or simply can't be found in handbooks. Students must use their intuitive knowledge of grammar or depend on native-speaking peers or teachers for support. Treatable errors can be corrected indirectly using a minimal marking technique, while untreatable errors generally require teachers to correct the sentence directly by writing in a more native-sounding way to express the same idea. With these errors, I usually end up saying, "That's just the way it is in English."

(continued)

FIGURE 10.4   *Continued*

Some examples of treatable and untreatable errors can be found in the following chart. It's based on Ferris (1999a) and Vann, Meyer, and Lorenz's (1984) study of the kinds of errors that most distract native-speaking readers (specifically college professors).

Classifying ELL Errors According to How Easily Their Underlying Rules Can Be Explained

←—————————————————————————————————————→

Treatable
Rule easy articulate.

Student can consult rule while editing.

Student is responsible.

Teacher marks minimally.

Untreatable
Rule difficult to articulate.

Student must know intuitively.

Teacher gives support.

Teacher supplies
native-sounding version.

- Unmarked plurals
- Wrong pronoun case
- Pronoun disagreement
- Subject-verb disagreement
- Verb tense formation
- Missing subject (*Is cold today.*)
- Comma splices

- Gerund/infinitive confusion (*enjoy to read* versus *enjoy reading*)
- Past/present participle confusion (*boring* versus *bored*)
- Spelling

- Missing/unnecessary/wrong articles
- Non-native choice of prepositions
- Phrasal verb confusion (*get up* versus *get on* versus *get out*, etc.)
- Word choice
- Word order

It's interesting to note that native speakers also have trouble with many of the treatable errors; several errors also appear on my priority list for native-speakers (See Figure 5.2). Treatable errors aren't necessarily easy to master, but because they're more concrete and rule-governed, they're easier for students to learn to self-edit than other kinds of errors.

This distinction between treatable and untreatable errors also guides me when I read the writing of my fluent bilingual students. For example, one of my students named Danny, a young Polish man who had immigrated to the United States as a teen a few years earlier, began an essay with the following sentence:

Sands I was little boy, I alway dream to be good in karate.

When it came time in the writing process to help him edit his work, I minimally marked *sands* and *alway* but didn't comment on them (See Figure 5.5). I thought he'd figure out what conventions he had violated and make the corrections on his own. However, above the phrase *dream to be* I wrote in *have dreamed of being* because I knew that there were two untreatable errors there that Danny probably couldn't correct: how to use the idiom *dream of* as a native would and whether *dream of* takes a gerund or an infinitive. (Imagine trying to explain why we use *of* with *dream* to talk about our aspirations or why *dream* takes an *-ing* word and not a *to+verb*. I don't know—we just do!) Both idioms and chained verbs are difficult for even fluent bilinguals. Normally, I wouldn't correct verb tense—that's a treatable error—but I wrote in the correct tense

FIGURE 10.4   *Continued*

because it was part of the idiom. When Danny handed in his next draft, he left *sands* as it was (his way of pronouncing *since* makes this spelling logical to him so he can't see that it's the wrong word here), but he corrected *always* and inserted it between *have* and *dreamed* on his own. And he copied over the phrase I suggested. It's possible that the act of copying this phrase will model for Danny how to use the expression *dream of being*, so he'll use it correctly next time.

This chapter explores strategies that mainstream English language arts teachers can use to support the writing development of fluent bilinguals and English Language Learners.

Exploring Your Own Language Experience

1. Before you begin the reading, spend five minutes or so writing in your journal about the following:

   Have you studied a foreign language? How much emphasis was placed on activities that encouraged you to communicate in the new language? Did you, for example, do small group discussions, role-playing, journal writing, etc.? What techniques that your teacher used did you find helpful in learning the next language?

2. Reread Daniels (Chapter 1) and Hagemann (Chapter 9) about how languages are learned.

Teaching Students to Self-Edit

Dana Ferris

This article originally appeared in TESOL Journal, *a quarterly journal focusing primarily on ESL teaching issues; it's published by Teachers of English to Speakers of Other Languages, a professional organization for ESL teachers. In this article, Ferris explains the process she uses to teach ESL students to become more independent self-editors. She recognizes that there's more to ESL writing than errors, but this is what mainstream readers tend to focus on. So she offers a strategy for helping students master at least some of their errors.*

Over the past 20 years, the process approach to teaching writing has greatly improved both L1 and L2 composition pedagogy. However, though students may be much better at invention, organization, and revision than they were before, too many written products are still riddled with grammatical and lexical inaccuracies. No matter how interesting or original a student's ideas are, an excess of sentence- and discourse-level errors may distract and frustrate instructors and other readers. Because this may lead to harsh evaluation of the student's overall writing abilities, ESL writing teachers, in addition to focusing on students' ideas, need to help students develop and improve their editing skills.

In the modern process approach composition classroom, editing refers to finding and correcting grammatical, lexical, and mechanical errors before submitting (or "publishing") a final written product. Recent studies claim that a lack of grammatical accuracy in ESL student writing may impede students' progress in the university at large (Janopolous, 1992: Santos, 1988; Vann, Lorenz, & Meyer, 1991; Vann, Meyer, & Lorenz, 1984). As a university-level ESL writing teacher, I know the high standard of accuracy in student writing the academic discourse community demands. My students will not succeed outside of the sheltered world of the ESL class unless they can learn to reduce their errors. Because I will not always be there to help my students, it is important that they learn to edit their own work successfully.

As shown by several recent ESL editing textbooks (Ascher, 1993; Fox, 1992; Lane & Lange, 1993; Raimes, 1992a) and a teacher's reference on responding to ESL writing (Bates, Lane, & Lange, 1993), researchers and teachers of ESL writing have become more aware of the need to help students self-edit their writing (Lane & Lange, 1993, p. xix). In response to this need, I have developed and used a semester-long editing process approach to help advanced ESL writing students become more self-sufficient as editors. The particulars of this approach follow.

Philosophical Assumptions

I based my editing process approach on the following principles:

- Students and teachers should focus on major patterns of error rather than attempting to correct every single error (Bates et al., 1993).
- Because not all students will make the same errors, it is necessary and desirable to personalize editing instruction as much as possible.
- The errors to focus on should be those that are most frequent, global (interfere with the comprehensibility of the text), and stigmatizing (would cause a negative evaluation from native speakers) (Bates et al., 1993; Hendrickson, 1980).

The Editing Process

Bates et al. (1993) and Hendrickson (1980) advocate teaching students a discovery approach through which they will become independent self-editors. I teach my advanced ESL students through a three-phase discovery approach to become self-sufficient editors.

Stage 1: Focusing on Form

Though some teachers assume that all ESL students are obsessively concerned with grammar to the detriment of developing and presenting their ideas, I have found that many students have little interest in and pay limited attention to editing their work. They find editing tedious or unimportant or they have become overly dependent on teachers or tutors to correct their work for them. A crucial step in teaching students to become good editors is to convince them of the necessity of doing so.

To raise awareness of the importance of editing, I use in-class activities in which the students look at sentences or short student essays that contain a variety of editing problems. Rather than simply finding and correcting errors, they discuss how these errors impede their understanding of the texts, as in the three examples below:

1. My *parent* always gave me a lot of love.
2. School is the place where I *learn* things such as reading and writing.
3. I like coffee: *on the other hand*, I also like tea.

The italicized portions of these three sentences contain common ESL writing errors: respectively, an omitted plural marker, a verb tense error, and a misused transitional phrase. However, none of the sentences immediately appears ungrammatical—*parent* can be singular, the two verbs in Example 2 are both in present tense and thus appear consistent, and *on the other hand* does signal a clause expressing a different viewpoint than in the one before it. But once the students look closely at the texts, they can see that the use of *parent* is confusing and nonidiomatic (if you really had only one parent, you would identify him/her as your father or mother), that they learned to read and write a long time ago in school, and that liking coffee is not the opposite of liking tea, as implied by the use of *on the other hand*. Even fairly minor errors can lead to problems in text processing and comprehension.

Another strategy I use to convince the students of the necessity of developing editing skills is to give them a diagnostic essay assignment and then provide them with written feedback about their ideas, detailed information about their editing problems, and an indication of what grade she would receive if still writing at this level at the end of the semester. Giving students an immediate sense of what their final grade could be is motivating, but does not seem to be intimidating if I make it clear that these initial grades are for their information only and will not be counted in their final course evaluation.

Stage 2: Recognizing Major Error Types

Research indicates that focusing on patterns of error, rather than individual errors, is most effective for both teachers and students, so at this stage, I train students to recognize various types of error. The categories may vary depending on the students' needs, but they should be selected from error types which are frequent, global, and stigmatizing. I sensitize students to these error patterns by going over the targeted categories, letting them practice identifying them in sample student essays, and then looking for these errors in peer editing exercises (See Activities 1 and 2). It seems to be true that it is easier to find mistakes in others' work than in one's own. Exercises in recognizing error patterns in other writers' work help students become more aware of similar problems in their own writing. They also help lead students away from the frustrating and even counterproductive notion that they can or should attempt to correct every single error in a given essay draft.

During this stage of the editing process, I may also give brief, focused instruction on major patterns of error if there are particular ones to which most students are prone. For instance, students may be confused about when to use the simple past tense and when to use the present perfect. In-class instruction should deal directly with this difficulty, rather than attempting to give students a complete overview of the English verb

ACTIVITY 1

Editing: Major Error Categories

Type 1: Nouns
- Noun endings:
  I need to buy some *book*
  I gained a lot of *knowledges* in high school
- Articles:
  I need to buy ^ *book*.
  A good *jobs* is hard to find.

Type 2: Verbs
- Subject-Verb Agreement:
  The boys *was* hungry.
  That TV show *come* on at 8:00.
  Many students in the class *is* failing.
- Verb tense:
  Last year I *come* to Sac State.
  I've never been to Disney World, but I *had been* to Disneyland before.
- Verb form:
  My car *was stole*.
  My mother *is miss* her children.

Type 3: Punctuation and Sentence Structure
- Sentence fragments:
  Wrong: *After I got home*. I washed the dishes.
  Right: After I got home, I washed the dishes.
- Comma errors:
  When I got home ^ I discovered my house was on fire.
  I studied hard for the test ^ but I still got a bad grade.
  I studied hard for the test, I still got a bad grade.
- Run-on sentences:
  I studied hard for the test I still got a bad grade.
- Semicolon errors:
  Although I studied hard for the test; I still got a bad grade.
  I studied hard for the test ^ I still got a bad grade.
  (Note: The categories for this activity were taken from Fox [1992].)

Type 4: Word Form Errors
  Examples:
  My father is very *generosity*.
  Intelligent is *importance* for academic success.

Type 5: Preposition Errors
  Examples:
  I do a lot of work *on* volunteer organizations.

For an American, I like baseball and hot dogs.

Editing Worksheet

Instructions: Read the sample essay. First, find all the nouns, and underline any noun errors. Then do the same with verbs, punctuation/sentence structure, word forms, and prepositions. Count the errors of each type and fill in the worksheet below. Turn in both your marked essay and this worksheet.

Type 1: Noun Errors

     Total number of noun errors in essay: ____

     Write one example from the essay below. Underline the error.

Type 2: Verb Errors

     Total number of verb errors in essay: ____

     Write one example from the essay below. Underline the error.

Type 3: Punctuation and Sentence Structure

     Total number of punctuation errors in essay: ____

     Write one example from the essay below. Underline the error.

Type 4: Word Forms

     Total number of word form errors in essay: ____

     Write one example from the essay below. Underline the error.

Type 5: Prepositions

     Total number of preposition errors in essay: ____

     Write one example from the essay below. Underline the error.

tense system or even of the various uses of the present perfect. (See Activity 3, which provides an example of an overview of noun error problems; this activity takes 15–20 minutes.)

Another alternative to whole-class instruction is to individualize editing instruction with an editing handbook (e.g., Ascher, 1993; Fox, 1992; Lane & Lange, 1993; Raimes, 1992a). A handbook is distinct from an ESL text, which attempts to provide comprehensive coverage of grammatical concepts, as opposed to focusing on specific writing problems students may have (See "Overview of Four Current Editing Texts.") In addition, many ESL writing textbooks include an editing section (e.g., Raimes, 1992b; Spack, 1990). When using an editing handbook, I give students homework assignments that correspond to their particular area(s) of need as shown in their essay drafts.

In the final phase, I require students to find and correct errors in their own essay drafts (see Activity 2). Also, throughout the semester, students keep a log of their error frequencies in the different categories so they can observe their progress.

ACTIVITY 2

Peer-Self-Editing Workshop

Your Name: _____

Writer's Name: _____

Instructions: Read your partner's second essay, looking specifically for errors in grammar, spelling, and punctuation. Mark the paper using the following symbols:

- If there is a spelling error, circle it;
- If there is a grammar error, underline the word or phrase that has the problem;
- If there is a missing word, put a ^ to show that something is missing.

  After you have read and marked the essay, complete the worksheet below.

Error Types

Type 1 (Noun Errors) Total number found in essay: ___
Example (from essay): _____

Type 2 (Verb Errors) Total number found in essay: ___
Example (from essay): _____

Type 3 (Punctuation and Sentence Structure Errors) Total number found in essay: ___
Example (from essay): _____

Type 4 (Word Form Errors) Total number found in essay: ___
Example (from essay): _____

Type 5 (Preposition errors) Total number found in essay: ___
Example (from essay): _____

As the semester progresses and the students get more and more editing practice, I gradually decrease the amount of editing feedback I provide and turn the editing task over first to peer editors and then to the writers themselves.

Does this Editing Approach Work?

I have developed the various components of this approach over several years. In order to assess its effectiveness, I have undertaken two small research projects (Ferris, 1994). The first showed that nearly all students analyzed (28 of 30) made significant progress in reducing their percentages of error in five error categories over the course of a semester.

ACTIVITY 3

Grammar Focus: Nouns

I. Definitions: A noun is a word that names a person, place, object, idea, emotion, or quantity.

Nouns may be concrete: physical, can be touched, seen, felt, etc. (book, table, gas).

Nouns may be abstract: nonphysical (friendship, sadness, hope).

Both concrete and abstract nouns can be classified into two types:
- count nouns: may be counted (apples, students, chairs)
- noncount nouns: are not counted (money, coffee, happiness)

II. Noun Trouble Spots for ESL Writers.
   A. Plural nouns must have plural markers:
   1. English teachers are good spellers.
   2. One of the ways to improve your spelling is to study hard.
   B. Subject nouns must agree in number with their verbs:
   1. *One* of the reasons I came here *is* to study English.
   2. *People* who emigrate to the U.S. *are* usually very happy.
   3. English *teachers are* good spellers.
   C. *Singular count nouns must* be preceded by a determiner (a/an, the, some, my, this, that, one, etc.):
   1. I have *a friend*.
   2. My friend owns *a car*.
   3. *The car* is old.
   4. She bought *her car a long time ago*.
   5. *Some people* think she should get *a new car*.
   6. *These people* have more money than she does.

Exercises: Find and correct the noun errors.
   1. One of the way teacher helps her students is to talk to them outside of class.
   2. Teacher in general are very hard-working.
   3. This is the reason that many people don't want to become teacher.
   4. Each of the students is important to a good teacher.
   5. Student should come to class everyday and always do homework.
   6. Students should treat their teacher with respect at all time.
   7. Student who come to United States have to learn English.
   8. Students is very nervous.
   9. A teacher who gives a lot of high grade is good teacher.
   10. All of student should give presents to their teacher at the end of the semester.

However, their degree of improvement varied across error types, essay topics, and writing context (in or out of class). As a result, I modified my instructional approach to editing during the following semester to allow for a more individualized treatment of student editing problems. Specifically, I gave the students individual editing assignments from a text (Fox, 1992) when each essay draft was returned, rather than providing

Overview of Four Current Editing Texts

1. **Ascher, A. (1993).** *Think about editing.* **Boston: Heinle & Heinle.**
   Description: Ten units; nine different editing topics (Verb Phrase, Sentence, Agreement, Verb Tenses, Determiners, Word Forms, Passive Voice, Conjunctions, Mechanics). Each unit has the following components: Pretest, Discovery, Summary and Review, Editing Your Own Writing, Suggested Writing Topics, and Answer Key.

   Comments: The pretest and discovery activities are nice features of the text. The organization of the chapters is a bit unusual, for example, comma splices and run-ons in the chapter on "Conjunctions," rather than the chapter on "Sentences"; Verb Phrases in Chapter 1 and Verb Tenses in Chapter 4. Is a whole chapter on passive voice really necessary? (It could perhaps be incorporated into one of the verb chapters.)

2. **Fox, L. (1992).** *Focus on editing.* **White Plains, NY: Longman.**
   Description: Six units; five editing topics (Articles, Nouns, and Noun Phrases; Verb Forms; Punctuation and Sentence Structure; Word Forms; Prepositions). Each chapter begins with a "What Do You Know?" activity, followed by Grammar Review, Exercises, Proofreading and Editing tips, and Editing Practice (paragraphs and a whole essay).

   Comments: The inclusion of whole essays for editing practice is helpful. The organization of the chapters into five large topics is helpful, allowing students to work intensively on areas in which they have major problems (e.g., with noun phrases, verb phrases). The chapter on sentence structure is a bit thin on problems student writers have—fragments, comma splices. Is a whole unit on prepositions really justified, given that there are so few generalizations that can be made about the use of them in English?

3. **Lane, J., & Lange, E. (1993).** *Writing clearly: An editing guide.* **Boston: Heinle & Heinle.**
   Description: Fifteen units; 15 editing topics (Verb Tense, Verb Form, Modals, Conditional, Sentence Structure, Word Order, Connector, Passive, Unclear, Subject-Verb Agreement, Article, Number, Word Choice, Word Form, Nonidiomatic). Each chapter has the following structure: What You Need to Know About Errors in . . . ; Common Problems, Rules, and Self-help Strategies; Exercises; Writing Activity; Applying What You Have Learned to Other Writing Assignments.

   Comments: This is the only one of the four texts with no answer key in the student text; thus it cannot easily be assigned for self-study. (The answer key is included in the accompanying teacher's manual, *Writing clearly: Responding to ESL compositions.*) There is a broad range of editing topics, so this could be a fine resource for teachers who want to develop their own in-class editing presentations. Editing exercises in the text are at the sentence- and paragraph-level; there are no complete essays for student practice. Teachers and students may find the system of marking advocated in the text cumbersome.

4. **Raimes, A. (1992).** *Grammar troublespots* **(2nd ed.). New York: St. Martin's Press.**
   Description: Twenty-one units containing 21 editing topics (Basic Sentence

Structure, Coordinating Conjunctions and Transitions, Subordinating Conjunctions, Punctuation, Verb Tenses: Tense and Time, Verb Tenses: Present-Future, Agreement, Verb Tenses: Past, Active and Passive, Modal Auxiliaries, Verb Forms, Nouns and Quantity Words, Articles, Pronouns and Reference, Adjectives and Adverbs, Infinitives and Participles, Prepositions and Phrasal Verbs, Relative Clauses, Conditions, Quoting and Citing Sources, Reporting and Paraphrasing).

Comments: Very comprehensive in its coverage of a variety of editing topics. Grammatical explanations are concise and clear. Well suited to self-study. Exercises are mostly at the sentence-level, with a few short paragraphs for students to analyze. Breaking the topics into 21 separate units could overload students and cause them to miss generalizations (e.g., the semantic similarities between "quantity words" and articles).

Ed. Note: At the time of this writing, Ascher's and Fox's texts are still available in their first edition. The second edition of Lane and Lange's text was published in 1999. The second edition of Raimes' text was reissued in 1998 by Cambridge University Press.

---

in-class grammar-focus presentations. Research on the effects of this change is ongoing, but preliminary results indicate that student improvement was even greater than with the prior approach.

Editing is an aspect of the writing process which has, until recently, been somewhat neglected by ESL writing teachers and researchers. With the introduction of new techniques and tools (such as editing handbooks) to help students edit better (and research and teacher training books to support these efforts), working on students' sentence-level needs is likely to become a more successful and satisfying enterprise than it has been in the past. Although we should not return to the excesses of previous generations (attempting to mark and eradicate every single error student writers make), our goal should be to have our students become skillful independent editors who can function beyond the ESL writing class.

The Teacher's Editing Feedback: From More to Less

Early in the Semester: Mark (by underlining, for instance) all examples of a particular error type in an essay draft, also pointing out in an end comment or on an essay feedback form that the student has a particular problem to work on ("Please go through your draft and try to correct all of the noun errors I have underlined.")

Midsemester: Underline a few examples of the error (perhaps only on the first page), again comment on the type of error, and ask the peer editor to underline the rest of the errors of this type.

Late in the Semester: You may want to make a verbal comment ("You still have too many noun errors—keep working on this!") but not mark any of them. Instead, ask the student writer to find them herself.

References

Ascher, A. (1993). *Think about editing*. Boston: Heinle & Heinle.

Bates, L., Lane, J., & Lange, E. (1993). *Writing clearly: Responding to ESL compositions*. Boston: Heinle & Heinle.

Hendrickson, J. (1980). Error correction in foreign language teaching: Recent theory, research, and practice. In K. Croft (Ed.), *Readings on English as a second language* (pp. 153–173). Boston: Little, Brown.

Ferris, D. (1994). *Can advanced ESL students be taught to recognize and correct their most frequent and serious errors?* Unpublished manuscript, California State University, Sacramento.

Fox, L. (1992). *Focus on editing*. London: Longman.

Janopolous, M. (1992). University faculty tolerance of NS and NNS writing errors. *Journal of Second Language Writing, 1,* 109–122.

Lane, J., & Lange, E. (1993). *Writing clearly: An editing guide*. Boston: Heinle & Heinle.

Raimes, A. (1992a). *Grammar troublespots*. New York: St. Martin's Press.

Raimes, A. (1992b). *Exploring through writing: A process approach to ESL composition* (2nd ed.). New York: St. Martin's Press.

Santos, T. (1988). Professors' reactions to the academic writing of nonnative-speaking students. *TESOL Quarterly, 22,* 69–90.

Spack, R. (1990). *Guidelines*. New York: St. Martin's Press.

Vann, R., Lorenz, F., & Meyer, D. (1991). Error gravity: Faculty response to errors in written discourse of nonnative speakers of English. In L. Hamp-Lyons (Ed.), *Assessing second language writing in academic contexts* (pp. 181–195). Norwood, NJ: Ablex.

Vann, R., Meyer, D., & Lorenz, F. (1984). Error gravity: A study of faculty opinion of ESL errors. *TESOL Quarterly, 18,* 427–440.

Questions for Discussion

1. What strategies do ELLs use to learn English? to develop their writing abilities? What implications does this have for teaching ELLs? for evaluating their writing?

2. Review what Rosen says about errors in student writing. How does their advice compare to Ferris's?

3. Return to the textbooks and state curriculum guidelines you examined in Chapter 2. To what extent do they discuss English Language Learners? What kind of support do they offer ELLs? (You may need to examine a teacher's edition, because suggestions for helping ELLs may appear only in the material meant for teachers.) If your state has mandated assessments to measure educational progress, are there any special policies for ELLs? If so, what are they?

4. Read the process essay by John (pp. 227–228). Imagine that John is your student. What comments will you give John—either in conference or in writing—to encourage him to revise his how-to essay? What do you think is strong about his essay? What advice will you give him about the content, organization, and tone of his essay? Are there places in his text that reveal he's a bilingual writer? Will you comment on these? Why/why not?

5. Read the draft of the literary analysis by Mario (pp. 228–230).
   a. Imagine that you're the trusted writing instructor Mario has come to for help

in proofreading his paper. What advice will you give Mario about his literary analysis? Since he hasn't asked you for help with the content, organization, and tone of his essay, will you make any suggestions about these higher-order concerns? Why/why not?

b. Minimally mark the surface errors you see in Mario's draft. What patterns do you notice in the errors? Do they tend to be "treatable" or "untreatable" errors? What advice can you give him to encourage him to be a better self-editor?

6. What have you learned about the teaching of grammar to language minority students? To mainstream students? Without consulting your previous responses, take the survey of attitudes about grammar and grammar teaching from Chapter 1. Compare your answers—to your previous responses, to those of your classmates, and to the responses of the general public. To what extent did your responses change? Why?

Part V

Student Writing

The sixteen pieces in Part V were written by a range of student authors. Along with each piece is a brief description of the context in which it was written and the assignment that prompted the authors to write. Granted, these pieces are taken out of context, and to know better what praise and advice to offer, you'd have to know much more about the authors as persons, as writers, as students. But I know of no way to provide you contextualized practice in evaluating student writing—short of inviting you into my classroom or vice versa.

I have a great deal of respect for each writer and each piece. I believe each has potential, but students and pieces may not always realize their potential without the feedback of peers and teachers. You might argue that as a teacher, I should avoid telling students what they should or shouldn't do in their writing because they should maintain ownership of their texts. I agree that any advice I give must help writers achieve *their* goals—and not mine. But I also believe, as Vygotsky (1962) does, that learning happens when teachers and students cooperate. Nancie Atwell (1998), a long-time middle school teacher and literacy researcher, agrees. She says, "Young writers want to be listened to. They also want honest, adult responses. They need teachers who will guide them to the meanings they don't know yet by showing them how to build on what they *do* know and *can* do" (p. 218). I would argue the same is true of adolescent and adult writers.

The sixteen pieces in this section help you explore the following questions:

- What ideas do these students want to communicate to us their readers?
- What hypotheses about the nature of written texts, of academic texts, do these developing writers seem to have formed?

Jasmine

This story was the final writing assignment of the fourth grade for Jasmine. It was not graded. When she read the story to her classmates during writing workshop, many students liked it so well they used it as a model for their own stories.

Writing Prompt: Write about one of your family traditions. Explain how the tradition came about. Who started this tradition? How long has it been in existence? Where does the tradition take place? What time of the year is it happening? Be sure to include specific details. Make sure your paper has a beginning, middle, and an end.

Something Tasty

¶1. "Hello, is anyone there? Okay, I see there is. Do you want something tasty? Just pull up a chair and listen. Oh since you want something tasty, I will tell you what it is and its history.

¶2. I really don't know when it started bat my mom said it was back in the 1980s. My great great Aunt this tradition. She passed a speacial recipe to my Aunt and then to her daughter than to her daughter's son and now to my mom. My great great Aunt said "it would make us remember our family. We make this speacial thing at every family get together. I will learn how to make it on my eleventh birthday like everybody else.

¶3. Can you guess what it is. Well I give you some hints. It can melt not being in the freezer, it can come in many different flavers and you can buy it Dairy Queen. If you haven't figured it out its homemade icecream. It's really tasty. So do you think it will be tasty. I guess you have to try it to know.

¶4. Well, I got to go now I hope you enjoyed my tradition. Are you still there will if your not you just don't know how good it is.

The End

The Kitchen Descriptions

These descriptions of kitchens are final drafts. They were written by fourth graders after a unit on descriptive writing. The students were encouraged to use all of their senses in writing descriptively.

Writing Prompt: Describe your kitchen.

Alexsandra

In My Kitchen

¶1. In my kitchen there is a clock it is black and white. I hate it because it goes tic, toc, tic, tac, really loud.

¶2. In my kitchen there are dishes, cups, silver wear, food and all kinds of other things like that. The floor is wooden and the walls are white. The wall mix in with everything else.

¶3. In my kitchen ther is cabinets they are wooden and thene ther is a refregerator wihene opens the door opens the at leades to heaven. That is why I love my nice clean kitchen.

Edgar

My Family Kitchen

¶1. Come take a look at. My Family Kitchen. When you walk in the brown door you will see a table. And it is brown it has four chares and we have parts to make it big. The color of the shairs are brown.

¶2. When you walk in the brown door you will see a regular stove and the color of the stove is green and black. It is on your right side. My mom wouldn't let me tuke it.

¶3. When you walk in the brown door you will see a refrigator and it is big. We can fit a lot of stuff in there and a lot of meat. There is a cavinit it has two doors.

¶4. When you walk in the brown door you will see the floor and the cloer of the floor is hounted green. They are siqeres and when you put the chair it will live a mark on the floor.

¶5. When you walk in the brown door you will see three cavinits and they are small cavinits. One is on the bottom two are one the top.

The Important Day Stories

These journal entries were written by fifth-graders in a multigrade classroom. Late in the school year, the class read excerpts from Facing History and Ourselves: I Promised I Would Tell *(1993, Facing History & Ourselves National Foundation), in which author Sonia Schreiber Weitz promises to keep the memory of her family and the Holocaust alive. As a follow-up, students were encouraged to tell about some important events in their lives.*

Writing Prompt: In the [excerpt from *Facing History and Ourselves: I Promised I Would Tell*], Sonia Schreiber Weitz uses diary entries to tell about important events in her life. If you could describe just three truly important days in your life, what would they be?

Alex

This is an untitled draft by Alex, a fifth grader in a multigrade class.

April 28, 1998. My father and I went to a sporting clay shoot for my birthday. It was one of the best times of my life because we actually got to spend quality time together. After the shoot was over, they had a lamb and pig roast. The food was delicious. The only bad thing that happened was that it started to rain about an hour after we got done with the shoot, so we had to leave right away. My father is taking me to another one this year, and I can't wait.

Nick

This personal narrative was written by Nick, a fifth grader in a multigrade class.

The Blizzard

¶1. The blizzard of March 19 was a scary day. When I woke up, all the power was out. My dad went to work, but when he got there all the power was out there too.

¶2. When I got up, my mom made me walk to the store and get some battery. When I got there the store was closed, but I saw that the roads were blowed, so I could go to my friends. When I got back home I got my mom to drive me over to my friends. We played board game for about three hours, we played Straptgo, Scrabble, and card games. It was so boring I wasn't having any fun until we went outside.

¶3. We a snowball fight, and we played football with a little kid down the street. My friend's graham made us shovel the snow. When we were done the power was back on at my house, my friend and I went back to my house and watch television and then went to sleep.

¶4. The blizzard was sort of boring, but when the power came back on it was fun. My friend and I played video games. I felt bad for all of the people that got suck in the snow. Some people I didn't feel bad for. This one gut got suck in the snow so my dad helped him out. Then he said "I'm going home and staying in". Then my dad saw him ten minutes later getting suck in front of my house.

The In-Class Essays

These papers were written in a tenth-grade English class. Near the end of the school term, students were given 115 minutes to brainstorm, draft, and edit an essay about one of three topics. Some students underlined their thesis statements before handing in their essays.

One topic was to explain what the writer would do if he or she had a million dollars.

Writing Prompt:	What would you do with 1 million dollars?

Matt

What I'd do with One Million Dollars

¶1. *One million dollars, what can I do?* Lets pretend I just recieved one million dollars. May be by winning a game or just luck. Well now I have this money but don't know what to do with it. There are tons of choices, I just want to make the right one.

¶2. I was thinking of putting it in the bank. This would be a good thing because I would not lose it, and I could make intrest off of it! I just don't think that is really what I was thinking of. So now I'm still tring to decide.

¶3. Wait I know, I could have my dream truck. Now that is a good idea. Something I have always wanted. It doesn't cost that much so I will have some more left over. That I could put in the bank.

¶4. No, I could buy a nice big house. On the perfect location. Just waiting for me when I'm ready. I could have it all paid off. Then with my nice new truck go live in it.

¶5. If I have any extra I think the smart thing would be to put it in the bank for a rainy day. You thought I would share with you.

Another topic was to imagine an ideal summer day.

Writing Prompt: | What my ideal summer day would be.

Yasmin

My Ideal Summer Day

¶1. My ideal summer day would be one worth remembering. At the crack of dawn I would get out of bed and run to the window to see the sun rise for the first day of summer. After enjoying the sensational view I will get ready and enjoy a well prepared breakfast. Then after devouring my meal I decide to burn it off by taking a stroll around my neighborhood.

¶2. Coming back from my stroll I figure I should take advantage of this beautiful weather and go swimming. I rush in the house put my bathing suit and took a relaxing dip in the pool. As I was swimming around I can feel the tremendous heat from sun shining on me. I took this time to get out of the pool to get dry.

¶3. Still having time to enjoy this beautiful day I decide to visit my godsister who conveniently lives down the street. I come to her door and asks if she would like to do driving around. And she said yes, so we drive everywhere and we notice that its starting to get a bit dark. And that means that the day is ending into night. My godsister drops me off and I got to my house.

¶4. Before I enter my house I look up to the sky and I say good bye for now, but I shall see you tomorrow. The reason why I say this is because when I look to the sky I feel that I could see my grandmother. And I swear I could see her smiling down on me. That is the reason why I love summer. And that is my ideal summer day.

N. Finklberry

My Summer Day

¶1. <u>My ideal summer Day would be like living in heaven.</u> I love the summer. The summer brings warm and happy feelings. It brings back memories never forgotten. My ideal summer day would like nothing in the world you can imagine.

¶2. Waking up with sun shinning bright in my face. While at a campground, I hear birds singing to me. The temperature is very warm and I'll prepare for a long wonderful day.

¶3. Leaving the campground off to ride on my boyfriend's boat. Jet skies on the back of his truck, and I'm all ready for fun. We get to the beach and we take the boat and jet skies out to the middle of the lake. While I'm having so much fun I'm getting a wonderful tan. Laughing and giggling the whole time, I couldn't have more fun.

¶4. Leaving back to the campground to eat a wonder dinner Mom has cooked. Sitting around the campfire while everyone tells how there day was. When I tell about my day to the family it was nothing compared to what they had done. As happy as I was things jut got better.

¶5. Sun starts to fall and my boyfriend and I decide to take a walk on the beach. Going to the beach while sun set was the most romantic thing ever. My footprints in the sand right next to his, and while we were passing the water washes then away. This day feels so good its like a wonderful dream.

¶6. In conclusion this wonderful day I lived. If all my day could be so warm this world wouldn't be such a cold dream.

Angie

Outline
I. Intro
   a. tell about essay
II. 1st para.
   a. tell everything step by step.
   b. times and what your doing.
III. 2nd para.
   a. repeat
IV. 3rd para.
   a. repeat
V. 4th para.
   a. repeat
VI. 5th para.
   a. repeat all main pts.

Final draft

My Ideal Summer

¶1. During the summer of 1999, I will have meny things to do, and a lot of time to do it all.

¶2. First, starting the summer right when I get out of school I will sleep in till 7:30. Then, I will take shower and go on the lake to ride my jet skis, and go boating in my boat. I will stay out there till 7:30 at night, go out to dinner, work out, and go to bed. While on the lake I will also get a tan.

¶3. Secondly, towards the almost middle of the summer I will wake up at 6:30, go running, go home and shower, and go on the lake till 7:30, go out to dinner, go home, work out, maybe watch a movie at theater, and go home and go to bed. I will work out up to two times a day and go higher as my awesome summer is on.

¶4. Next, in the middle summer I will wake up at 6:30, go running, shower, go on the lake till 7:30, and while on the lake, I will run and do aerobics in the water, then go home, eat dinner, workout, and go to bed.

¶5. Lastly, toward the end of summer I will wake up at 6:30, go running, shower, go on lake till 7:30, eat dinner, work out for 2 hrs., go to sleep. While on the lake I'll swim and do different exercises.

¶6. So, during my summer, I will work out a lot, go on the lake everyday, because that is my life, but during some days I'll rollerblade instead of running, I'll also tan a lot. I will also be going to Florida for 3 wks. in the middle of summer, so I'll get a nice tan.

I'll come back to school with a great tan, and lots of stories to tell about my great summer.

Jennifer

Pre-Writing

¶1. My ideal summer day is going to be lots of fun.

¶2. First, when I wake up, I'm going to tan for a little bit. Then when the time get around noon. I'm going to call my friends, and were all going to go somewhere and hang out. When I get hungry I'll eat, and when I'm tired I'll sleep.

¶3. Then somedays I'll have to work. But that should only be 2 days out of the week, for only 4 hours.

¶4. I'm also going to stay out really late. And spend the night over my friends house with about 10 other people. Its going to be great.

Final Draft

My Summer

¶1. My ideal summer day is going to be lots of fun.

¶2. First, when I wake up, I'm going to tan for a little bit. Then when the time gets around noon, I'm going to call my friends, and were all going to go somewhere, and hang out. When I get hungry I'll eat, and when I'm tired I'll sleep.

¶3. Then somdays, I'll have to work. Bat that should only be for 2 days out of the week, for only 4 hours.

¶4. I'm also going to stay out really late. And spend the night over my friends house with about 10 other people. Its going to be great. And I can't wait.

Louray

Louray is a student in a "Fundamentals of Writing" course at an urban, regional college. Below are two drafts of the first essay of the semester. The first one is her handwritten first draft. This draft was reviewed by one of her peers. The second is a later, typewritten draft. By the time she had written the later draft, Louray had gotten feedback from her instructor, her peers, and a Writing Center tutor.

Writing Prompt:	Take an abstract concept, such as *courage* or *friendship*, and define it by telling a story that demonstrates the concept.

First draft

Friedship

¶1. Friedship mean more than just saying your someone friend. but you have to show that person by giveing them adivce when they need it or just by being. there for them. when they have a problem. Or someone to talk to when they can't go anywhere else, someone, that would lift them up when there feeling sad should be able and all alone. Which you to always count on each other when you need help. Which you should always trust in one another. And your friend should never lead you in the wrong way or Never let you down. friendship should last forever. you should never Give up on your friend. If you have one. Because am the kind of person that would listen to anyones problems you don't Have to be my friend. to ask me for help. Im there for anyone you don't have to know me to talk to Me. Kindness is always In my heart. Because Im that kind of person you can always call on when your in need of anything I. would never let you down. I'm also not the kind of person. Here for you one minute And not there for. you the next minute. I know some people Are like that.

Later Draft

Friendship

¶1. Friendship means more than just saying your someone friend but you have to show that person by giving them adivce when they need it or just by being there for them when they have a problem. A friend is someone to talk to when you cant go anywhere else, someone that would lift you up when you are feeling sad and all alone. You can always count on each other when you need help. You should aways trust in one another. Your friend should never lead you the wrong way or never iet you down. Friedship should last forever. You should never give up on your fried if you have one. I am the kihd of person that would listen to anyone problem. You dont have to know me to talk to me. Kindness is always in my heart. You can always call on me when your in need of anything. I would never let you down. Im also not thekind of person here for you one minute and not there for you the next. Iknow some people are like that. I am a good friend to my sister because when she needs help with her baby, I will always be there fore her. She has a handicapped baby; she needs a lot of help with him. I also babysit him. I feed him and I also chance his clothers. My sister is also my best friend. we goshopping and we can talk about anything. she also listen to me when I have a promblem with my home work. she also helps me a lot. we lives in the same house and we do things together. she is a beautiful person.

The Creativity Papers

These two analyses were written in a basic writing course at an urban, regional college in response to the first major writing assignment of the semester. First the class brainstormed attributes they believed were part of being creative. For homework, they wrote journals on a time when they or someone they knew was creative. Then students read an excerpted chapter from Daniel Goleman, Paul Kaufman, and Michael Ray's book The Creative Spirit *(1992, Dutton). In this reading, the authors distinguish between what they call Big "C" creativity and Little "C" creativity. The former refers to achievements that have changed the world, such as those by Mozart and Einstein. The latter refers to ordinary creative moments by ordinary people. According to the authors, "The everyday expression of creativity often takes the form of trying out a new approach to a familiar dilemma" (p. 25). Students were then asked to revise their papers to incorporate a definition of creativity.*

Writing Prompt: | **Assignment for Analyzing.** Tell about a time when you believe you (or someone you know) acted in a creative way. Using the definitions of creativity by Goleman, et al., analyze the event, explaining why your actions could be defined as creative. Use information from the sources to support your definition and provide enough details so that your readers, who are not familiar with the event, can understand what happened.

Adam

> *Adam wrote a draft of this essay as a homework journal assignment and then it was peer reviewed by members of the class, who focused exclusively on the content of his essay. The class also talked about introductions and conclusions before he was asked to revise it to hand in. On the day the essay was due, the class discussed and practiced proofreading strategies, and Adam was given time to proofread his paper.*

"Creative Person"

¶1. The assignment is to write about a person that has been creative. The person I have chose to write about is creative everyday of his life. His name is Trent; he is a tattoo artist in Michigan City. Trent has done five tatoos on my brother an two on me, as a matter of fact he will be giving me my third tattoo this coming Friday.

¶2. First of all, Trent has been a tattoo artist for about two and a half years. When Trent draws a tattoo for someone it is his own design, most tattoo artists take other people's work and then gives the tattoo, but not Trent he wants people to know that his art is unique and original. When he gets behind the needle (or the tattoo gun) he makes a drawing, a work of art on a persons body. A person could ask Trent to draw a cross, and the person would expect just a normal cross, but not when he draws it. Trent would put designs and crazy colors in the drawing that would catch the eye of people. I have seen many tattoo artists perform their work. Every artist that I have witnessed is very normal and does not use any form of imagination in their work. With Trent everything is different from color to combination of designs. When Trent performs his tattoos he tries to make the tattoo as lifelike as possible. Trent can take a drawing and make it look like a work of art that has ever seen before.

¶3. Trent is so creative that he even performs tattoos on him self. For example, on the inside of his lip he tattooed a dragon. What Trent did is he stood in front of a mirror held his lip down with his left hand and with the right hand he did the tattoo. To be honest the tattoo cam out really good and it was even showed in a tattoo magazine. If the reader does not think that is creative then I do not know what creative is.

¶4. So basically I am saying that the way Trent draws and tattoos is just unique and crazy, because his imagination is so diverse when he gets behind a pencil or the tattoo gun.

Drew

> *This version is Drew's second version. He had feedback from his peers and his Writing Center tutor as well as extensive written comments from his teacher before handing in this version. Most of the feedback on his first version had been on the content and organization of his essay.*

Becoming A Good Black Jack Dealer

¶1. Black Jack is something that I enjoy doing. It takes a lot of practice to become good. Let's go on a journey of how I learn how to deal this fun and great game that we call black jack. So sit back relaxes and get ready to take this journey into B.J. dealing through Drew's eye take off.

¶2. In the first week for two hour a day all we did was play with the chips so that we could get use to them. We did things like getting the feel of twenty chips in both hands. Than we learn how to size into the customer's bets (pushing one stack of chip into the bet and sliding your finger across the bet and leaving the same amount as the bet) and cutting the chips in stacks of five.

¶3. The second week we had to learn the way that the casino wanted their cards shuffled. The deferent between the way you shuffle cards at home and the way the casino wants the cards shuffled. We are not allowed to bend the cards at the casino because they got to last the all day. When at home we tend to bend the cards. It took me a little while to learn how to do the casino shuffle I had to break my bad habit of shuffling like I was at home. This meant that I had to change the way I shuffle where I shuffle cards and it work well.

¶4. After the second week I felt like I knew the game good enough to win some money so, I went gambling. That was not true knowing the game from top to bottom do not mean a thing because when I went to the casino I lost five hundred dollar with one hour.

¶5. Back to class now we are in our third week of class it was time to speed up. When I say speed I mean how many hands per hour can you deal. They want about 350 hands per hr. we took all the ten and face cards out of the decks of cards and started to deal the game of black jack to each other we where in groups of five. This will help us see add the deferent ways to make twenty-one. Most of us got our hands up to about 280 hand this week. In the next two week everybody was close to the goal that the casino wanted us to reach put out there. After finishing with class we were ready to go to work.

¶6. What we did not know was there was more to dealing then knowing how to deal the cards. In order to make some tips the most important part of the job was for you to focus on your customers and make them feel special and give great service. This was the hardest part me because before I got the job I was petty much shy and too myself. In order to get over this problem I just imagine I was someone else it was easy when I act like a clown.

¶7. Since I do not deal BJ that much any more I got a little slow most of the dealer who only deal BJ can deal up to 440 on average per hr. But I deal around 360 hands on average per hr. We are evaluated twice a year on speed, neatness of cards placement and how we focus on our customer. If you do good both of your evaluation you get a very small raise of $.25. We make most of our money from tips they average about $13.00 per hr.—$5.00 per hr. base pay.

¶8. I had this doctor and lawyer at my table I know that they were because they played at my table many times. One night while playing together they said they had lost about 30,000 but most lie about what they lost. So they don't feel bad when they don't tip. When the doctor and lawyer left my table they where up about 27,600 so my boss told me after they left. Because I did not change my shuffle is the reason that's I don't get to deal BJ that much any more. Instead I deal this game call mini baccarat this is another card game. Matter of fact it is one of the best game in any casino. I like this game but the people smoke to much.

¶9. The value of chips we had on our boat is $1, $2.5, $5, $25, $100, $500, and $1000. There is a $5000 chip but we never had to bring them out so I do not know if this is true.

¶10. The classroom definition of creative was to create something that was not there. The reason that I feel that this was a creative time in my life is that without creating this job skill, I would still be doing the things I use to do. I would have never been able to go back to school or got over some of my shyness.

¶11. To sum it up it takes skill and a lot of personality to be a good dealer.

Amy

This is a graded version of a paper written by Amy, a basic writing student at an urban, regional college, late in the semester. She had read a number of articles about date rape and had synthesized them into an essay. Before her teacher graded this draft—Amy was given a "Pass" on this paper because there are only "pass"/"not pass" grades in this class—she had commented extensively on two previous versions.

Writing Prompt:	**Assignment for Synthesizing.** In class, you have chosen a social problem to investigate and have read carefully at least one published source that will give you information about the problem. Write a paper in which you define the problem in your own words, drawing on your own experience and your sources.

Date Rape

¶1. Date rape is a very serious problem in society today. Date rape has many different causes that are always followed by some kind of solution.

¶2. Rape is when a man forces himself upon a women sexually after a woman says no. In the article "Sex on Campus," Sarah Glazer states that one in every four women will be victims of rape or attempted rape (963). There are many things that cause a man to rape a woman. One is the consumption of alcohol. "In one study 75 percent of acknowledgd date rapists said they sometimes got a woman drunk to include the likelihood of having sex with them" (How to Protect Yourself From Rape, 41). This quite shocking to women. More startling is that when a man drinks alcohol in his system he interprets things differntly. A woman may be acting friends towards the man, but the man will think the opposite, SEX (. . . Rape, 41). Another cause of date rape is that of a drug. This drug is called rohypnol or "ruffies." This is a drug that is commonly used. It is put into drinks that the woman will drink. The drug will make the woman lose all control of what happens to her. She will not be able to speak, and she will not remember what has happened to her (Van Buren, 7).

¶3. There are some solutions to the problems of date rape. This one for example is one: In a court scene the victim of a date rape has said she was also drinking the night that she was raped. When saying this she can now be held accountable for a lead on to the rape (. . . Rape, 41). This example helps the woman to remember to keep her mind clear, and not too drink more than one drink when on a date. There are many types of solutions to the drug rohypnol. These are: 1.) "Do not exchange or share drinks with any one. 2.) Do not take a drink from a punch bowl. 3.) Do not drink from a bottle being passed around. And 4.) If a man offers a woman a drink from the bar, the woman should go with the man" (Van Buren, 7).

¶4. With all of the causes and the solutions this should help solve the serious problem of date rape.

Works Cited

John

John is an underclassman at a technical institute. John grew up in India and went to English-medium schools his whole life. He had two years of high school in the United States before coming to college. In addition to English, John reads, writes, and speaks Hindi and Bengali (two northern Indian languages); he also speaks, but doesn't read or write, Malayalam (a southern Indian language). He speaks Malayalam with his parents and English with his younger sister. This is the final draft of a process essay he wrote for his first-year composition course, about midway through the term. Before he had finished his first draft, he showed what he had written thus far to a writing faculty tutor, who suggested some reorganization of his paragraphs.

| **Writing Prompt:** | In this paper you will write a process essay . . . for a general audience. |

How to Play Chess?

¶1. There are several indoor games that we cherish to spend our pastimes. On is Chess which needs a lot of practice to know the choices to make. Chess was originally a game played by kings and noblemen in India during their leisure time; now it is played almost in every country. In Chess we account the probability of every move made and yet to make. The player has to have a visual pattern already set in his or her mind before making any kind of move on the chessboard.

¶2. In the past several years Chess has gained world popularity. It is now considered as a game which helps to increase an individual's IQ level. Players have to austerely adhere to the set rules and also have a mind map or perception of the different patterns. Gary Kasparov, a well-known grandmasters in chess, who had been playing chess since his childhood had to admit defeat to the super computer Deep Blue by the third round. Thus we see that not only practice but also visual perception leads to victory or winning a game.

Chessboard and its components

¶3. A typical chessboard comprises of the board itself and different kinds of chessmen, which function differently. Of the chessmen, the *king* is the sole important figure; it's the job of the other chessmen to defend the *king* from the brutal pinions of the enemy team. The front row is comprised of the *pawns* or soldiers who confront their foes valiantly by even risking their lives. They can only move straightforward, but they can only kill their adversaries diagonally on the chessboard. The back row is comprised of the *King, Queen, Bishops, Knights, and the Rooks*.

¶4. The *King* can move forward, backward, or sideways but by one step on each move. The *Queen*, on the other hand, can move forward, backward, and sideways, but also diagonally. She can take as many steps at one time on each move if none of her soldiers are guarding her path, and she can kill her foes any way she wants. She is the ultimate lethal weapon that the *King* uses to suppress his invincible foes.

¶5. At the extreme corners of the back row are the *Rooks*; they move forward and sideways only, and they can take as many steps they want if none of the team members are guarding them. They are one of the predominant figures comprising of the *King* and *Queens'* strength. Next in line are the Bishops; they are the *King* and *Queens'* personal bodyguard; they move only back and forth diagonally and they too can take as many steps at one time if not guarded. On either side of the *Bishops* are the *Knights*, the most ferocious of warriors who attack their puny enemy like a giant mammoth. They move and kill following an "L" pattern.

Strategies to follow while playing Chess

¶6. Always have a visual pattern made in mind before commencing the game. Judge the pros and cons of each move. Be alert and vigilant, aware of the deceiving pattern set by the enemy. Time is not a priority in most cases and there are no second chances for each move.

¶7. I would go with the *pawns* first to strike the opposition. The *pawns* are of less significance compared to other chessmen. Never move your *King* forward till the last move because it is more prone to unpredicted attacks than to victory. The two Rooks and the *queen* are the ultimate strength of the *king*, so never try to lose them early in the game. When things look a little out of hand, move the *knights*; they attack the opposing team even without its knowledge. Thus they are the secrets to quick victory.

¶8. The *bishops* also contribute a lot to strengthen the *kings'* powers. They are almost invincible against any chessmen except the *queen*. So I would rather lose one or two of my *pawns* in the process of defending the *king* than any of my *bishops* because they are always a threat to the opposition ; their taking as many steps at one time diagonally if they are unguarded enhances their usefulness. Next if I wasn't able to save my *bishops* , I would go for my knights; they can behead the enemy without leaving it any trace to escape. Their taking as many steps at one time if they are not guarded enhances their motive.

¶9. The *rooks* and the *queen* protect the *king* from further attacks. If my *king* is helpless at this point, I can use my queen to do a little stunt. By placing her by the *king* and having one of the *rooks* guard the *king* in front I would be able to kill any of my adversary trying to kill my *king* either from front or back or diagonally after it gets rid of my *rook* Thus it kills the opposing chessmen before it are about to make the *king* its prey. If the *king* is left solely by itself then it has to make its own decision on how to defend itself from the vindictive grips of its enemy.

Conclusion

¶10. Thus we see that Chess is not just another game but rather a circle of reality which revolves around choices to make out of innumerable options which yield to ultimate victory or defeat. Playing Chess has been helpful to various people I have known. It moulds the mind into practicality and makes it shrewder.

Mario

Mario is an upperclassman at a technical institute. He was born in the United States, but lived in Mexico from the ages of 18 months to 10 years. He went to school in Mexico from kindergarten to fifth grade; he has attended American schools since the sixth grade. He reads, writes, and speaks Spanish and English. With his family, he speaks a mixture of Spanish and English. For this paper, the final project for a literature class on Shakespeare, Mario had a number of different topic choices; the one he chose is shown below. This is the draft Mario showed a trusted writing instructor. Because he felt comfortable with the organization and development of his ideas, but not about his punctuation and grammar, he asked for help editing his surface errors.

| **Writing Prompt:** | Compare the main characters of several of Shakespeare's plays. |

Overview of Shakespeare Characters

¶1. It is believed by many scholars that good characterization is what brings Plays to life. One writer that followed this belief was William Shakespeare. Even thought most of his characters are generated by his artistic imagination, they unfold the meaning of the action. To show how Shakespeare manages to steal you away through the use of his characters. I will summarize some of the major and most memorable characters used by William. I will mainly focus on Hamlet, Henry Prince of Hail, Richard II and Richard III.

¶2. Prince Hamlet is probably the hardest character to understand and foresee. If I was to describe Hamlet to anyone who has never neither watched or read the play. I would say that Hamlet is a 35-year-old *kid*, who wines and cries a lot. He is also full of vengeance and waiting for the right time to kill Claudious. He is rude to his all that people around him; his own mother, his love Ophlia, Polonious and his friends Rosecrantz and Guildenstern. You might me asking you self, how can anyone be so focus on such a person. Well this is where Shakespeare comes in; he does an excellent job of presenting Hamlet to his audience. Hamlet is a very open-ended character it is very hard to interpret and predict him since his is unable to interpret himself (McLeish 108). Which always leaves the audience wondering what Hamlet would do next. Hamlet the son, when the play starts he arrives to a very uncomfortable situation. He's father has just died, he later finds out that he was murder by Claudious and his mother has just remarried. Hamlet the lover, due the devastating death of his father; he is unable to devote his love and affections towards Ophelia. Hamlet the friend, other then Horatio he doesn't have any true friends. The above examples are the reason why Hamlet is a mad man looking for revenge. But Shakespeare would not send Hamlet straight for the kill, instead he has the Prince plot a plan and deliver several soliloquies to help build his character. By the middle of the play you realized that Hamlet has every right to do what he does and you will be on his side for the rest of the play.

¶3. Many Shakespearean characters make appearances in more than one play, but none of those characters show as much consistent line of development as Henry Price of Hal (McLeish 113). At a first glance you can classify Henry as a dishonest rascal, who enjoys making a mockery of the English Language. You can also classify him as a cherry party animal that follows Falstaftf around. However, through the use of a soliloquy Henry lets us know that this is not the case. The speech marks the beginning of his development cycle. In *Henry IV Part Two*, Henry establishes the play's climax with the reconciliation with his father. This is a clue that Henry is growing up even more, he is longer an arrogant juvenile but becoming a worthy candidate of his father's crown. Finally in *Henry V*, the young Prince has fully mature and has obtained the role of King (McLeish 114). There were many speculations about having such a young and inexperienced King; many believed that Henry would escalade the differences with his father's enemies. As a result of Henry's motivation speech; his army was able to win *The Battle of Agincourt*. This was an example that King Henry deserved the throne. Every hero and majesty should have a significant other to share his victory with. Henry did not just win the war against France, but also the love of Katharine. This is another character that Shakespeare successfully imposes upon you, to admired and cherished.

¶4. *In Richard II*, Shakespeare uses a slightly different approach to capture the attention of the readers and viewers. In his particular play he converts King Richard from a self-centered, arrogant villain to a dramatic hero. Richard is introduced with great physical glamour and elegancy; this is a method of illusion used by Shakespeare to make the audience overlook the bad deeds performed by the King. Another great aspect of Richard is the dramatic reactions towards his followers. "When he abdicates it is like an archbishop dispensing the Host at some glittering State Eucharist" (McLeish 212). This charm is what wins him our sympathy every time he speaks, but it also foreshadows the fall of his kingdom. Yet another victory for Shakespeare, he has capture our attention and made us turn a villain into a hero.

¶5. King Richard III the villain of all villains. Richard has got to be Shakespeare's most cruel characters, he is cruel, manipulative, insensitive and a murderer. The obsession of becoming King makes Richard commit some of the most despicable acts imagine. His lists of victims include his brother Clarence, who he sent to the tower and later order his death. Richard's two nephews were also victims; the children were a threat to Richard's crown. Therefore he had then imprisoned and murder. Richard knew exactly how to manipulate people to achieve his dream of becoming king. And any who dare to oppose his requests or question his authority would not live to talk about it. Lady Ann is a prime example of how manipulative Richard could be. Thanks to Richard she had recently lost her husband. Some how the evil King was able to sweet-talk her into becoming his Queen. Although Richard is a wicked character, Shakespeare still manages to catch the attention of his audience. Shakespeare does something very impressive he shows the readers that Richard has a conscious and tries to portrait him as a good person. The night before the battle against Richmond and his troops, Richard has a dream. It's more like a nightmare where all of the people that he has hurt one way or the other come back to hunt him. When Richard wakes up he pauses for a brief moment and recaps what he has done. Another instance of showing Richard's feelings happens towards the end of the play. In the battle Richard looses his horse and becomes scare for his life. He says "thy horse, thy horse, I'll give thy kingdom for thy horse", this shows that Richard is actually afraid of death.

¶6. In conclusion I think that Shakespeare does a great job in his characterizations. He is able to take many different types of characters and still catch to readers attention. Weather the characters are childish, cry babies, young, immature, manipulative, glamorous, or villains. You will focus all of your attention on these people because they make the play some to life.

References

Andrews, L. (1995). Language awareness: The whole elephant. *English Journal, 84*(1), 29–34.

Andrews, L. (1998). *Language exploration and awareness: A resource book for teachers* (2nd ed.). Mahwah, NJ: Lawrence Erlbaum Associates.

Atwell, N. (1998). *In the middle: New understandings about writing, reading, and learning.* Portsmouth, NH: Heinemann Boynton/Cook.

Bartlett, M. (2001). Good e-mail communication requires hard work—study. *Newsbytes,* July 31, 2001. Retrieved August 23, 2001 from http://www.newsbytes.com

Baugh, J. (1998). Linguistics, education, and the law: Educational reform for African-American language minority students. In S. S. Mufwene, J. R. Rickford, G. Bailey, & J. Baugh (Eds.), *African-American English: Structure, history and use* (pp. 282–301). New York: Routledge.

Beason, L. (2001). Ethos and error: How business people react to errors. *College Composition and Communication, 53,* 33–64.

Berger, M. I. (n.d.) *Teach standard too: Teach oral and written Standard English as a second dialect to English-speaking students.* Chicago: Orchard Press.

Braddock, R., Lloyd-Jones, R., & Schoer, L. (1963). *Research in written composition.* Urbana, IL: National Council of Teachers of English.

Calkins, L. (1980). When children want to punctuate: Basic skills belong in context. *Language Arts, 57,* 567–573.

Cameron, D. (1995). *Verbal hygiene.* London: Routledge.

Christensen, F. (1967). *Notes toward a new rhetoric.* New York: Harper & Row.

Coffin, S., & Hall, B. (1998). *Writing workshop: A manual for college ESL writers.* New York: McGraw-Hill Primis Custom Publishing.

Collins, J. L. (1998). *Strategies for struggling writers.* New York: The Guilford Press.

Conference on College Composition and Communication. (1974). Students' right to their own language [Resolution passed by the assembly at its annual business meeting]. Urbana, IL: NCTE. Retrieved September 7, 2001 from http://www.ncte.org/ccc/12/sub/state1.html

Conference on College Composition and Communication [CCCC]. (1998). CCCC statement on Ebonics [Resolution adopted by the CCCC Executive Committee]. Urbana, IL: NCTE. Retrieved September 7, 2001 from http://www.ncte.org/ccc/12/sub/state7.html

Connor, U. (1996). *Contrastive rhetoric: Cross-cultural aspects of second-language writing.* New York: Cambridge University Press.

Connors, R. J., & Lunsford, A. A. (1988). Frequency of formal errors in current college writing, or Ma and Pa Kettle do research. *College Composition and Communication, 39,* 395–409.

Cooper, C. R., & Odell, L. (1999). Introduction. In C. R. Cooper & L. Odell (Eds.), *Evaluating writing: The role of teachers' knowledge about text, learning, and culture* (pp. vi–xii). Urbana, IL: National Council of Teachers of English.

Cordeiro, P. (1998). Dora learns to write and in the process encounters punctuation. In C. Weaver (Ed.), *Lessons to share on teaching grammar in context* (pp. 39–66). Portsmouth, NH: Boynton/Cook.

Crystal, D. (1995). *The Cambridge encyclopedia of the English language.* New York: Cambridge University Press.

Daiker, D. A., Kerek, A., & Morenberg, M. (1978). Sentence-combining and syntactic maturity in Freshman English. *College Composition and Communication, 29,* 36–41.

Danesi, M. (1993). Whither contrastive analysis? *The Canadian Modern Language Review, 50*(1), 37–46.

Danesi, M., & Di Pietro, R. J. (1991). *Contrastive analysis for the contemporary second language classroom.* Toronto: The Ontario Institute for Studies in Education.

Danielewicz, J., & Chafe, W. (1985). How "normal" speaking leads to "errorneous" punctuating. In S. W. Freedman (Ed.), *The acquisition of written language: Response and revision* (pp. 213–225). Norwood, NJ: Ablex Publishing.

Daniels, H. A. (1983). *Famous last words: The American language crisis reconsidered.* Carbondale: Southern Illinois University Press.

Donnelly, C. (1994). *Linguistics for writers.* Albany, NY: State University of New York Press.

Ellis, R., Basturkmen, H., & Loewen, S. (2001). Preemptive focus on form in the ESL classroom. *TESOL Quarterly, 35,* 407–432.

Faltis, C. J., & Wolfe, P. (Ed.) (1999). *So much to say: Adolescents, Bilingualism, and ESL in the secondary school.* New York: Teachers College Press.

Ferreiro, E., & Teberosky, A. (1984). *Literacy before schooling.* London: Heinemann Educational Books.

Ferris, D. (1999a). The case for grammar correction in L2 writing classes: A response to Truscott (1996). *Journal of Second Language Writing, 8*(1), 1–11.

Ferris, D. (1999b). One size does not fit all: Response and revision issues for immigrant student writers. In L. Harklau, K. M. Losey, & M. Siegal (Eds.), *Generation 1.5 meets college composition* (pp. 99–118). Mahwah, NJ: Lawrence Erlbaum Associates.

Ferris, D., & Roberts, B. (2001). Error feedback in L2 writing classes: How explicit does it need to be? *Journal of Second Language Writing, 10,* 161–184.

Finegan, E. (1992). Style and standardization in England: 1700–1900. In T. W. Machan & C. T. Scott (Eds.), *English in its social contexts: Essays in historical sociolinguistics* (pp. 47–68). New York: Oxford University Press.

Flower, L. (1979). Writer-based prose: A cognitive bases for problems in writing. *College English, 41,* 19–37.

Freedman, S. W. (1985). Introduction: Acquiring written language. In S. W. Freedman (Ed.), *The acquisition of written language: Response and revision* (pp. x–xv). Norwood, NJ: Ablex Publishing Corp.

Glencoe/McGraw-Hill. (2001). *Glencoe writer's choice: Grammar and composition: Grade 6.* Columbus, OH: Glencoe/McGraw-Hill.

Goleman, D., Kaufman, P., & Ray, M. (1992). *The creative spirit.* New York: Dutton.

Graddol, D., Leith, D., & Swann, J. (1996). *English: History, diversity and change.* New York: Routledge.

Great Source Educational Group. (n. d.). *Daily oral language* [Promotional Information Packet].

Wilmington, MA: Great Source.

Hagemann, J. (2001). A bridge from home to school: Helping working class students acquire school literacy. *English Journal, 90*(4), 74–81.

Hairston, M. (1981). Not all errors are created equal: Nonacademic readers in the professions respond to lapses in usage. *College English, 43,* 794–806.

Hakuta, K., Butler, Y. G., & Witt, D. (2000). *How long does it take English learners to attain proficiency?* Retrieved September 14, 2001, from University of California Santa Barbara, Linguistic Minority Research Institute Web site: *http://www.lmrinet.ucsb.edu.*

Hall, N. (1996). Learning about punctuation: An introduction and overview. In N. Hall & A. Robinson (Ed.), *Learning about punctuation* (pp. 5–36). Portsmouth, NH: Heinemann.

Harklau, L. (1999). The ESL learning environment in secondary school. In C. J. Faltis & P. Wolfe (Eds.), *So much to say: Adolescents, bilingualism and ESL in the secondary school* (pp. 42–60). New York: Columbia University Teachers College Press.

Harklau, L., Losey, K. M., & Siegal, M. (Eds.). (1999). *Generation 1.5 meets college composition.* Mahwah, NJ: Lawrence Erlbaum Associates.

Hartman, B., & Tarone, E. (1999). Preparation for college writing: Teachers talk about writing instruction for Southeast Asian American students in secondary school. In L. Harklau, K. M. Losey, & M. Siegal (Eds.), *Generation 1.5 meets college composition* (pp. 99–118). Mahwah, NJ: Lawrence Erlbaum Associates.

Hartwell, P. (1985). Grammar, grammars, and the teaching of grammar. *College English, 47,* 105–127.

Haswell, R. H. (1983). Minimal marking. *College English, US,* 600–604.

Hollie, S. (2001). Acknowledging the language of African American students: Instructional strategies. *English Journal, 90*(4), 54–59.

Hudson, R. (2000, Autumn). Grammar teaching and writing skills: The research evidence. *Syntax in the Schools* [The Assembly for the Teaching of English Grammar] *17*(1), 1–6.

Hull, G. (1987). Constructing taxonomies for error (or can stray dogs be mermaids?). In Theresa Enos (Ed.), *A sourcebook for basic writing teachers* (pp. 231–244). New York: Random House.

Hunt, K. W. (1965). *Grammatical structures written at three grade levels* (NCTE Research Report No. 3). Urbana, IL: National Council of Teachers of English.

Hunt, K. W. (1977). Early blooming and late blooming syntactic structures. In E. White (Ed.), *Evaluating writing: Describing, measuring, judging* (pp. 91–104). Urbana: IL: National Council of Teachers of English.

Hunt, K. W., & O'Donnell, R. (1970). An elementary school curriculum to develop better writing skills. (Report No. OEG-4-9-08-0042-010). Washington, DC: Office of Education. (ERIC Document Reproduction Service No. ED050108).

Ivanic, R. (1996). Linguistics and the logic of nonstandard punctuation. In N. Hall & A. Robinson (Ed.), *Learning about punctuation* (pp. 148–169). Portsmouth, NH: Heinemann.

Joos, M. (1961). *The five clocks: A linguistic excursion into the five styles of English usage.* New York: Harcourt, Brace and World.

Kerek, A., Daiker, D. A., & Morenberg, M. (1980). Sentence combining and college composition. *Perceptual and Motor Skills, 51*, 1059–1157.

Killgallon, D. (1998). Sentence composing: Notes on a new rhetoric. In C. Weaver (Ed.). *Lessons to share on teaching grammar in context* (pp. 169–183). Portsmouth, NH: Heinemann.

Kolln, M. (1996). Rhetorical grammar: A modification lesson. *English Journal, 85*(7), 25–31.

Kolln, M. (1999). *Rhetorical grammar: Grammatical choices, rhetorical effects* (3rd ed.). Boston: Allyn & Bacon/Longman.

Kolln, M., & Funk, R. (2002). *Understanding English grammar* (6th ed.). New York: Longman.

Kress, G. (1982). *Learning to write.* London: Routledge and Kegan Paul.

Kroll, B. M., & Schafer, J. C. (1978). Error-analysis and the teaching of composition. *College Composition and Communication, 29*, 242–248.

Landers, Ann. (1999, February 13). Who'da thunk we'd sink this low? *Chicago Tribune*, p. 28.

Lane, B. (1993). *After "the end": Teaching and learning creative revision.* Portsmouth, NH: Heinemann.

Lester, M. (1990). *Grammar in the classroom* (1st ed.). Boston: Macmillan.

Lester, M. (2001a). *Grammar and usage in the classroom* (2nd ed.). Boston: Allyn & Bacon.

Lester, Mark (2001b). Teaching grammar and usage. In Glencoe/McGraw-Hill. *Glencoe writer's choice: Grammar and composition: Grade 6.* Columbus, OH: Glencoe/McGraw-Hill.

Lightbown, P. M., & Spada, N. (1999). *How languages are learned* (Rev. Ed.). Oxford: Oxford University Press.

Linguistic Society of America. (1997). LSA resolution on the Oakland "Ebonics" issue. Retrieved September 7, 2001 from http://www.lsadc.org/web2/resolutionsfr.htm

Long, M. H., & Robinson, P. (1998). Focus on form: Theory, research, and practice. In C. Doughty & J. Williams (Eds.), *Focus on form in classroom second langauge acquisition* (pp. 15–41). New York: Cambridge University Press.

Madraso, J. (1993). Proofreading: The skill we've neglected to teach. *English Journal, 82*(2), 32–41.

Meier, T. (1998). Kitchen poets and classroom books: Literature from children's books. In T. Perry & L. Delpit (Eds.), *The real Ebonics debate: Power, language, and the education of African-American children* (pp. 94–104). Boston: Beacon Press.

Miner, B. (1998). Embracing Ebonics and teaching Standard English: An interview with Oakland teacher Carrie Secret. In T. Perry & L. Delpit (Eds.), *The real Ebonics debate: Power, language, and the education of African-American children* (pp. 79–88). Boston: Beacon Press.

Mufwene, S. S., Rickford, J. R., Bailey, G., & Baugh, J. (1998). *African-American English: Structure, history and use.* New York: Routledge.

National Council of Teachers of English [NCTE]. (1986). *Expanding opportunities: Academic success for culturally and linguistically diverse students.* [Statement prepared by the 1986 Task Force on Racism and Bias in the Teaching of English]. Urbana, IL: NCTE. Retrieved September 7, 2001 from http://ncte.org/positions/exp-opp.html

National Council of Teachers of English [NCTE]. (1996a). *Guidelines for the preparation of teachers of English language arts.* Urbana, IL: Author.

National Council of Teachers of English [NCTE]. (1996b). *Standards for the English language arts.* Urbana, IL: Author.

Neman, B. S. (1995). *Teaching students to write* (2nd ed.). New York: Oxford University Press.

Nicklin, J. L. (1994, April 20). 'Switching' between Black and Standard English [Electronic version]. *The Chronicle of Higher Education.* Retrieved December 30, 2001 from http://chronicle.com/

Noden, H. R. (1999). *Image grammar: Using grammatical structures to teach writing.* Portsmouth, NH: Heinemann Boynton/Cook.

Noden, H. (2001). Image grammar: Painting images with grammatical structures. *Voices from the Middle, 8*(3), 7-16.

Noguchi, R. R. (1991). *Grammar and the teaching of writing: Limits and possibilities.* Urbana, IL: National Council of Teachers of English.

Oakland, California, Board of Education. (1996/1998). Resolution of the Board of Education adopting the report and recommendations of the African-American Task Force [resolution adopted December 18, 1996]. Reprinted in T. Perry & L. Delpit (Eds.), *The real Ebonics debate: Power, language, and the education of African-American children* (pp. 143–145). Boston: Beacon Press.

Odell, L., Vacca, R., Hobbs, R., & Irvin, J. L. (2001). *Elements of language: Introductory course.* Austin, TX: Holt, Rinehart and Winston.

O'Hare, F. (1979–1980). In praise of sentence-combining, chunks, and messiness: Interview with Frank O'Hare. *English Quarterly, 12*(4), 9–19.

Olszewski, L. (1996, December 19). Oakland schools OK Black English: Ebonics to be regarded as different, not wrong. *San Francisco Chronicle.* Retrieved December 30, 2001 from http://www.sfgate.com/cbi-bin/article.cgi?file=/chronicle/archive/1996/12/19/MN11848.DTL

Patterson, N. G. (2001). Just the facts: Research and theory about grammar instruction. *Voices from the Middle, 8*(3), 50–55.

Peregoy, S. F., & Boyle, O. F. (1997). *Reading, writing, & learning in ESL: A resource book for K–12 teachers* (2nd ed.). New York: Longman.

Raimes, A., & Sofer, N. Z. (1996). *Instructor's support package for keys for writers.* Boston: Houghton Mifflin.

Ray, K. W. (1999). *Wondrous words: Writers and writing in the elementary classroom.* Urbana, IL: National Council of Teachers of English.

Reid, J. M. (1998a). "Eye" learners and "ear" learners: Identifying the language needs of international students and U.S. resident writers. In P. Byrd & J. M. Reid (Eds.), *Grammar in the composition classroom: Essays on teaching ESL for college-bound students* (pp. 3–17). New York: Heinle & Heinle Publishers.

Reid, J. M. (1998b). Responding to ESL student language problems: Error analysis and revision plans. In P. Byrd & J. M. Reid (Eds.), *Grammar in the composition classroom: essays on teaching ESL for college-bound students* (pp. 118–137). New York: Heinle & Heinle.

Rickford, J. R. (1999). *African American vernacular English: Features, evolution, educational implications.* Malden, MA: Blackwell Publishers.

Rosen, L. M. (1998). Developing correctness in student writing. In C. Weaver (Ed.), *Lessons to share on teaching grammar in context* (pp. 137–154). Portsmouth, NH: Heinemann.

Rueda, R., Saldivar, T., Shapiro, L., Templeton, S., Terry, C. A., Valentino, C., et al. (2001). *English.* Boston: Houghton Mifflin.

Schaffer, J. (1996). Peer response that works. *Journal of Teaching Writing, 15*(1), 81–90.

Siegel, J. (1999). Stigmatized and standardized varieties in the classroom: Interference or separation? *TESOL Quarterly, 33,* 701–728.

Shaughnessy, M. P. (1977). *Errors and expectations: A guide for the teacher of basic writing.* New York: Oxford University Press.

Shurley, B., & Wetsell, R. K. (n. d.). *The Shurley method: English made easy* [Promotional Information Packet]. Cabot, AR: Shurley Instructional Materials.

Sommers. N. (1982). Responding to student writing. *College Composition and Communication, 33,* 148–196.

Smith, F. (1988). *Joining the literacy club: Further essays into education.* Portsmouth, NH: Heinemann.

Smith, J. J. (1992). The use of English: Language contact, dialect variation, and writing standardisation during the Middle English period. In T. W. Machan & C. T. Scott (Eds.), *English in its social contexts: Essays in historical sociolinguistics* (pp. 47–68). New York: Oxford University Press.

Spolsky, B. (1998). *Sociolinguistics.* Oxford: Oxford University Press.

Straub, R. (2000). *The practice of response: Strategies for commenting on student writing.* Cresskill, NJ: Hampton Press.

Task Force on Educating African-American Students. (1996/1998). Recommendations of the Task Force on Educating African-American Students [recommendations adopted January 21, 1997]. Reprinted in T. Perry & L. Delpit (Eds.), *The real Ebonics debate: Power, language, and the education of African-American children* (pp. 151–153). Boston: Beacon P.

Teachers of English to Speakers of Other Languages [TESOL]. (1997). *ESL Standards for Pre-K–12 Students.* Alexandria, VA: Author.

Town, C. H. (1996, October). An overview of traditional, cognitive, and social perspectives on error. Paper presented at 1st Thomas R. Watson Conference on Rhetoric, Louisville, KY.

U.S. Bureau of the Census. (1990). *Language use and English ability, Persons 5 to 17 years, by state: 1990 census.* Retrieved September 13, 2001 from http://www.census.gov/population/socdemo/language/table2.txt

Vail, N. J., & Papenfuss, J. F. (1989). *Daily oral lan-*

guage. Wilmington, MA: Great Source Education Group.

Valdés, G. (1992). Bilingual minorities and language issues in writing: Toward professionwide responses to a new challenge. *Written Communication, 9*(1), 85–136.

Valdés, G. (1999). Incipient bilingualism and the development of English language writing abilities in the secondary school. In C. J. Faltis & P. Wolfe (Eds.), *So much to say: Adolescents, bilingualism and ESL in the secondary school* (pp. 138–175). New York: Columbia University Teachers College Press.

Valdés, G. (2001). *Learning and not learning English: Latino students in American schools.* New York: Teachers College Press.

Vann, R., Mayer, D., & Lorenz, F. (1984). Error gravity: A study of faculty opinion of ESL errors. *TESOL Quarterly, 18*, 427–440.

Vygotsky, L. (1962). *Thought and language.* Cambridge, MA: MIT Press.

Walqui, A. (2000, September). *Contextual factors in second language acquisition.* Retrieved September 14, 2001 from http://www.cal.org/ericcll/digest/0005contextual.html

Warner, A. L. (Sept. 1993). If the shoe no longer fits, wear it anyway? *English Journal, 82*(5), 76–80.

Weaver, C. (1996). *Teaching grammar in context.* Portsmouth, NH: Heinemann Boynton/Cook.

Weaver, C., McNally, C., & Moerman, S. (2001). To Grammar or Not to Grammar: That Is *Not* the Question! *Voices from the Middle, 8*(3), 17–33.

Weitz, S. S. (1993). *Facing history and ourselves: I promised I would tell.* Brookline, MA: Facing History & Ourselves National Foundation.

Widdowson, H. G. (1996). *Linguistics.* Oxford: Oxford University Press.

Williams, J. (1995, Summer). Focus on form in communicative language teaching: Research findings and the classroom teacher. *TESOL Journal, 4*(4), 12–16.

Williams, J. M. (1981). The phenomenology of error. *College Composition and Communication, 32*, 152–168.

Wolfram, W. (1998). Linguistic and sociolinguistic requisites for teaching language. In J. S. Simmons & L. Baines (Eds.), *Language study in middle school, high school, and beyond* (pp. 79–109). Newark, DE: International Reading Association.

Wolfram, W., Adger, C. T., & Christian, D. (1999). *Dialects in schools and communities.* Mahwah, NJ: Erlbaum.

Wolfram, W., & Schilling-Estes, N. (1998). *American English: Dialects and variation.* Malden, MA: Blackwell Publishers.

Yorio, C. (1989). Idiomaticity as an indicator of second language proficiency. In K. Hyltenstam & L. K. Obler (Eds.) *Bilingualism across a lifespan: Aspects of acquisition, maturity and loss* (pp. 55–72). New York: Cambridge University Press.

Yule, G. (1996). *Pragmatics.* New York: Oxford University Press.

Acknowledgments

Larry Andrews. Language Exploration and Awareness exercises. From *Language exploration and awareness: A resource book for teachers*, 2nd ed. (pp. 116, 230 and 252–253). Copyright © 1998 by Lawrence Erlbaum Associates Publishers. Reprinted by permission of Lawrence Erlbaum Associates Publishers.

Mary I. Berger. (1997) *Teach standard too: Teach oral and written Standard English as a second dialect to English-speaking students*. Text copyright by Orchard Press, Inc. Used with permission of the publisher.

Stephanie Coffin and Barbara Hall. *Writing workshop: A manual for college ESL writers* (pp. vii–ix). Copyright © 1998 by McGraw-Hill. Reproduced with permission of the McGraw-Hill Companies.

Harvey A. Daniels. "Nine ideas about language." From *Famous Last Words: The American Language Crisis Reconsidered*. Copyright © 1983 by the Board of Trustees, Southern Illinois University Press. Reproduced by permission.

Dana Ferris. "Teaching students to self-edit." From *TESOL Journal* 4(4) (1995). Copyright © 1995 by Teachers of English to Speakers of Other Languages. Reprinted with permission.

Julie Hagemann. "A bridge from home to school: helping working class students acquire school literacy." *English Journal* 90(4) (2001). Copyright © 2001 by the National Council of Teachers of English. Reprinted with permission.

Don Killgallon and Jenny Killgallon. *Daily sentence composing*. Text copyright © 1999 by Great Source Education Group, Inc. Reprinted by permission of Great Source Education Group, Inc. All rights reserved.

Martha Kolln and Robert Funk. Excerpts pp. 313–320, 323, 325, 332–333 and 335–338. From *Understanding English Grammar*, 6th ed. by Martha Kolln and Robert Funk. Copyright © 2002 by Pearson Education, Inc. Reprinted by permission of Pearson Education, Inc.

Rei R. Noguchi. "Run-ons, comma splices, and native–speaker abilities." *Grammar and the Teaching of Writing: Limits and Possibilities* (1991).

Copyright © 1991 by the National Council of Teachers of English. Reprinted with permission.

Nancy G. Patterson. "Just the facts: research and theory about grammar instruction." From *Voices from the Middle* 8(3) (2001). Copyright © 2001 by the National Council of Teachers of English. Reprinted with permission.

Lois Matz Rosen. "Developing correctness in student writing: Alternatives to the error hunt." *English Journal* 76(3) (1987). Copyright © 1987 by the National Council of Teachers of English. Reprinted with permission. Adapted and revised in *Lessons to share: On teaching grammar in context* by Constance Weaver. Published by Boynton/Cook, Heinemann in 1998.

Richard Straub. "Guidelines for responding to student writing." From *The practice of response: Strategies for commenting on student writing*. Copyright © 2000 by Hampton Press, Inc.

Neil J. Vail and Joseph F. Papenfuss. *Daily oral language and daily oral language plus*. Text copyright © 2000 by Great Source Education Group, Inc. Reprinted by permission of Great Source Education Group, Inc. All rights reserved.

Guadalupe Valdés. "Incipient bilingualism and the development of English language writing abilities in the secondary school." Reprinted by permission of the publisher from Christian J. Faltis and Paula Wolfe (Eds.) *So Much to Say: Adolescents, Bilingualism, & ESL in the Secondary School*, New York: Teachers College Press, © 1999 by Teachers College, Columbia University. All rights reserved., pp. 168–169.

Constance Weaver, Carol McNally, and Sharon Moerman. "To grammar or not to grammar: That is *not* the question!" From *Voices from the Middle* 8(3) (2001). Copyright © 2001 by the National Council of Teachers of English. Reprinted with permission.

Walt Wolfram, Carolyn Temple Adger, and Donna Christian. "Dialects and Written Language." From *Dialects in Schools and Communities*. Copyright © 1999 by Lawrence Erlbaum Associates Publishers. Reprinted with permission of the publishers.

Index